CW00545336

BSA
MOTOR CYCLES
SINCE 1950

Other books by the same author:

British Motor Cycles Since 1950

Volume 1: AJW, Ambassador, AMC (AJS and Matchless) and Ariel roadsters of 250cc and over

Volume 2: BSA, Cotton, Douglas, DMW, Dot, EMC, Excelsior and Francis-Barnett roadsters of 250cc and over

Volume 3: Greeves, Hesketh, Indian, James, Norman and Norton roadsters of 250cc and over

Volume 4: Panther, Royal Enfield, Scott, Silk, Sunbeam, Sun and Tandon roadsters of 250cc and over

Volume 5: Triumph Part One: The Company

Volume 6: Triumph Part Two: The Bikes; Velocette, and Vincent-HRD

Practical British Lightweight Two-Stroke Motorcycles

Practical British Lightweight Four-Stroke Motorcycles

BSA
MOTOR CYCLES
SINCE 1950

Steve Wilson

Patrick Stephens Limited

© Steve Wilson, 1983, 1991 and 1997

All rights reserved. No part of this publication
may be reproduced, stored in a retrieval system
or transmitted, in any form or by any means,
electronic, mechanical, photocopying, recording,
or otherwise, without prior permission in writing
from the publisher.

This book substantially comprises material first
published in 1983, with revisions in 1991, in
BRITISH MOTOR CYCLES SINCE 1950
Volume 2 – BSA, Cotton, Douglas, DMW, DoT,
EMC, Excelsior and Francis-Barnett roadsters of
250cc and over

British Library:
A catalogue record for this book is available from
the British Library

ISBN 1 85260 572 3

Library of Congress catalog card no. 96 78553

Patrick Stephens Limited is an imprint of Haynes
Publishing, Sparkford, Nr Yeovil, Somerset,
BA22 7JJ

Typeset and printed in Great Britain by
J. H. Haynes & Co. Ltd, Sparkford

Contents

Acknowledgements

Grateful thanks are due to Polly Palmer, Nick Kelly and Paul (Clockwork Mouse) Heritage of the BSAOC, to Triples expert Norman Hyde, and especially to J. Gardner of the Gold Star Owners Club, for unstinting checking of the relevant sections of the manuscript, and for photographs, advice and encouragement, to the late Ivor Davies and Bert Perrigo, and to Bert Hopwood. To Mick Woollett at the old *Motor Cycle Weekly* my thanks for kind permission to use the majority of the photos; and now thanks to *Classic Bike* magazine and *The Classic Motor Cycle* magazine for kind permission for the use of pictures which are currently copyright of EMAP National Publications Ltd. Once again to hyper-typist Sandra den Hertog without whom none of it would have come together. And once again the bottom line, to the original scribes and illustrators of the Fifties and Sixties motor cycle press, whose work I have drawn on so heavily.

Introduction

It is over fifteen years since the first edition of this work was written. The main outlines of the BSA story, which effectively ended in 1972, remain unaltered, and as sad as ever. Naturally I am relieved that nothing which has subsequently emerged has challenged, in my view, the book's principal interpretations as to what happened in the post-war period to this once-great motorcycle producer. But from my own and others' work subsequently, some further fascinating details have emerged about the life and death of the giant factory which used to stand at Armoury Road, Small Heath, Birmingham.

BSAs at their best were solid, workmanlike conveyances, and twenty-five years after the last ones were built, many models have stood the test of time. The BSA Owners Club with around 4,000 members is only the tip of an iceberg of riders whose enthusiasm keeps the wire wheels turning. The volume of BSA production runs—well over a quarter of a million machines were produced even in Small Heath's final troubled decade—makes BSA the second most popular, after Triumph, of classic British motorbikes. Everyone has their preference, and there are separate clubs for owners of the sporting Gold Star singles and their Rocket Gold Star twin cylinder cousins at one end of the spectrum, and for the workday Bantam two-strokes at the other.

I must confess an interest. Though I started out on Nortons, the three machines in my bike shed today are BSAs, two twins and a single. A likeable '56 A10 Golden Flash, reimported from South Africa, which we call Anneka (she was a bit of a challenge to put to rights); a rather nippy '72-registered oil-in-frame A65, one of the last, which has benefited from the extensive attentions, inside and out, of twin specialists SRM; and finally a brush-painted maroon '55 M21 side-valve 600 cc single, my bike for all seasons, which recently completed a 1500-mile round trip to the Shetland islands. Two from the '50s against one

from the tail end of the '60s: I'll let you draw your own conclusions from that.

Like these durable machines, BSA was substantial, worthy of respect. Photos let you contemplate the rank-upon-rank of side-valves for the Army and the AA; and the King and Queen, Churchill and de Gaulle visiting in wartime, when with a workforce of 12,000 Small Heath and its 72 satellite factories produced over half of Britain's armaments. Later, over the acres of maple-wood floor in the 'New' Building (originally erected in 1915 to build Lewis guns) came more exotic visitors, from King Farouk to Roy Orbison (a BSA twin rider), and robed African dignitaries under fringed parasols, parading across the wet Birmingham cobbles. All gone. And still regretted. As BSA sidecar champion Chris Vincent said to me, 'it probably wasn't run very well, but us in Birmingham that had to do wi' 'em were soft on the place'.

As the war had drawn to a close in 1945, and the works planned for the immediate post-war boom, £80,000 was spent with a view to enabling annual production to reach 100,000 machines. However, problems which would dog the factory over the next two-and-a-half decades were already emerging. Not just the government-imposed shortage of raw materials, but of shortfalls in the workforce. Lack of 'predictable supply of labour' worried factory boss James Leek, with female labour having to be 'inexperienced girls' from outside the Birmingham area. Though it was far from politically correct, or fair, the female element in the workforce—there were for instance all-female teams to assemble Bantams at Small Heath after their parts had been made at Redditch—was crucial to cost-effectiveness, as women, however skilled, were paid only twice the rate for juniors, and thus well under the rate for men.

By 1951, with a largely prosperous and successful decade underway, the labour shortage

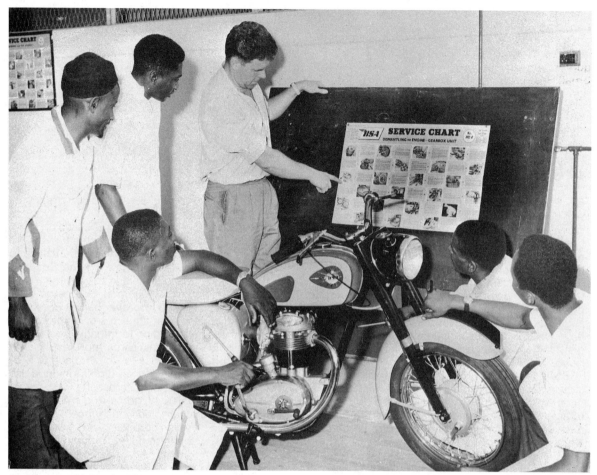

Service school in on the BSA C15 in Tanganyika in the late Fifties. But for the company such markets were shrinking along with the Commonwealth.

was still widespread, if more selective. Draughtsmen went to the better-paid aircraft industry, while labourers, storesmen and production counters were 'practically unobtainable' thanks to the car industry, whose higher wages were an ongoing lure away from the rabbit warren of Small Heath's 17 acres of buildings on the 26 acre site. (One's perception of the works could change, however. As Chris Vincent put it, 'when I started out, you could get lost in the dinner hour. By the end, I had friends all over the factory, the place seemed to have shrunk.')

For there were benefits beyond cash ones to working at Small Heath, which the company had built up deliberately over the years. They engendered a family atmosphere to the place, and many families did work there, with up to eight or nine members spread through two or three departments. By the '50s there was a full-time works doctor and dentist, and on-site eye clinics. Social clubs included an amateur dramatic society, and there was a full-time recreation officer to co-ordinate the excellent sports and hobby clubs. Another reflection of this positive side of Small Heath was that from the '50s there was a fair amount of immigrant labour, both male and female, who were integrated with no major problems.

The benign paternalism which all this represented may well have been a large factor in Small Heath's outstanding record for industrial relations with a stoppage-free record which contrasted strongly with both the car industry and with another motorcycle factory which became part of the BSA Group in 1951, Triumph at

Meriden. I am indebted to an academic study by Canadian Steve Koerner comparing labour relations at the two factories for much valuable research material on this topic. Among it are quotes from an interview with H. W. Robinson, a Small Heath representative of the TGWU, the dominant Trade Union post-war among the nine or so active within the factory; although unlike Meriden, Small Heath was never a closed shop ie one with compulsory Union membership.

Robinson recalled the '40s and '50s as a time of weak Union organisation at the factory, and one when the tone at the place for the shop-floor workers was 'do what you're told or you're out', and 'stay on the good side of the gaffer'. And Koerner himself points out the failure of the Unions to derive any financial leverage from the ongoing shortage of labour. Most wages were based on a rate for piece-work, but Koerner observes that it seemed the company via their staff (foremen) dealing with the workers directly, could unilaterally set the all-important piece-work rate and wage levels, without negotiation, though admittedly with a degree of consultation, with the Union shop stewards.

Not too important, you might think, if everyone was relatively satisfied. But as well as the sharply increasing turnover in labour, which we shall see in the '60s was mainly due to the comparatively low wages, and which was to be accompanied by a marked decrease in the quality of the product, the Small Heath workers' 'poor labour morale' would be cited as a major consideration in a report by consultants Coopers, which was the basis for the end of the BSA name, the run-down of Small Heath and the shifting of the bulk of the Group motorcycle production from there to Meriden from early 1972, rather than vice-versa. The Group's overall slide, from mismanagement and the Japanese competition, was probably the principal reason for this demoralisation. But the Small Heath workers' lack of a sense of self-determination from effective collective bargaining, and of self-worth when they were earning between 25 and 50% less than their Meriden rivals within the Group, must have been a major contributor.

As with men, so with machinery. The Group's failure to invest in new plant is well known, but the details can still fascinate. At the beginning of the period, swords were beaten into plough-shares; one example of how wartime production equipment was adapted directly to motorcycle manufacture was the new Val Page/Herbert Perkins telescopic fork, which had been specifically designed so that it could be produced on otherwise redundant gun barrel drilling machines.

The wartime machinery in general lingered on; after the company collapsed and Small Heath's 5,000 machine tools were auctioned off in the early '70s, the vast majority were found to be ones bought in from the wartime dispersal factories. In addition there was machinery far older than the 'new' gun-making gear of 1936. The majority was belt-driven. There were over thirty deafening miles of belting in the factory, and 'beltman' was a specialist trade. The belts used 'stickyjack' on them, a mixture of shellac and other ingredients to make them grip, and each maintenance man had his own formula.

The money was there to retool: net profits rose from £522,450 in 1951 to £936,000 for 1954. But BSA was a public company with an accountable Board, and so, in the way of the British system, the bulk of these profits went not to the workplace or the workers, but to the shareholders, who in 1954 for instance were enjoying a particularly juicy dividend of 17.5%

Over in faraway Japan, meanwhile, they did things rather differently. The *Zaibatsu*, the big trading companies who bank-rolled actual industrial firms, would settle for annual profits of ½%, in the interests of corporate growth rather than short-term profit. Their liaison with their government was also excellent, which was hardly the case in the UK, where throughout the post-war period, 'Stop-Go' economy measures were undertaken in abrupt steps, via variation in purchase tax, HP deposits and repayment periods, petrol tax, the Bank Rate etc. These fluctuations were particularly damaging to BSA in the '50s, who at home sold largely to the utilitarian end of the market. Stop-Go made for an unstable industrial environment which further demoralised both workers and management, and above all made forward planning with any degree of certainty almost impossible, even for a giant like BSA.

Whatever the reasons, Works Manager Al Cave had pointed out that the failure to spend money on new machines was crucial, because operating costs and times, which determined profit, were dependent upon the mostly manually operated machines. Only as late as 1967 did BSA begin to introduce compressed air and hydraulic tools to begin replacing the many hand ones. Not only did this failure soon put the company at a disadvantage against foreign competition, but the quality of manual work, though remaining generally high, did become uneven as the '60s blossomed; it often related, as Al tactfully put it,

Natives in the Himalayas appreciate world traveller Sean Hawker's BSA M21 outfit, 35 years after it was made in Birmingham.

to what an operator had been doing the night before.

Even the good operators who stayed on were limited by the machinery. Before the Group acquired their first specialist cam-grinders in 1968 (which anyway went to Meriden for the Trident), all cams had been made on old-fashioned spring-loaded machinery. In the '50s BSA's own pistons, though diamond-cut and sturdy, were made on twenty-year-old solid turners, which could allow 10 thou differences in ovality.

In special cases this could be turned to advantage: Chris Vincent, as a popular sidecar TT winner, had the run of the factory as he built up his race engines. He told me how he would sight up castings and pick ones off the line before work on them had gone too far. (Some castings were bought in, but some, such as Bantam chaincases, BSA made themselves.) That way Vincent could grade and control cylinder heads, con rods, cranks and pistons for his own purposes. As he put it, 'the gaffers were the last to recognise me —the ordinary people knew what I was doing first, and they'd always help'. Operators would

leave a little extra metal on if required, or machine to the tighter tolerances he wanted. Other in-factory competitors like Mick Boddice, the Hanks brothers and current classic race champion Bob Heath also did this.

The antiquated machinery goes some way to explaining why even in the '50s when home market sales were healthy, Small Heath production figures fell short of their potential. As mentioned, a total of 100,000 machines a year had been envisaged, but despite the calls in 1951 from Chairman Sir Bernard Docker for 'production and still more production', in the best years of the mid-'50s the actual annual total never rose above the mid-50,000s. Yet the best week in 1953 reached a figure of 1,750, which if it had continued throughout the year would have given a total of nearly 90,000.

Motorcycle production then, however, was a seasonal affair. The cycle began in August at the end of the summer holiday, by which time the following year's design prototypes and drawings had to be in, so that production could commence in time for reaction to new models to be gauged at the Earls Court show in October/November. Up to Christmas, stocks were built up for the home market and for those in the temperate southern hemisphere, though as the book describes, those traditional Empire and Commonwealth markets like Australia declined sharply from the beginning of the '50s.

Immediately after Christmas, production began for the US market. Shipments would have to start leaving the factory at the end of January at the latest, as the trade route to the States was lengthy, and it took at least two months for machines to reach dealers. And although our image of US export centres on shirt-sleeved riders gripping cowboy-curl handlebars in the Californian sun, the reality was that the West Coast took only 25% of BSA's American export total. The rest went to the East Coast, with its hard weather and brief Spring selling season. Missing this for three years in a row was what brought the Group down.

Before the war this production cycle had meant seasonal redundancies after the Spring. Post-war it was usually a matter of heavy overtime and occasional extra recruitment up to April/May, and short-time after it. BSA were never to be so successful as Triumph in evening out production in the slack times with military and institutional fleet orders such as those for the police, despite determined efforts led by Al Cave to do so in the late '60s.

As the '50s came to a close, despite culminating—after a drop in orders to BSA and Ariel of £1 million in 1958—with the wonderful peak sales year of 1959, the overall pattern was one of decline. In 1943 the Group had acquired New Hudson autocycles for £90,000 and the Sunbeam name for £50,000; both had been shut down in 1957, the autocycles wilting in the face of the continental scooter boom. The loss-making BSA bicycle side was sold to Raleigh also in 1957, and Daimler went to Jaguar soon after. Profits remained healthy as a result of these sell-offs, and the remaining Group motorcycle producer, Triumph, was a consistently strong performer. In 1944 the Group had bought Ariel for £310,000, but Ariel were moved from their Selly Oak home to Small Heath in 1963, and the name effectively expired two years later.

The Small Heath tradition of doing things in-house was changing too. From 1958, specialist functions such as the manufacture of pistons went to Hepolite, chains to Renolds and springs to Terrys. With sales declining, economies of scale diminished, and the BSA products were no longer price-competitive against these specialists with their more up-to-date machinery.

The main reason for the problems which increased dramatically in the early '60s was, again, Britain's Stop-Go economy. 1959's record sales were the direct result of the MacMillan government's pre-election cuts in Purchase Tax plus the elimination of HP restrictions. (How's this for an instant profile of motorcycling as a blue-collar pursuit—at that time only 25% of cars were bought on hire-purchase, but 75% of motorcycles.) But by 1960 the boom had gone, as HP restrictions had been reintroduced that April. The effect was really dramatic: by 1961 the British motorcycle industry's production had been cut by 50%. That year, despite having undertaken contract work for Dowty and Massey Ferguson to cushion the blow, BSA's new Chairman Eric Turner refused to host a visit of Commonwealth Prime Ministers to Small Heath, not wanting to show politicians round a Birmingham factory that was largely standing idle.

The fear which this market collapse put into the Group explains a great deal of what followed in the erratically swinging '60s. Triumph continued to make money largely because of their brilliantly developed organisation in the United States, one of the only markets where the 'youth dollar' created a bulk demand for large, powerful machinery. It was also one which the famous Japanese publicity onslaught was to help lift from the steady sales plateau in the '50s of around 12,000 British motorcycles overall, to hitherto unknown heights. Out of a total of 43,436 BSAs built in 1966/67, 23,302 went to America, part of a total near 70,000 for the whole industry. Since 1963 Group motorcycle exports had grown by 50%, and as Harry Sturgeon had intended, production itself had increased by 50%.

Of the BSA Group's turnover in 1957, 23% had derived from machine tools, 18% from steel and titanium, 18% from small arms and general engineering, and 14% from Daimler. That left 27% from the two-wheeled side. By 1966 motorcycles constituted 53% of the Group's turnover—a dangerous, and growing, dependence, but one warmly embraced after the nightmare of the '60–'63 slump.

To help with this production spurt came the ICT 1902 computerised assembly line. As long ago as the late 1920s, the lack of a proper mass production line at Small Heath had been noted critically, and it was hoped that the computer-controlled system of parts delivery would counter the rambling nature of the works, where part-completed units had to be moved in lifts, and then in trucks between buildings.

A BSA for the Nineties? This Seymour-Powell designed prototype for a four-stroke 125 Bantam looks good.
(Photo: Martin Christie)

Previously too the production process itself had often involved a juggling act. Until the twins, the same machinery had been used on the ohv B-group, middleweight C-group and side-valve M-group singles, with the machinery appropriately re-jigged after several thousand of each; not mechanically re-jigged, as on a rotary multi-driller, but by hand. While the automatic part of the operation of, say, skimming a crankcase top was being done, the worker himself had to be doing something else, so often three, four or even seven machines were in one person's care. Each would be different, and it had been a matter of coupling machines and operations so that everyone was occupied as much of the time as possible.

The computerised line, installation of which started in 1965, was intended to be part of a more streamlined production process, with nine integrated conveyors servicing five different assembly tracks. However the claim of its makers Fisher and Ludlow in the mid-'60s that it made

Small Heath 'the most modern motorcycle plant in Europe', was misleading, since it was not until 1970 that the system was completely installed! One symbolic side-effect had been that the sheer weight of the old and new machinery had caused the windows of the New Building to start bowing, so that during 1967/68 all their support columns had to be rebuilt.

Furthermore, even in the '60s peak year of 1966/67, production was often hampered, and on occasions the line actually brought to a standstill, by component suppliers like Smiths and Lucas failing to provide the parts necessary to complete machines. This contributed to the fact that Small Heath that year only met 60% of its projected production target. Much of the actual manufacture was still done on worn machinery by labour intensive methods; and the labour supply problem, far from going away, had worsened. A 1964 report identified a more than 40% yearly labour turnover, with 817 leaving out

Author Steve Wilson enjoys his 600 cc BSA single in all weathers.

of a total of 1,650 employees. Two machine shops actually suffered 100% turnover, and the probable cost to the company in retraining was £30,000. The cost in the quality of the product can not be calculated, but it's no wonder that management were prepared to put up with Meriden's wage demands, to keep their skilled labour force. For wages were the key; in 1966 a Small Heath labourer on £18–20 a week could get £24–26 at a BMC car factory. The '60s Unions at Small Heath did become more militant, with steady pressure to increase piece-work and day rates. Eventually the wage structure was revised, with piece-work calculated no longer by 'value' but by 'time'; and in contrast to '50s practices, the timing connected to the setting of piece-work rates, which had previously been a matter between foreman and workers, after around 1967 was always done in the presence of a shop steward.

It could not be concealed from the workforce, however, that things were not well with the Group. (One '60s ex-employee noted that 'BSA had probably the best jungle telegraph. If anything happened in the Boardroom, the works cat knew within two hours.') Another part of the problem, dealt with in the book, was that the motorcycles being produced were increasingly both old-fashioned and unreliable, sometimes dramatically so. For instance, the more powerful versions of the C15-based unit 250 single, released for 1967, were initially known as the C25 Barracuda. But by 1968 it was known in the UK as the B25 Starfire. Officially this was because of the name conflicting with an American car, the Plymouth Barracuda; but the Starfire name had already been in use in the US since C15 days, and an ex-BSA employee told me that in fact the decision to call it the B25 had been taken because the C-series had been so thoroughly discredited by the grenade-like C25.

Despite the new assembly system, and the Small Heath workforce increasing so that by 1971 it stood at a record 3,292, production actually fell steadily, from 39,809 for 1967/68 to 33,000 for 1970/71. Here the errors and incompetence of management, and consequent disorganisation, were principally to blame. The new MD Lionel Jofeh's insensitive style was the cause of the single day lost at Small Heath due to industrial action, when he attempted to contract out casemaking and packing work without prior consultation. Strategically management errors are dealt with in the book, but a few more tactical examples can be added.

There was the failure to do homework on the Ariel 3 trike, which turned out to be street-legal only in the UK and the Bahamas! Also the ill-fated Fury/Bandit dohc twin; despite chairman Turner being fixated on its 350 capacity as an entry-level one for America, Al Cave knew it could never make money because its design did not allow for it to be enlarged to a 500. And East Coast BSA man Don Brown has written in *Classic Bike* of a meeting with Chairman Turner in 1968, as the BSA/Triumph triples were about to be launched, when Turner asked him how many Rocket 3s he could sell. When Brown replied 1,800 in the first year, Turner 'went into shock'. He hadn't read Brown's 37-page analysis on the matter, and 'had bet his corporate life on the triples . . . (hoping) to get a return on their tooling investment in *one year*—obviously an incredible proposition.' He doesn't seem to have talked to Al Cave either, who could have told him that with the outdated manufacturing methods employed, plus the frequent need to laboriously change things from the BSA to the Triumph versions and back again, production was both not economical, and limited at first to just fifty triple engines a week, or some 2,500 machines a year. With management capable of overlooking something like that, the rest was very soon history.

So much for the BSA factory; but on a happier note, what of the machines produced there in those often troubled times? Many of them were, and still are, a credit to the men who designed and built them. Again I don't have too many reservations about what I wrote: though experience, both of my own bikes and while road-testing for *Classic Bike Guide*, has modified a few things. I under-rated the M-series side-valves, both in terms of the plunger's frame handling and of the engines' quite surprisingly satisfying pick-up. I probably over-rated the '71-on conical hub brakes. I did not differentiate quite enough between the various A65-series chassis; the rather cramped early ones, the more satisfactory '66–'68 versions, and the top-heavier '69–'70 jobs. And I definitely under-rated the '67–'70 B25/B44 all-welded chassis, which I have found delightful.

But overall, if what I wrote conveys that most post-war BSAs were thoroughly likeable motorcycles, then I don't want to change a word of it. Which is just as well, since unfortunately production considerations have meant that what has been reprinted is pretty much the original text, warts and all. So apologies for the odd glitch, and I can only hope that you enjoy the book as much as I do the bikes.

Wantage
Oxfordshire
September 1996

The author with his 1962 BSA A65 twin on a trip to southern Portugal

How to use this book

The book is arranged in the following way:
1 A brief history of the marque.
2 More detailed consideration of the major categories within the factory's road-going output during the period (ie usually broken down into single and twin cylinder machines, but with separate sections for unusual and exceptional designs like the Gold Star).
3 These are followed by a table of *Production dates*. Here, though production generally shifted during August and a new machine would usually be on display in November at the annual Show of say, 1950, I have followed the makers' intentions and referred to it as the 1951 model or model for 1951. Next come some necessarily brief *Technical specifications* for each range of machines.
4 These are followed by a detailed *year-by-year survey* of each range, noting developments and modifications. (Like the book, these are 'British', as with information available it has not been possible to include export specifications.) This should help with the identification of particular models, but it should be noted that sometimes there were changes made either gradually or mid-year.
5 A final section with details of the marque's *engine and frame numbers* (where available), and *colour schemes*.

The following further points should be borne in mind. The *Production Dates* quoted are in general those for availability in the UK rather than for export. *Weights:* all weights quoted in the technical specifications are the weight dry (unless otherwise stated). They have usually derived from *Motor Cycling* magazine's Buyer's Guide section, and occasionally inaccuracies have come to light, either from a failure to update or from optimism by the factory which supplied the figures. *Speeds:* top and cruising speeds for most models are to be found in the text not the specifications, and are approximate figures. This is because not all machines were road-tested, and not all those tested underwent timed runs at MIRA. Also the author feels that top speeds on road test machines were not always representative, as they could feature non-standard high-performance parts fitted by the factories. *MPG:* petrol consumption figures are also approximate, being subject to the variables of state of tune, prevailing conditions and the hand at the throttle.

Owners Clubs. For up-to-date information on Owners Clubs, please phone the BMF (British Motorcyclists Federation) in London on 0181-942-7914.

BSA

BSA Motor Cycles Limited, Armoury Road, Small Heath, Birmingham 11.

BSA, Birmingham Small Arms, was the biggest. Not only as a Group, for during our period the parent company included many subsidiaries, from gun and bicycle manufacturers to steel works, as well as a motor cycle division which incorporated the Ariel, New Hudson, Sunbeam and Triumph names. The title BSA Motor Cycles Ltd, incidentally, was first used when the motor cycle side was segregated from the bicycle manufacturing during 1953.

But the marque name BSA, and the BSA machines made at the massive Armoury Road complex at Small Heath in South Birmingham, then featured the largest volume production of any British motor cycle factory—one machine every four minutes was claimed in the early '50s, and compare the figure of over 75,000 machines produced annually for the peak years of the '50s with barely 80,000 produced by Norton-Villiers (later Norton-Villiers-Triumph) during the *ten* year period from their launch in 1966 until the time when the last Commando was made in 1976.

BSA was the principal supplier of machines to the British Army, as well as many domestic and foreign police and armed forces, and production runs were large. Some 58,000 A65 twins were built between 1962 and 1972, and 126,334 M20

side-valve singles manufactured during the years of World War II alone, together with more than half a million Bantam lightweights. Volume production of motor cycles was initially coupled with a conscientious service department—they guaranteed, for instance, the supply of spares for the Gold Star singles for ten years after production had ceased—and even the chaos of the late '60s and early '70s produced plentiful, if unwanted, supplies of spares, as the ultramodern computer in charge of ordering them blindly obeyed its over-programming. Fortunately, this means that generous quantities of both the machines themselves, and spares for most models, including the older ones, are still readily available.

The very size and scope of BSA makes their decline seem that much worse. After all, their fall represented the descent of something that had been a part of most riders' motor cycling experience and a household name for half a century. Blunders and false starts characterised the '60s until, by the time of the group's collapse in 1973, BSA had become something of a bad joke. Proof of the abiding power of the name,

Below left *1955, and it was all true.*
Below *War work—some of the 126,334 M20s leaving the factory.*

To you, these trademarks represent past progress— present endeavour—future promise.

however, has been its revival in April 1979 by Dennis Poore's NVT, which had inherited it when Norton-Villiers took over BSA-Triumph in 1973. The name has again changed hands recently and is now (1996) owned by BSA-Regal. There is no continuity whatsoever between the 'new' BSA foreign-engined lightweights and the products of the once mighty Small Heath factory, which itself has been demolished. The name is now a promotion aid, and as such has been good for hefty sales of mopeds to Nigeria and to India. BSA-Regal currently plan to launch an all-new 125 cc BSA Bantam, and other models.

Many words have been devoted to that fall of the mighty. For as Dave Minton said in his piece on 'The Rise and Fall of BSA' (*Bike* magazine, winter 1972), one of the best pieces of truth-telling journalism ever written on the British bike-producers: 'BSA was only a small example, one we can understand, of what was going on throughout British industry. Hasty, myopic top management, frustrated, overlooked middle management, and a shop floor resentful of their lack of communication.'

As a summary of the company's ills that would be hard to better, but more recently two excellent books have analysed the crash. They are Barry Ryerson's *The Giants of Small Heath* and Bert Hopwood's *Whatever happened to the British Motorcycle Industry?* The following portion of this book inevitably owes much to their work. The two men adopt different approaches, naturally — for while Ryerson was a long-time motor cycling journalist and enthusiast, Hopwood, who was responsible for the Norton Dominator and the BSA A10 twin engines, refiner of the Gold Star, and originator of innumerable other projects, was arguably the greatest designer at work in the field during this period. However, both are lucid writers, and dispassionate; though reading Hopwood with his dry, sometimes acid wit, and measured, objective style with example after

Above left *Designer, industrialist and now historian — Bert Hopwood is seen here in his BSA days.*
Above *A reputation for reliability — the 493cc Sloper single of 1930.*

example of short-sightedness and waste, often confirmed by contemporary documents and drawings, it is hard not to share in his cumulative sense of frustration and sadness.

Ryerson, on the other hand, deliberately presents both sides of the question, reconstructing the complexity of the problems confronting the decision-makers in reality, rather than trotting out the solutions which now, with hindsight, seem so obvious. He puts both the decisions and the deterioration of the 1960s in the context of the diminishing home market of that time. He modifies the traditional criticism of BSA's unwillingness to reinvest profits in the works by sketching a long record of financial prudence, represented by carefully maintained revenue reserves and suggests that in the mid-'60s the fault may have been due to *over*-investment than the opposite, though admittedly this was, possibly unwisely, in assembly systems rather than new production machinery. He points out the difficulty of the choice that had to be made between the benefits of a large range against the disadvantages of the multiplicity of components such a range involved. However, this was a problem for which Hopwood had an elegant, but repeatedly ignored, solution to hand, namely his modular range of designs — machines with engine capacities multiplying from an initial basic single to a superbike V-five, with the bikes using as many interchangeable components as possible throughout the range. Ryerson's central theme is unassailable as, again and again, he pinpoints failures of communication within the company as its 'fatal sickness'.

It may seem superfluous to dwell, as we will have to, on long-past and irretrievable errors of judgement and on office politics, but the downfall of the entire British industry related directly to them. And while the guidelines for this work remain the machines themselves, it is difficult not to find interest in examining developments in factory and boardroom that can now be seen to have directly affected the bikes.

The full story goes back a long way. The basis of the Small Heath factory had been created by a consortium of Birmingham weapon-makers in 1866, the gun connection emphasised by the traditional 'piled arms' insignia. The first motor bicycle, a 499 cc single, was produced in 1910. After World War 1, BSA machines, while lacking the charisma of racing involvement following a disastrous entry in the 1921 Senior TT, instead built up an enviable reputation for reliability. This was spectacularly demonstrated by the ACU-monitored test of 1925, where complete new machines were assembled out of spares gathered from different dealers, and then successfully subjected to a stiff test ride. This process was then repeated, again successfully, with an 11-year-old model! With machines like the 1920 1,000 cc V-twin, often with own-brand BSA sidecar attached; like the ubiquitous 249 cc two-speed sidevalve 'Round Tank' model of the '20s; or the 493 cc ohv single 'Sloper' from 1927 on, the company rode out the Depression.

This was also due to other traditions within the factory. The directors, several of whom were substantial national figures like Neville Chamberlain or Sir Edward Mandeville, after refusing personal pay-rises during the Great War, adopted a conscious attitude of co-operation with the labour force, providing decent pay, working conditions and hours, by the standards of the day. Indeed until the Depression struck, they could guarantee a wage even in slack periods. As a consequence the trade unions were moderate in their demands, strikes were unknown, and the works was a place where son followed father into employment, and where standards of skill and efficiency were high. Dealers, plus bodies like the Post Office, the AA and the police, as well as the public, were quick to respond and the true slogan 'One in four is a BSA' was coined during these years.

When World War II came it could easily have been 'one in three', as BSA won a bulk contract to produce military machines, and of the total 425,000 motor cycles that the British industry produced for the Allied forces, partly as a result of the early destruction of the Triumph factory in the

Coventry Blitz, no less than 126,334 were BSA 500 cc sidevalve M20s. A 1937 MOD specification had ensured that the major Forces bike would be a sidevalve—not the most suitable engine, and with its great weight and low ground clearance the M20 was not the most suitable machine. But possibly the War House was recalling that World War 1's 'trusty Triumphs' had been 550 cc sidevalves, and certainly whatever else they may have been, the M20s were rugged. BSA personnel also co-operated in training their riders.

In addition, the company, with foresight and altruism, had invested in the necessary machine-tools and building, and kept weapons-making facilities on at their own expense, in the national interest. When war came, they developed and produced hundreds of thousands of rifles and automatic weapons like the Lewis, the Bren, the RAF Brownings and 20 mm cannon guns in a network of 67 factories. But not without paying the price, for on the night of November 19, 1940, over 50 employees lost their lives in the Blitz and many of the original Small Heath's buildings were bombed out. These were extensively rebuilt, the fusion of new and old forming a rabbit-warren covering several acres. And as the war drew to a close, the works, under James Leek, managing director since 1935, prepared to meet the boom that would follow, as it had done after World War 1.

So at the start of our period, emblazoned with the winged BSA insignia adopted during the war, Small Heath stood poised on the brink of a decade of expansion. In many ways they were well-equipped to take advantage of it. To begin with they were more fully self-sufficient than any of their competitors, with a side-car works and the famous Competition Shop, a drop forge and huge press shop, a steel works and a Group research company, as well as testing facilities within the factory grounds. Direct benefits can also be seen to have come from other branches of the Group. The exhaust valves of the post-war B31 350 cc single, for example, were the first to employ austenitic high nickel-chromium G2 alloy, which had been produced by Jessops, a BSA Group steel company, previously mostly for use in aircraft engines. As Bert Hopwood, who joined the company from Norton in 1949, points out, all this 'invariably made possible huge savings in time during the manufacture of new components, especially experimental versions of new products'.

As Hopwood goes on to emphasise, with such a huge operation, organisation of the parts and effective co-operation were essential. By 1950 the team at Small Heath was impressive, and working

well together. At the head, James Leek was a formidable figure, an ex-production engineer from Daimler (another Group holding) who, despite dressing like a member of the board, was also a rider, given to testing bikes personally. He had ironed out some of the customary differences between the design, sales and production sides; and above all, though abrupt in manner, was accessible to anyone from any level of the company. Bill Nicholson, the works trials ace responsible for much of the early development of the Gold Star singles, went directly to Leek in 1950 after Perrigo, the competitions manager, while tacitly approving the extensively modified and lightened frame which Nicholson had built and was using, would not go further and secure official approval for it. Leek gave Nicholson's work the thumbs-up, and it was in production by the end of 1951. The outcome of the MD's intervention was not always so happy, as in the case of an experimental racer designed by Hopwood's partner Doug Hele, the 250 cc four-valve MCI, which after an enthusiastic test by Geoff Duke, on the point of entering its first race was stopped from doing so because Leek demanded something impossible—an absolute guarantee that it would win. However, Hopwood endorses this cautious approach to going GP road-racing, which was at any rate natural for BSA with its record of failure in the field up till then; and both stories show Leek as a man deeply involved with his product—motor cycles.

Other members of the Small Heath team in the '50s included Alan Jones, the works director;

Above left *Distinguished wartime visitors to Small Heath. Escorting the present Queen Mother is MD James Leek.*
Above *War work again—Oerlikon 20 mm cannon under assembly in one of the many BSA Group dispersal units.*
Below *Trials ace and Gold Star developer Bill Nicholson, on a 1948 A7 in off-road trim. Leek listened to him.*

Arthur Lupton, who was to be responsible for instruction manuals and service sheets; Bill Rawson, Sales Director and head of a service department with the motto 'Service is the Keyword'; Bert Perrigo, competitions manager and a distinguished competitor himself, who after leaving for a brief spell with Ariel in 1953 developing the Red Hunter singles, returned in 1956 as chief development engineer until his retirement in 1968; and Perrigo's successors in the Competition Shop, Dennis Hardwicke and Brian Martin. These men, and the company's wealth and prestige, attracted the brightest and best of competitors in every branch of motor cycle sport, except in Grand Prix road-racing. The Gold Star's domination of the Clubman's TT event will be dealt with later, and the history of trials and scrambles in the 1950s was mainly the story of a ding-dong battle between AMC and Small Heath, with BSA emerging as the winner. It was important that the company did attract the talent, argued Don Morley in his series on four-stroke trials machines in *Motor Cycle Sport*. He claimed that 'the riders make the real story; the experts would have won on *anything* and in my opinion in

Brilliant ex-competitor Bert Perrigo, post-war BSA competition manager, later chief development engineer.

BSA's case did just that'. He went on to point out that BSA were the *least* successful trials marque in private hands. The comparatively non-specialist nature of even the works BSA trials and scrambles machines during the '50s was a result of company policy, for like the road-racing Gold Star variants, for commercial reasons it was decreed that the off-road competition machines had to deviate as little as possible from the production roadsters. All of this benefited the ordinary road rider by resulting in exceptionally strong and proven roadster mounts.

At that time, BSA offered an ever-improving range of robust and practical road machines; and as in pre-war days, it was designed to be a complete range, from small to large capacity—or 'From the Bantam to the Golden Flash', as the publicity put it. The design for the two-stroke Bantam, in 125 cc, then 150 cc and finally 175 cc form, had been acquired complete as war reparations from the German DKW factory (in former East Germany, and till recently the home of MZ) and, built in mirror image to bring the kick-start and gear pedal to the right was introduced to the British market in late 1948. It was dogged by electrics which were sometimes poor and by detail faults, as well as being for the most part criminally under-developed. Indeed for many years BSA waited for DKW to uprate the little bike and then simply copy the changes. The bike's competition potential, too, was sadly under-exploited, for as late as 1967 a works competition Bantam variant achieved second place in the Scottish Six Days Trial. Nevertheless, nice looking, low revving and with an agriculturally robust engine, the Bantam was an ideal learner, commuter and fleet machine, as the GPO discovered for themselves, and an estimated 500,000-plus were manufactured at the nearby Redditch works and assembled at Small Heath before the end came for them early in 1971.

The then management, despite the continuing potential indicated by several fleet orders during 1970, including one (as late as October) from the Post Office worth £90,000, declined to take advantage of a redesigned Autolube version kept on ice since 1968, or to uprate the stroker to 250 cc, or even to take the offer of a consortium, including Competition Shop chief Brian Martin and the fine old Birmingham dealer Len Vale-Onslow, who wanted to buy the Bantam rights and tooling. The company, as Bob Currie revealed, settled the matter once and for all by putting a sledge hammer through the little bike's tooling jigs. They could then sit back and watch the oil crisis and recession of the '70s gather momentum, and budget East European CZs,

Above *Bantam beginnings—a 1948 D1.*
Above right *Bantam as part of the Boom. The 100,000th machine being unveiled by PM Sir Anthony Eden at 1953 Earls Court Show.*

Jawas and MZs—one, the MZ TS 150 Eagle, a direct heir to the DKW—flood the streets of Britain, while our industry lacked a single viable lightweight with which to respond. But back in the '50s and '60s, the Bantam set many young learner riders on a course of brand loyalty to the BSA marque.

The other two mainstays of the '50s range were the B31 350 cc single and its larger B33 500 cc brother, together with the great A10 Golden Flash twin and its smaller 500 cc A7 sister. From basic concepts by Val Page, the latter machines had been transformed rather than developed by Bert Hopwood on his arrival in 1949, from the basis of Herbert Perkins' original and less satisfactory A7. The full story can be found in the 'Twins' section, but here it can be said that both A10 and A7 became exceptionally robust and well-loved machines, equally at home with side-car attached or solo—strong, quiet, reliable and eminently saleable—all the qualities that Hopwood had striven for. Spectacular proof of the twins' 'rightness' was provided by the famous 1952 Maudes Trophy test, for which three plunger A7 Star Twins were selected at random from the production line, ridden to the International Six Days Trial in Austria, competed without dropping a mark, took gold medals and the manufacturer's

team award and then were ridden home, a near-5,000 mile trip taking in ten countries, with no problems. The singles in their turn benefited from this, the Gold Stars for instance adopting a modified A-type gearbox for 1953 and the whole B-range of singles following for 1954. The whole range also benefited from Gold Star development work, in the matter of cycle parts such as the very convenient single-bolt petrol tank mounting adopted for 1954.

The BSA works was a good place in which to be employed at this period. The great scrambler Jeff Smith MBE has described his experience as a 'promising' apprentice at Small Heath (his major competition successes began early in 1951 when he was just 17, and from 1953, after a brief defection riding for Norton, though still working for BSA, he rode for Small Heath without a break until the end). 'The plant was full of work and BSA was expanding with a sound business base. Motor cycles poured from the factory . . . My five years as an apprentice ran its appointed course through the service department, mechanical test, toolroom, E section, heat treatment, Gold Star engine and machine build, and finally to the Competition Shop.' Admittedly this was the experience of a youngster of obvious talent, but it does indicate a flexible approach involving apprentices in as many aspects of production as possible.

But despite the good machines, the favourable market conditions and the strong factory team, there were darker sides to the picture. For a start,

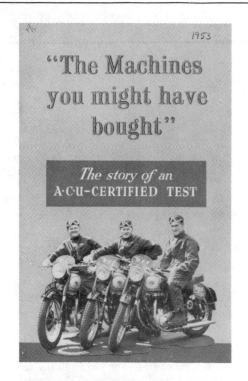

with the exception of the Gold Star (and less than 2,000 a year of these were sold even in the best years), to the British public and especially young people, the range always seemed on the bland side—'thoroughbred hacks', as the cooking singles were described in retrospect by Royce Creasey in *Bike* magazine. The lack of grand prix road-racing charisma obviously contributed, and in general, it was a case of Norton for handling, Triumph for style and rorty engines, and BSA—somewhere in between.

Then there was the team: good men and true, but by the mid-'50s scarcely in the first flush of youth. Fred W. Hulse was Small Heath works manager until his death in 1956, at which time he was 72 years old. Bert Perrigo had joined in 1927, Arthur Lupton in 1929, James Leek himself had been MD since 1935 and was in his late 50s. Hopwood summed it up when he characterised even for the most part excellent motor cycle engineers as 'older, not hungry'. This was a factor in deterring some of the best men; Bill Nicholson left in 1954, and Hopwood went back to Norton in 1956. The same age factor was echoed in the increasingly antiquated manufacturing machinery, jigs and tools. However, for the reasons behind the apparent unwillingness to replace them, one must look higher.

As already mentioned, the BSA parent company embraced many more interests than the motor cycle side, in fact 20 other companies, including gun and bicycle manufacturers and concerns such as Daimler cars and commercial vehicles, all came under the BSA umbrella. The parent board sat in St James Street, London SW1, which is a long way from South Birmingham whichever way you look at it, and even at this date Hopwood remembers the board as distant, patronising, 'self-satisfied and lethargic'—especially in relation to a forward plan for the motor cycle industry, despite the fact that motor cycles were a particularly profitable concern for the Group. At their head was Sir Bernard Docker, a wealthy man in his own right and a good publicist for the BSA name, who for the most part simply allowed James Leek to get on with the motor cycle side of things.

The first major post-war managerial problem for the company was to arise not from Sir Bernard but from his wife, Lady Docker. Norah was a flamboyant figure, an ex-barmaid who had three

1952 Maudes Trophy Victors (from left) Norman Vanhouse, Fred Rist, Brian Martin (future competitions manager)—and their A7 Star Twins, picked at random from the production line.

times married money while retaining the genuine common touch. However, as Ryerson convincingly suggests, her life itself must have taught her that money did not come from hard work and from producing manufactured goods of excellence—she referred to Docker's BSA products as 'your wretched nuts and bolts'—but from ostentation, like the gold-plated Docker Daimler, and from money itself. To this end she attempted, vigorously, to gain control of the board. She became a director of Hooper's, another BSA Group company, and also began to interfere directly with the motor cycle side, a fact Ryerson perhaps plays down.

Anyone doubting her pernicious influence in this sphere should refer to a chilling incident recounted in Robert Condon Champ's excellent history of the Sunbeam marque. BSA had acquired the Sunbeam name from AMC in 1943, and were using it to market their prestige in-line twins, the S7 and S8 models. It was also intended that the Sunbeam name would be used for a new 250 cc single, developed by Hopwood from half an A7 engine and featuring many parts in common with the twin, yet also with interesting new features, including simple rear enclosure. Three prototypes had been built and after extensive testing, culminating in three days on the Montlhery circuit, Bill Nicholson lapped the track there on one of the new machines at just under 100 mph. The bike, dubbed the MC4, was due to be exhibited at the 1955 Earls Court show and as a Sunbeam, it was finished in the same paint as the S7 and S8 and the D1 Bantams—Mist Green, a rather drab, but not unpleasant shade roughly the colour of tinned pea soup.

Just before the BSA group bikes were due to be despatched to London, Sir Bernard and his wife arrived to look them over. They returned from the inspection to announce that Lady Docker had developed an aversion to the colour Mist Green, and that consequently the new bike was not to go to the show. There was probably more politics to it than that, and Hopwood confirms that it was the parent board which turned down the MC4— thereby laying BSA open to the subsequent new 250, the C15, developed from Edward Turner's Tiger Cub and, as will be examined in the 'Singles' section, a fatally flawed burden to the company for the 14 years that versions of it continued to be produced.

Shortly afterwards, the struggle for control of the board came out into the open. A counter-attack on the Dockers was launched, led by Jack Sangster, the man who had breathed life into the Ariel marque in the early '30s. He had

Above *Happiness is a bulb horn and suede shoes.*
Below *Prentice boys. Fathers watch their sons being indentured.*

Above *Sir James and Lady Docker and the first Docker Daimler.*
Left *War paint. 1955, Sir James and Norah leave to launch a counter-attack on the board which toppled them. They lost.*

subsequently acquired the Triumph Engineering Co, and had sold both concerns to BSA disposing of Ariel in 1944, and announcing the Triumph deal in March 1951, before taking up a seat on the BSA Board in 1953. In 1956, when Norah Docker tried to get a place on the board for her sister's husband, horns were locked, and Sangster was able to convince the biggest 'institutional' shareholder, Prudential Assurance, that Docker, under Norah's persuasion, had been keeping trade figures from them. Unfortunately for Sir Bernard, 1955 had been a loss year for the transport side to the tune of £700,000, but no mention of this had been made at the annual general meeting, and no action was taken, it was claimed, on the Prudential's subsequent demand for an investigation. After a brisk boardroom struggle, the board voted Docker out in late 1956, and the shareholders backed them up three to one. The last Docker, Bernard's cousin Noel, left the board at the end of 1958.

At first sight this would appear to have been a victory for right thinking and the interests of motor cycling. Sangster was an engineering executive whom Hopwood described as 'a needle-sharp man' with no time for 'anything but conclusive and convincing comment' and the actions he took following Docker's departure appear to endorse this view. For once Sangster became managing director, he immediately restructured the entire group. In Ryerson's words: 'the parent board became a holding company responsible for major aspects of finance and policy, with a series of wholly-owned operating subsidiaries, each with its own active board entrusted with management of the individual business.' Initially, this rearrangement was successful, but as Ryerson points out, Sangster 'had created a ready-made tool for successors interested only in financial acquisition', rather than turning out decent products for profit. The ghost of Norah lingered on, the brassy, acquisitive side of the post-war years.

The second result of this new structure and its orientation was to make it completely impossible, after the initial appointment of Edward Turner, for the upper echelons of middle management to be able to entertain any realistic hopes of achieving the highest posts. This must have been disheartening, and by 1960, as Hopwood put it, the parent board 'now seemed very remote from the business of motor cycle production'. It makes a contrast with the career of the outgoing James Leek, who had begun his working life as an engineering pupil at Daimler, and was eventually promoted from general works manager to managing director with a seat on the board.

As far as Small Heath and the motor cycle side were concerned, the reorganisation meant that the bicycle side, already separate, was sold to Raleigh (and continues to exist today), and Daimler cars disposed of to Jaguar. Meanwhile, Sunbeam and New Hudson were registered as individual companies and an automotive division formed, embracing all the motor cycle and other vehicle concerns. James Leek, who had stepped down as chief executive in 1956, retired from the board in October 1957, and from Triumph, Edward Turner who had been brought in to replace him, at first as managing director of the Midland Group, now became the first managing director of this new automotive division on its formation in 1957.

Edward Turner was undeniably a motor cycle man, but despite his new title, in Hopwood's words: 'the Triumph company seemed still to be run as a private company, with Turner at the helm.' Ryerson said Turner could never 'get hold of' BSA, in the sense of get a grasp on its multitudinous operations, the tradition at Meriden being to buy in and assemble, rather than keep as

many operations as possible in-house. So with his appointment for the first time the strains within the Ariel/Triumph/BSA conglomerate surfaced, turning from healthy rivalry to bitter in-fighting, and damaging the range in the process.

The first casualties were in an area over which the industry has been much criticised for inadequate response to the market, namely lightweight machines. The BSA pair were a 75 cc two-stroke 'scooterette', the Dandy, and an electric-start 200 cc four-stroke side-valve scooter, the Beeza. Designed and developed by Hele and Hopwood, the Beeza was a gutless machine and the Dandy's original design meant that the crankcase had to be split to get at the contact-breaker. But by Hopwood's account they were machines made to impossible time factors, exhibited at a foolishly early stage for the 1955 show and then, with insufficient engine development time spent on it, because of the good response at the show, the Dandy was rushed into production in 1956 (the Beeza was abandoned). At this time Hopwood went back to Norton, worn out by alternately stalled and frantic activity resulting from the lack on the part of BSA management of a forward plan, frustrated by the rejection of his and Hele's MC1 and MC4 designs, and no doubt aware of the imminent arrival of Turner with whose ways he was all too closely acquainted, having worked with him at Ariel and Triumph from 1935 until 1947. Hopwood's assistant Ernie Webster took over his design duties.

But after his own departure the Dandy, says Hopwood, 'suffered the loving care of a dozen or so "chief engineers",' most of whom were out of their depth. Cast iron was substituted for the light alloy originally specified as cylinder material, with consequent loss of heat dissipation and attendant problems; while no advantage was taken of something the designers had pressed for, the coating of the light alloy cylinder bores with hard chrome — another process which a Group subsidiary had pioneered. The Dandy's release was delayed until October 1956, and it faded fast, while the 200 cc Beeza never reached the public at all. The official reason was that it would have been 'uncompetitive in price in overseas markets', but Hopwood had another, blunter explanation and one which carries a distinct echo of Parliamentary party political practice: 'Top management had now become very Triumph oriented,' he wrote, and they made 'the picture at Small Heath look as bleak as possible, with the usual trick of writing off, forthwith, much of the work carried out by their supposedly clueless predecessors . . . [this]

BSA DE LUXE TOURER Model 22-47

Finished in Black, Maroon or Beige.

BSA SINGLE SEAT SALOON Model 22-54

Finished in Black, Maroon or Beige.

BSA proprietary side-cars. Purged by the new broom in 1958.

has the advantage of indicating to the hapless shareholders how fortunate they are that the new management arrived just in time.'

In truth, the shareholders could have been forgiven for thinking just that, as vigorous action appeared to bring about immediate benefits. The pruning of the range had begun with the demise of the civilian M20 in 1955, and by 1958 all the side-valves bar the M21, together with the antiquated C11 and C12, were gone, to be replaced by the apparently spanking-new C15. In a basic eight-model range every machine bar the M21 now featured pivoted-fork rear suspension, and twins, singles, and the Gold Star all reached their high point of development with sporting successes continuing. The year of 1958 also saw the closing of the side-car works, as well as the demise of the Sunbeam twins. The proof that reorganisation, perfecting and trimming were effective seemed to be shown conclusively in the company's profits. After the 1955 loss, the automotive side, once Daimler had gone, could take advantage of a motor cycle market booming as never before.

A large part of production was going for export to over 150 countries. The Commonwealth, particularly Australia and New Zealand, had been strong markets from the start, and America became increasingly important. Here, too, success was very largely attributable to the new men, Sangster and in particular Edward Turner,

who since his first visit there in 1939, had become convinced of the USA's customer potential. Triumph distributors there, in particular Bill Johnson, fought the Harley-oriented American Motorcycle Association for fairer importing conditions, and opened up the market for British bikes. BSA too had not been idle and their West Coast distributor, Hap Alzina, had again personally and successfully fought for BSA's right to enter the 1954 prestigious Daytona 200 race, where Star Twins and Gold Stars were eventually to take five out of the first six places. Further details of the US organisations, and the export market there, will be found later in this account; suffice it to say for now that it was lucrative and growing.

Production of British machines in the '50s hit an all-time high of 21, 840 machines for the month of July 1957 alone, and that year BSA Group profits were up by around a third, bank loans were paid off and dividends increased, all despite the Suez crisis, and petrol rationing. Furthermore, much of this was directly due to the motor cycle side, which with the shedding of various subsidiaries now represented 41 per cent of the Group's total activities.

But closer scrutiny reveals a less happy picture. There was Sangster, a motor cycle man of proven business sense, who might have been expected to curb Turner's temperamental excesses. However, Turner, during his period with Triumph, had been an unquestionable, meteoric success, and in some ways Sangster's protégé since the Ariel boss had first hired him in the early 1930s. But even without that, for Sangster, a millionaire industrialist, BSA was an acquisition, not home base. Whatever Sir Bernard Docker's faults, his father Frank had been a BSA board member as long ago as 1912, and Sir Bernard had been chairman since 1940 — he was a Small Heath man through and through, which could not be said of the new chairman Sangster, who also, as Hopwood points out, 'had indicated that he was willing to take [that] office for a short time only', and indeed was to retire as chairman in 1961. In the meantime, the parent board numbered ten, with an average age of 60, and the only members with interest or experience in the motor cycle world were Sangster himself, and Turner.

Edward Turner was at best a mixed blessing. It must be acknowledged that the man was a designer of genius, who had an outstanding rapport with the aspirations and dreams of the young men who made up the bulk of the market for his machines. As the father of the Speed Twin he had set the trend of big bike building for 30 years, and was also an astute businessman, well able to balance returns and expenditure on a project at the well equipped and productive Meriden works. Or as Ivor Davies, first Triumph and then BSA publicity man put it; 'With Turner, the name of the game was to make money, and Triumph Engineering made a hell of a lot of money.' A full consideration of his achievements will be found in the Triumph section of a later volume.

But it must be noted here that Hopwood states decisively: 'As an engineer, Edward Turner seemed to lack the technical knowledge which must be embraced if engine design is to be anything but guesswork . . . His original designs were, to me, dangerously lacking technically and always needed "vetting".' This view is supported by several specific examples which Ryerson gives from Turner's time as supremo at Small Heath, where he also sometimes lacked the safety-net provided by his Triumph subordinates, in particular his drawing office chief, Jack Wickes. The most telling anecdote is possibly the following. Dennis Hardwicke, the one-time BSA Competition Manager, while working in the development department, was given a specimen clutch and a set of drawings to work from. Upon finding that the drawings did not relate to the

Above *Export or die, but this is ridiculous. Bantam and feathered friend in New Guinea.*
Below *New governor. Triumph's Edward Turner, head of the BSA Automotive Division from 1957.*

specimen, he was told apologetically that he had been given Edward Turner's own drawings by mistake and not the 'proper' (ie corrected) ones. This indicates a) that many of Turner's original designs, unmodified, were unworkable and b) that astonishingly, this fact had to be concealed from him. As Ryerson points out, this trait did nothing to encourage communication within the factory.

The reason for this seems to have been connected with his personality, which even his admirers had to agree was egotistical to the point of being megalomaniacal. Ryerson argues persuasively that this was probably the result of a fundamental insecurity, a feeling, also concealed from himself, that he was inadequate, a small boy masquerading in a man's job. Something of the flavour of his mind is conveyed by a Hopwood-reported lofty utterance which Turner delivered while temporarily at odds with an erstwhile employer. He spoke of this unfortunate as 'the faceless one who prospered by my brilliance'. It was 1942, and the man he was referring to was Jack Sangster.

An example of faulty design work which directly affected BSA was the Group's next stab at the

scooter market in the shape of the BSA Sunbeam/Triumph Tigress models. These scooters were launched at the 1958 Show and there were 175 cc Bantam-engined versions of each, as well as models with a 250 cc four-stroke twin-cylinder engine of Turner design, with or without optional electric start. The latter were £20 dearer and 40 lb heavier than the 150 cc Lambrettas and Vespas, and though Robert Condon Champ argues in the Sunbeam history that they were aimed at the heavy scooter market, the domain of the Heinkels and Zundapps, as he says, in this case they were 'entering a limited market at a late stage'. And though the 250s at around 240 lb and £187 were in fact no heavier and slightly cheaper than the top wops, the Lambretta TV 175 and the Vespa GS, they certainly looked bulkier, sounded wrong and were not, in the parlance of the day, 'neat'. The scooter boom may have been fading but it was far from over — *the* Mod Summers were from 1963 to 1965, but these machines weren't relevant to those days with their razor-sharp sense of style. And while the machine handled well, and the 250 engine contained many interesting features, the bikes also suffered from overheating. For Turner had failed to estimate the loss of cooling due to enclosure correctly, which lead to vapour locks in the fuel system and burnt legs on the hot side panels. The scooters did not sell well, though they lingered until 1964.

Turner, despite his title, continued to spend most of his time at Meriden and took little interest in Small Heath. For beneath the board-room manoeuvring and the market forces, one fact remained — with the exception of the scooters, no completely new machines were coming from the motor cycle division. Sangster had made reorganisation a substitute for genuinely new designs and products. The apparent exception in 1958 was the 250 cc C15, but this was derived from Triumph's 200 cc Tiger Cub. Having been developed from the original 150 cc Terrier, neither the Tiger Cub nor the C15 were fundamentally reliable machines. However, initially this was not apparent. With Bert Perrigo masterminding the C15's sports development, and top riders like Smith, Arthur Lampkin and the new Competition Shop chief Brian Martin aboard, the lightweight 250 was very much in tune with the times and performed well in trials and scrambles from the start.

It was also not entirely to be sneezed at as a roadster. Genuinely light, unlike the AMC 'lightweights', at 280 lb dry, with ac electrics and true unit construction, its only real home-grown

Below left *Sales were less scintillating. Sunbeam scooter with all Motoplas accessories for 1961.*

Right *Don't smile, lady, for BSA this is the birth of the blues. Triumph origins of BSA's unit single range, 150 cc Terrier.*

Below right *Birth of the blues II. New for 1958, the 250 cc C15 Star.*

TRIUMPH 150 c.c. TERRIER

competitors were the faster but even oilier Royal Enfield 250s. I had an unusual opportunity to sample a low-mileage C15-derivative in recent years, when I bought as second owner a 1965 350 cc B.40 which had been crated up for Civil Defence and sold off brand new nearly ten years later. It was smart, compact, easy to ride around in town and its crisp rather noisy exhaust note relished by all who sampled it. However, that was probably the best variant and year, and a near new machine; the many faults of the earlier pre-'65 versions will be found detailed later. The post 1967, hotted up C25/B25 variants merely exposed the inherent weaknesses of the design, which lacked true robustness. The bike needed considerate riding, regular attention and luck if it was to stay oiltight and in one piece for a reasonable working life.

With learner riders restricted to 250 cc from 1960, a lightweight 250 was certainly a must for the time, but Turner, in pushing a version of one of his own designs, ignored a wealth of viable and interesting alternatives available to BSA. The Hopwood-designed MC4 had been rejected already, but from 1958 there existed within the group the excellent Ariel 250 cc two-stroke twin engine, which as already related in the Ariel section of the previous volume, was made the basis of two conventionally framed prototypes. This was one possibility, but since these were the

simply marvellous

the NEW
BSA 250
O·H·V
STAR

brain-child of Ariel's Bernard Knight, inter-group rivalry apparently damned them.

And since 1956 there had been another direction in Roland Pike's Gold Star of 250 cc, on which Terry Cheshire took a gold in the ISDT that year. It became the basis of a quite successful road racer, the GMS (Geoff Monty Special). Imagine the charisma a pukka 250 Gold Star would have had for a learner — it would have been the Yamaha LC of its day. It can be argued that weight would have been a problem, but Bill Nicholson's work on the Gold Star, and Sammy Miller's weight-saving work on his 500 cc Ariel, another heavy four-stroke single which he reduced to 240 lb, suggests what could have been done, even if one excludes expensive trick parts like the Miller titanium wheel spindles. Another objection might have been that ac electrics were a must, since Lucas were phasing out volume production of magdynos and doing everything they could to induce British manufacturers to adopt crankshaft-driven alternator systems. But the B31 and B33 singles, the basis of the Gold Stars, successfully adopted Lucas ac electrics for 1958. This move did not ensure their survival, however, and with the cooking version of the singles gone, the Gold Stars were not long in following. Their production ceased in 1963. The rationale was cost, and that they tied up unjustifiable amounts of skilled workmen at a time when export was a prime concern. But as to export, the story goes that the Goldies' life was actually prolonged by the fact that some US dealers refused to take their quota of roadster twins and singles without a leavening of 500 cc Gold Stars. Indeed Bruce Main-Smith, a motorcycling journalist at the time, recounts in his publication *The Book of the Gold Star* how David Munro, who had been BSA's Technical Liaison Officer, told him that it was Edward Turner's belief in 1958 that the Gold Star represented a threat to his Triumph Tiger 100s, and it was this which really accounted for the single's lack of development from then on, and for its eventual demise.

This left Small Heath without a flagship, and the end of the A7/A10 range, plus its replacement by the unit A50/A65 twins from 1962 on, left the company without a machine, as Dave Minton put it, that a man would sell his soul for. The victims of lacklustre styling, the new twins were rush jobs, the decision to go unit having been taken apparently in response to demand from the USA. Dave Minton also mentions an intriguing rumour concerning the sale of rights to the pre-unit twins, and of a visit to Small Heath by a Japanese representative. What is certain is that the Japanese Meguro company produced their KI 500 cc twin, a very near duplicate of the A7, in 1960; and following the takeover of Meguro by Kawasaki, their W-range bored-out versions of this highly esteemed machine, continued to be produced as late as 1976, and in many areas were an improvement on their A7/A10 originals. (Details can be found in the 'Twins' section.) This may have been straight copying, which had been a very widespread Japanese practice in the 1950s. Certainly in 1968 BSA's then managing director Lionel Jofeh in a TV interview on 'The Money Programme' accused the Japanese of pirating BSA twin designs — but then, as we shall see, if a deal had existed, he could easily have been the last to know.

The new A50/A65 twins were plagued with teething troubles. Ironically they replaced a near-perfected A10, the mighty and desirable 46 bhp Rocket Gold Star which was initially only about £20 dearer and 20 lb heavier than the new 38 bhp

Birth of the blues III. New for 1962, the A65 650.

A65. The excuse of ac electrics was offered for the redesign, but once again the alternator conversion of the B31/33, which shared much of its bottom end with the A7/A10, gave the lie to that, and conclusive proof was offered by an article in the magazine *The Classic Motor Cycle* describing five A10s built as late as 1962 for the Shropshire Police, which though retaining a magneto, featured crankshaft-driven alternators. It could have been done. Once again, it would be folly to deny the necessity of at least the appearance of modernity and progress. Unit construction was also much cheaper in terms of machining and casting and by 1960 BSA needed something cheaper. But since the name of the game was still the vertical twin, and the A65 range shared much in common internally with the A10, progress should have incorporated the best features of the older model, in particular its bullet-proof bottom end.

It was true that the new twins, with their triplex primary drive chain and short stroke engines, were a purposeful response to demands from America for an unburstable mount of that sort, with short-track racing particularly in mind. But unfortunately, there was a serious flaw in the redesigned engine which could nullify those advantages after a comparatively low mileage under hard use. This was the drive side main bearing, which when it failed, savaged the crankcase before seizing the engine. Details will again be found in the Twins section, but though a solution had been developed, it was never implemented, and this fault, coupled with oil pumps made of inferior material and electrical problems, caused losses of hundreds of thousands of pounds' worth of warranty work. Dave Minton estimated that over 60 per cent of A65s received more than one guaranteed servicing. And in general as the power output of the Group's vertical twins increased, the problems became worse. As an example, by the beginning of the '70s warranty work was costing Meriden £40,000 a month.

The building of the A65 as a response to US demand comes as no surprise when it is found that automotive chief Edward Turner had it written into his contract that he was to spend six months of each year in the United States. As already mentioned, Turner and Sangster, first with Bill Johnson in Los Angeles and then with the Triumph Corpn of Baltimore, had been very instrumental in exploiting the US market for British bikes. While, as Hopwood says, Turner 'never got through on visits to BSA dealers, for whom he didn't feel responsible,' he undoubtedly did play a large part in shifting the emphasis of the Group's products to suit American markets. And for some years events were to vindicate and reinforce this direction. The US from the mid '50s on was a booming motor cycle market while the Group's home sales, by contrast, shrank dramatically from their 1960 peak. This contraction, which will be found discussed in the introduction to Volume One, was chiefly due to the availability of cheap cars through increasing affluence, to the fluctuations of government economic policy particularly as they resulted in a number of credit squeezes, and to the inroads of reliable and sophisticated Japanese light- and middleweights had made into the home market. As we have seen, since the war the Group had been export-oriented, and the number of countries they sold to was to increase, until by the end of the '60s it stood at no less than 288. By then, 90 per cent of their products were for export, with 70 per cent of that total going to the United States.

This trend had begun for BSA in 1945 when Alfred Childs had arrived unsolicited at Small Heath and secured 'the agency for the 48 states' from James Leek. By the '50s this had grown to a large, efficient dealer network divided between the Rich Child Cycle Corpn of New Jersey for the Eastern States, and the Hap Alzina Company in San Francisco for the west. At the beginning of the '50s a visit from Bert Hopwood, accompanied by Competition Manager Perrigo, led to meetings, or rather confrontations, with a number of dealers angry about spares and reliability problems. This resulted, as seemed customary with Hopwood, in prompt, positive action once he had seen for himself the scope and ruggedness of the terrain and the service problems this involved. As a direct consequence, the plunger A-range acquired a triplex primary drive chain and the Gold Stars got the necessary strengthening of gearbox and valves which allowed their participation in the 1954 Daytona 200 victory. Short-track racing was also a good showcase for BSA ruggedness, and the name established a strong following. So from the beginning of the 1960s, it was natural that the US, with its market for predominantly big capacity bikes, was the one to encourage, in order to extricate the company from the difficulties at home.

The man who was to preside over the exploitation of that market to the hilt arrived at the company early in 1960, the last major appointment made by Jack Sangster. This was Eric, not to be confused with Edward, Turner, who came from

Above *Bert Hopwood (right) and Perrigo returning on the* Queen Elizabeth *from a 1951 jaunt to the USA. News greeting them was the merger with Triumph.* **Below** *Two Turners, Edward (left) and Eric Turner who became chairman in 1961.*

the Blackburn group, just 42 years old and one of the first of the immigrants from the aircraft industry to BSA. He arrived as deputy chairman, was groomed as the new leader and took over the top post in June 1961, only a week after the celebrations for the centenary of BSA's formation, and with a record profit shown for the previous year, Sangster retired as chairman at 65, though he was to remain as a director until the end of the decade.

Eric Turner, a trained accountant, was a businessman pure and simple. He was ambitious, and as Ryerson points out, had no prior commitment to motor cycles, and failed to develop one over his period of office. Not necessarily a disaster, perhaps, for the chairman of a Group which then comprised over 30 companies covering a wide variety of activities. But it must be remembered that the motor cycle side represented an ever-increasing percentage of the Group's total business, having risen to 41 per cent in 1960, then dropping back to 25 per cent in 1963 due to a resurgence of machine and tool interests, but after that climbing consistently from 1964 to 1967, at which time, due to the sale of other interests, motor cycles and associated light engineering represented no less than 71 per cent of BSA Co Ltd's total Group turnover.

At first Edward Turner was the new chairman Eric's motor cycle mentor, a charismatic figure with the ever-growing profitability of Meriden to vindicate him. Triumph had exceeded all previous profits for 1959 and 1960, and 45 per cent of their products went for export. In line with the new US-oriented thinking, the BSA A50/A65s were duly launched at the beginning of 1962.

Later in that same year, Edward Turner launched another attempt to enter the lightweight market with the 75 cc BSA Beagle and a 50 cc version, the Ariel Pixie, as well as with the Triumph Tina automatic scooter he had designed. As Hopwood reveals, the Tina was the subject of a dealer launch earlier in the year before it had been properly prototype tested, 'ET' having got it past the board of directors without prior checks, despite large tooling costs and the construction of a new wing and a semi-automatic assembly line. Hopwood, who had returned to the Group as general manager at Triumph in May 1961, was left holding the baby as Turner departed for California—the day before the launch. Hopwood soon discovered serious design faults that resulted in frame bending, difficult starting and a jamming automatic transmission, and by the time he had sorted it out, the end of the large volume scooter market for them had come about and despite an expensive revamp of its appearance by the new chief executive Harry Sturgeon, the Tina was never a success.

The Beagle and the Pixie, for both of which Edward Turner personally had laid down the basic design of the engines (further Tiger Cub derivatives) and much of the cycle structure, were expensive bad jokes made all the more bitter by the fact that Turner, also personally, had vetoed a genuine Ariel lightweight project in favour of his own brain-children. It took him a while to find out about the rival project and development, in the fraught atmosphere of inter-factory fighting within the group, had been well-advanced by Ariel's Director, Ken Whistance, before any reference had been made to the parent Board, for reasons that by now should be obvious. The machine in question was a promising design, a 100 cc ohc machine with toothed rubber belt camshaft drive, and was one of a number of projects which might have saved the Ariel marque. However, they were all cut short, Ariel was moved to Small Heath in 1963 and the name effectively killed off two years later.

The Beagle and the Pixie failed to meet their production dates, and their motors were characterised by Hopwood as the results of 'Mickey Mouse engineering'. Costing the same as the infinitely superior Honda step-through equivalents then available, they were ridiculed by dealers, and when they did trickle through to the showrooms, caused so many problems that orders dried up, and both were withdrawn. This did nothing for BSA Group credibility, both with dealers and the public, in the face of the Japanese challenge, now highlighted by Honda's performance during these years in the Lightweight TT races. Indeed this costly and ignominious failure must have influenced the Group's decision to abandon this end of the market to the Orientals. Aside from the Ariel-3 (of which more later), the continuing sporadic development of the Bantam, available from 1958 as a 175 cc, and the 1965 move to Triumph Tiger Cub production from Meriden to Small Heath where the Cub would be married to Bantam cycle parts and rapidly expire, this was the end of the Group's effort in the light-weight field of endeavour.

Edward Turner at the beginning of the new decade had better reason than most to be aware of the gathering Japanese onslaught on the commuter and mid-range market. In 1960 he had visited Japan, toured the motor cycle factories there, and had seen 'the quality machine tool equipment, advanced techniques, scientific ability and keen commercial enterprise'. He knew about

Above *A dog. The Beagle, for 1964, an Edward Turner brainchild.*
Below *BSA technical author Arthur Lupton and designer Ernie Webster consider a sectioned Beagle engine with, perhaps, a hint of scepticism.*

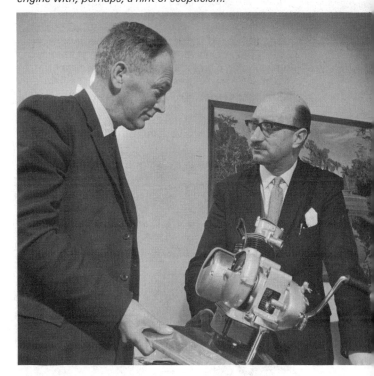

the half-million-and-rising new units a year that were then being produced, competitively priced and comprehensively equipped for a solid captive home market of 1.5 million (six times what was available in Britain). He also knew about the protective import tariffs. He knew that Honda alone were building nearly a quarter of a million units annually which amounted to more motor cycles than the whole of the British Industry put together, and he expressed this knowledge in an incisive report to the Board, though he admitted: 'answers are going to be hard to find'.

His tentative conclusion was that it might be necessary 'to have the courage to reduce our variety of manufacture so as to produce larger requirements for [a] single model.' This attitude appears to have hardened and to have been adopted by the decision-makers, and by the middle of the decade Turner was making self-congratulatory statements on how the proliferation of smaller Japanese machines was actually a benefit, as they introduced more youngsters to motor cycling who would then graduate to big British twins. Possibly he was simply rationalising, making the best of what he saw as inevitable; for at the base of his report was a philosophy of despair and a knowledge that 'the motor cycle industry has never been big business in Britain', 'never attracted big capital and enterprise', and that by comparison with the Japanese 'we have not now nor ever have had the quantities of any one product which would justify [the Japanese's] highly desirable methods being used'. His vision, while realistic, was inevitably influenced by the comparatively modest dimensions of the Triumph Engineering Co's success story. But even allowing, as he did, for Japanese low wages compared to the West, and for their generous government and private investment and

incentives, and even though events would seem to have proved him right, the wealth and scope and the experience and capabilities of the BSA Group, on whose board he sat—as well as those 288 export markets—permit one to imagine an alternative scenario. If different philosophies had been embraced, and above all if a long-term strategy involving new alternative products like the Ariel 100 cc and above all, like Hopwood's projected modular range, had been adopted, things could have been different.

As mentioned, Hopwood, with Hele following 18 months later, had returned to the Group during 1961, the former as director and general manager of Triumph, though with no seat on the board. He had given in to Edward Turner's request and consented to work with him again because Turner had confided that he was a sick man, suffering from diabetes (which incidentally, while it remained undetected, may well have accounted in part for his violent swings of mood), and that he intended to step down as chief executive shortly. In fact, he was to do so in 1964, though he remained on the board in an advisory capacity. In the meantime, Hopwood found much with which to busy himself. Though now resented as a Triumph man by Small Heath, he was able to help sort out the spares situation in Birmingham, which had deteriorated largely as a result of the management emphasis on machine production for export. He was shocked to find that Edward Turner and the board, while blaming the multiplicity of components necessary for a large range, felt themselves powerless to correct the situation. It was an early instance of the fatal lack of communication within the company.

He was also aware, despite the efforts of older stalwarts such as Bob Fearon, Small Heath's general manager, of a new and alarming factor. 'Bad quality,' he wrote, 'became a disease in most industries . . . bedevilling the product line at BSA in particular.' The process had begun in 1956, and this was now the '60s, a materialistic, acquisitive, hedonistic and easy-going decade. The attitudes of a money-oriented managerial class had permeated to the shop floor. BSA had become unionised during the '50s, but although no strikes had occurred, more active and militant trade unionists were not slow to point out that BSA's

Left *Spares, old style. The BSA Motorcycle Service Department in 1960. An average 50,000 components were despatched worldwide every day.*

Right *Production line. C15s leave the end of the line during the mid-'60s.*

post-war success had been built on low wages and on a workforce willing to make extraordinary efforts with worn and outdated machinery in a factory that was now a rabbit warren, but without a proper share in the profit that resulted from those efforts. The fact that, by the '60s, the Meriden men were earning up to half as much again as they were, did not help. To a new and more cynical generation appeals to the wartime values of pulling together rang increasingly hollow, and pride in craftsmanship and the BSA name were hard to sustain in the face of top management's palpable indifference to the product, with a range based largely on the C15 and the A65. As the decade progressed, large numbers of skilled men on the floor left. Fiddling became widespread, with very slightly imperfect components finding their way out of the factory for private re-sale. And the BSA reputation for reliability was eaten away.

Ryerson has a chilling example, revealed by a spot check, of a worker, who when he ran out of circlips, substituted a piece of bent wire for one to save time because, if the substitution had gone undetected, by the time the engine had seized it would have been too late to blame him. A friend of mine bought a new Bantam on which the timing slipped while the mileage was still in single figures. More than £80,000 of warranty work was carried out on the A65 before an electrical fault was traced and corrected. And with a fine irony, Doug Hele himself was thrown and cracked an ankle when he was running in a new Bantam for his son and it suddenly seized. It was all quite a contrast to the reliability demonstrated by those earlier Maudes Trophy wins.

Back at boardroom level, in 1964 when Edward Turner stepped down, chairman Eric Turner made what was at first sight not a very promising appointment. He chose Harry Sturgeon, another ex-aircraft industry man who, after leaving De Havilland, had moved to the BSA subsidiary of the Churchill Grinding Machine Company as managing director, and now came to the motor cycle side, not only as managing director but also with responsibility for the vacant post of marketing director, which was to prove his strong point. Hopwood, initially angry at the way in which existing and experienced BSA management talent was passed over for this post, canvassed the other divisional directors and with Charles Parker, financial director with Triumph, drafted a letter to chairman Eric Turner, protesting that the appointment should have been made from within the company. Eric Turner, angry himself, gave as his reason for bringing in an outsider the fact that appointing anyone of the existing staff would have made the others jealous. That does not seem, in retrospect, as if it would have presented an insuperable problem.

Earlier in 1964, Eric Turner's business orientation had led to the Board calling in McKinseys, the US Management Consultants. It was the beginning of what Hopwood was to call 'the age of the sophisticated organisation chart', and by his account the consultant's presence depressed the motor cycle division and, as time-and-motion men invariably will, damaged morale. Following the appointment of Sturgeon, the McKinsey recommendations were adopted and another restructuring of the management took place. BSA and Triumph were integrated into a single division, with a simple management structure and just four directorial posts. Sturgeon doubled up for two of them as already described, Hopwood was appointed deputy managing director and engineering director, and Charles Parker took over as division financial controller.

This meant that two out of the four were Triumph personnel, and left three former directors unplaced. Bob Fearon, the ex-BSA General Manager, chose early retirement. Bill Rawson the ex-BSA Sales Director, who could have been marketing director and coached a successor, was demoted from director to sales manager and retired shortly afterwards. And Ariel's Ken Whistance, a distinguished ex-competitor, whom Hopwood described as 'a ready-made divisional managing director', not only had his Selly Oak factory shot from under him in 1963, but now was relegated to BSA quality control manager, a post which, though as the above remarks indicate was highly necessary, he too quit shortly afterwards to become managing director of Concentric Steel Pressings. Hopwood himself, despite the deputy managing director tag, knew well that he was unacceptable to Eric Turner as a really top executive, for the latter had 'a firm non-acceptance of practising engineers' as he believed they lacked business gumption, and that 'the board looked on the motor cycle division as a cross to bear.'

And yet from these inauspicious beginnings a brief new golden age was inaugurated. Sturgeon, the new chief, may not have had one hundred per cent commitment to Small Heath and to motor cycles—he was a farmer as well as businessman, and Ryerson describes how he would retire to his Hertfordshire farm if the weather was favourable—and his attitude may have been to sell anything that was to hand, with its quality being

Harry Sturgeon (on right), supersalesman, seen here with William J. Ceder, President of West Coast's Johnson Motors Inc in 1965.

of secondary importance, but he did get things done and he was an outstanding salesman. As such he knew his market; it was he who let BSA know as early as 1964 that Honda were working on a 750–4, and who authorised work to continue and prototypes to be built of Hopwood and Hele's projected riposte, BSA-Triumph's last great bike, the 750 cc three-cylinder Rocket III/Trident. Sturgeon was a triple fanatic, and up to his tragically premature death early in 1967, work was progressing on a prototype three-cylinder 250 cc as well.

However, Sturgeon's real flair was for selling, and with the slump in the home market, this inevitably meant America. He understood the facts of life of the US market, where the bottom line was an inflexible selling season lasting just ten weeks from April to the middle of June. Virtually all US sales took place during this brief period so production had to be geared to it, with designs finalised and work on the following year's range beginning immediately the workforce returned from their annual holiday in August. By aiming clearly at the US market and spreading production more evenly, he helped increase production levels and sensibly worked for an integrated range of BSA and Triumph, but without too much badge engineering.

But one unobtrusive aspect of this process was thought to be extremely unfortunate by men in a position to know, such as Bert Perrigo. Under Sturgeon there was a merging of the BSA and Triumph sales reps, and in some cases dealerships. By deliberate policy since the pre-war days, communication between BSA dealers and reps had been exemplary, and quite good over at Triumph as well. In the USA competition between Triumph and BSA was understood and relished by all involved. Now the personal touch and the feeling that the reps would faithfully relay problems and complaints back to the specific home factory was gone for good.

However, profits soared, and Sturgeon's success had the added bonus of leading to Queen's Awards for Industry being given to both BSA and Triumph individually for 1965 and 1966. For between 1964 and 1966 the proportion of machines exported rose to 75 per cent, extra manpower was employed, and BSA-Triumph production increased by 40 per cent.

Cash flowed, and not just one way, for Sturgeon's success persuaded the board to release cash for modernising Small Heath to cope with the boom. From 1965, new equipment worth £750,000 was installed, including a new plating plant and in particular a computer-controlled car-

'The Most Modern Plant in Europe'—Small Heath's newly installed assembly tracks with loaded containers running alongside.

type assembly process. With the latter system, wheels, frames and engines were fed directly to the assembly tracks but all other parts converged on a marshalling stores, from where separate containers, one for all of each machine's parts, were carried down the tracks by overhead conveyors until removed and fitted. The computer, an ICT 1902 costing £100,000, issued data for the drawing and issue of parts by the stores, as well as for spares programming. Another new and useful installation was a rolling-road for testing new machines, thus sparing them from the ravages of English weather and cutting down on the numbers of machines returned from abroad due to deterioration in crate. All this made Small Heath the largest and most up-to-date

motor cycle factory in Europe, with a potential production capacity of 1,600 machines a week, over 80,000 a year, or one every 1.5 minutes of each working day.

However, it will be noted that what was not included was new production equipment, or re-tooling for new models. Indeed, the installation had taken place against the advice of the Group's own US consultants, McKinseys, who had advised the firm to wait until further growth before computerising. For as Ryerson points out, growth in a company carries its own problems, especially growth of this type, with returns restricted to a limited period, leaving 9 months virtually without income. The inevitable response to this for the growth-hungry and increasingly profligate Group was an increasing reliance on

Small Heath's answer to the computer from 2001 — A Space Odyssey — *the ICT 1902 computer room.*

bank loans from both British and American banks. This was to be the basis of the Group's demise, the fault apparently being their failure to restrain growth and keep it in line with their working capital, ie, the cash available from sales. In this the motor cycle side took their cue from the parent board, who had given themselves over to 'acquisition opportunities' in a large way, in accordance with a financial climate which saw big, quick money being made increasingly from asset-stripping and speculation, particularly property speculation, rather than investment in the production of manufactured goods.

The parent board, isolated from Small Heath by the structure Sangster had initiated, and now made up of accountants, financiers, merchant bankers and consultants, went at it with a will. For example, they had earlier acquired the unprofitable Churchill Grinding Machine Co. for £6 million (a sum which, as Hopwood observed, would have been sufficient to save the motor cycle industry). They let their own industrial engines be sold off to Villiers of Wolverhampton, only to see Villiers soon afterwards acquired by a company who were to become their rivals, Dennis Poore's Manganese Bronze Holdings. Probably their costliest deal was, as Bob Holliday describes is his BSA marque history, the sale in 1966 of the Group's entire Tools Division (including the aforementioned Churchill concern) to the Alfred Herbert Company, a deal which as Holliday wrote 'went sour because payment had been accepted in Herbert shares which when later turned into cash cost BSA several million pounds.'

In 1967 the steel-making subsidiary Jessop-Saville went to Firth-Brown and the J.S. Titanium business to Imperial Metal Industries, and it was deals of this kind which left the motor cycle side representing 70 per cent of total group turnover, just at the time when, after Sturgeon's death in April 1967, the parent board contained not one man who possessed the necessary specialist knowledge of or interest in motor cycles. From then on, as Holliday wrote, 'a series of acquisitions, disposals and mergers followed, linking BSA with such organisations as SMC Sterling Ltd., Tube Investments and the British Steel Corporation', with management 'preoccupied with diversifying the Group's operations' into 'central heating, sintered metal production and powdered-iron foundry work in fields that had nothing to do with motor cycles.'

But back in the Sturgeon years from 1964 to 1966, things had looked quite hopeful. One jewel in the Small Heath crown was the scrambles team which continued on its highly successful way

under the guidance of Brian Martin, who had become head of the Competition Shop in 1958. Martin had been one of the three Maudes Trophy ISDT riders back in 1952, and he remained an active member of the squad as well as a real leader. As Jeff Smith wrote, Brian 'recognised before anyone else that horsepower was not the answer in off-road racing, anticipated the lightweight two-strokes by three years and provided four-stroke machines that were 50 and 60 lb lighter than their rivals'. With just five men working under him on the scrambles side, he often got around fairly tight financial constraints by having work done for him quietly and unofficially by other department heads within the factory complex. The work benefited the roadster range, with the twins adopting the Jeff Smith-developed front fork for 1966. Martin's team was close knit and knowledgeable, and included Ken Sprayson at Reynolds Tubes who, consulted after earlier problems with breaking frames, was responsible for the oil-bearing Victor frame based on a 2¼ in diameter 18 gauge top-tube, and in 1964 and 1965 he was to see Smith on Victor Mk I and IIs take the World Motor-Cross championship. Sprayson was left to wonder, however, at the absence of professionalism in a major factory that would 'send (Smith) out with just a truckload to spares and then leave him to fend for himself (when) other factories' riders (were) surrounded by mechanics and helpers.'

As some felt happened with the Gold Stars, success had come despite, rather than because of the bosses, and the point was underlined in 1966 when top management, now eager for a hat-trick, decided to lend a hand. As Frank Melling described it in the magazine *Motor Cycle Mechanics*, 'the budget limit was cancelled and BSA's senior designers formed a committee . . . the committee's reasoning was simple . . . if a lightweight 440 cc won races, then an even lighter 500 cc would do the same job even better'. So they decided to 'build virtually the whole bike from titanium . . . 65% lighter than steel . . . and only 80 times more expensive!' Brian Martin was then given responsibility for turning the committee's drawings into metal and he went to Speedwell Gearcase, one of the few companies anywhere which had experience in working with titanium.

Speedwell immediately pointed out one of the major problems—they were being asked to make titanium copies of an oil-bearing steel frame. The exotic metal's different properties meant that the frame, rushed out with no time for testing, flexed badly, wallowed in corners and pitched over bumps, before eventually cracking at its welds.

The Most Modern Plant in Europe II — computer-controlled plating vats, with exhausts and silencers emerging.

Rocketing to stardom. 1965 A65 with mock launchertubes and James Bond Aston Martin DB5. A driveon part in Thunderball.

The BSA comp shop squad on production Victor Mk II scramblers with their bosses, Hawkstone Park, August 1965. Brian Martin (second from right) chats with Arthur Lampkin. Jeff Smith is third from left.

Jeff Smith takes off on the 1968 Victor scrambler. Who needs titanium?

Here the second major problem surfaced. Titanium's properties are such that all welding work on it must be carried out in a sealed chamber, and since one was not available in moto-cross paddocks, no running repairs were possible. Melling estimates the cost of this failure at around £120,000, a very large sum in 1966. Ironically even the weightsaving was rapidly overtaken since the 212 lb all-up weight of the titanium machine was followed by the 1969 Mk III Victor of just 224 lb. Indeed, when produced in steel the chassis was excellent and the 39.5 bhp 500 cc (84 × 90) engine with its good wide spread of power took Smith and others to further victories in 1969 and 1970, though not the World Championship.

But in 1965, as well as the scrambler's successes, the existing road models were all improved. This applied to the C15 and B40 singles in their electrical department (see Singles section) especially, and in 1967 the resulting B40 in a scrambler-derived frame, won bulk orders from the War Office to replace their ageing M20s. The all-conquering scramblers were able to yield an excellent roadster in the shape of the 1967-on 441 cc Victor. And from 1965 there was a choice of several powerful variants of the twins, most of which acquired twin carburettors and highly tuned engines, and shook off the stigma (or virtue) of being the flexible-but-workaday counterparts to their Triumph stablemates. Mike Hailwood's June 1965 victory on an A65 Lightning in the Hutchinson 100 production race at Silverstone nicely highlighted the change.

On a more fundamental level, Harry Sturgeon seemed capable of getting to grips with forward planning. As Hopwood says, he recognised the merit of the projected modular range and 'seemed to understand the urgency of the situation far more clearly than any of this Board colleagues'. He had also promised Hopwood that talented up-and-coming youngsters at Small Heath would be in line for more responsible positions. It was therefore all the more tragic when, early in 1966, illness removed him from work. He was to return briefly later in the year after convalescence, but his sickness turned out to be the result of a brain tumour, from which he died in April 1967.

His removal was a major blow, for the situation with regard to the model range was urgent. In the 250 cc class, increasingly important and profitable at home after learners had been restricted to it since 1960, the singles, while benefiting in 1966 from a stronger engine derived from the still-successful scramblers, for 1967 with further strengthening had their output and compression raised dramatically, with an equally spectacular fall-off in reliability from a soon clattering and oily because chronically overstressed engine. And the twins might now have a higher theoretical top speed, but they too vibrated and leaked oil; the unreliable crankshaft configuration and oil pump were still there also, and neither responded well to the stresses of steeper compression ratios and high revs. Though a pleasant enough all-rounder when they did hold together, as Dave Minton later wrote despairingly, 'Who could cruise *fast* on an A65 Spitfire?'. After one long-distance high-speed dice with some BMW-mounted Germans, the bike was 'a clanking ruin' and the shape of Minton's hands forced him to visit his doctor who diagnosed 'Wimpey fist', a common complaint

Right *'I'll give yer (Wimpey) fist.'*
Super vibrator. 650 Spitfire Mk II of
1966.

650 Spitfire Mk II Special Model A65SS

Below right *Hype. Tony Newley
and Lucille Ball chose a twin carb
A65 Lightning outfit for personal
transportation.*

among road-drill operators, caused by inflamed
tendons due to excessive vibration.

In the US however, the BSA twins were still
valued for their excellent low-down torque for dirt-
track racing. And when Hunter S. Thompson,
journalist and chronicler of the California Hell's
Angels in the book of that name, needed a
machine to run with the outlaws but didn't feel
committed enough for one of their Harley
Sportsters, he chose not the Triumph twin that
Marlon Brando had ridden in the original biker
movie, *The Wild One*, but a BSA A65 Lightning
Rocket. It was a decision in which both the
Lightning's speed and power, and a certain
raunchiness of image for the Angles' benefit,
must have played a part. For Stateside bikers the
big BSAs had a reputation as potentially 'strong
runners' for long, lazy cruising, and it was from
that side of the pond that one of the problems
with the bike was sorted. This was piston seizure
primarily due to a 'rogue' spark which roved and
re-ignited, causing over-heating and eventual
seizure. Peter Colman, the BSA Technical
Director in the USA, was the one to pinpoint the
problem, and a service bulletin was sent round to
the dealers with the details of a new contact-
breaker cam designed to overcome it. More use of
American feedback could have been very
beneficial.

But instead American influence of a different
sort was to guide the company's direction. Early in
1966, with Sturgeon off sick, Eric Turner returned
from a visit to the States. He had formed various
impressions from his contacts with dealers there,
with whom relations had improved during
Sturgeon's reign. And apparently on the basis of

these impressions, he made several choices which decisively influenced the company's direction until its eventual crash. In a report he made following his return, he confirmed that US prospects were good, but saw the financial problems inherent in the 10-week market. To exploit the market properly he emphasised the importance of the 350 cc class, a genuinely strong seller in the States at that time, over both 500 and 250 cc classes. The 250s he felt could be coped with by a simple, hot, single; he rejected the 250 cc triple which Hopwood was designing, on the grounds of cost and development time, and went ahead with the already-mentioned 1967 C15-derived C25/B25s, for which he saw a potential US sales figure of 16,000 per annum.

The 350 cc market on the other hand he read as potentially far more lucrative, with an initial 15–20,000 sales rising to a possible 30–50,000 per annum. This was the basis of his decision to commission Edward Turner in a freelance design capacity to begin work on what would be the BSA Fury/Triumph Bandit dohc twin, though the dealers had wanted a triple. Since Hopwood's 250 cc triple was already underway, and it is hard to believe that it could not have been enlarged to a 350, and since Turner's 350 following heavy modification was only to appear after five years and massive tooling costs, the 'delay and expense' factors cited for dropping Hopwood's design seem difficult to justify.

Another piece of feedback from the sales

Above *Strong runners for good ol' boys? Not quite — these are BSA and Triumph triples in dirt track trim at Santa Rose National 1970. It was the twins which did best on the dirt.*

Left *Yankee doodle Brit. US-styled A50 Royal Star for 1969 — high bars, small tank, skimpy mudguarding 'only fit for cowboys and short trips in the sunshine', they snorted, north of Watford.*

outlets was the demand for machines with overhead camshaft engines such as the Japanese were then producing. This led to development staff being ordered to stop working on the 750 cc triple and start a conversion of the A65 engine to the ohc configuration. In a recent piece in *Motor Cycle Weekly* Bob Currie quoted Les Mason, later of BSA twin's specialist Devimead, but at that time working in the Small Heath drawing office. Mason says they dubbed the engine that emerged 'the Rabbit' because of the long 'ears' sticking up from the timing case which were needed to carry the ohc chain drives. 'It was a right hotch-potch . . . it never did get made and after nine wasted months we were to drop everything and finish off the three-cylinder'. As Currie pointed out, the wasted time could well have cut down the lead gained by the triple's rival, the Honda 750–4, which in the event was to appear just after the triple did, and ate into its market before it had had time to become established.

But back in 1966, with figures to show that BSA-Triumph dollar earnings for 1965–6 exceeded those of any single British car firm, America was the promised land and the US tail wagged the Birmingham dog. As a result, for 1966 the USA and home motor cycle ranges were merged, to the accompaniment of an announce-ment that 'integration such as this permits longer production runs and avoids temporary hold-ups which changes in specification, to suit various markets, can bring'. The shadow of the ICT 1902 was looming. In the event it was not so much a merging as a take-over by US specifications. Grab-rails and side-reflectors were harmless innovations but now fully enclosed rear chains were out, and in came chrome mudguards, truncated and ineffective, high and wide bars impractical at speed, low gearing and, increasingly, minimal-sized petrol tanks. In no time, the range was under attack in Britain as 'only fit for cowboys and short trips in the sunshine'. As we shall see, with regard to delays, the new computer-controlled methods were to do more harm than good. And despite the fizzing trendiness of the late '60s, ignoring the European markets and the enthusiasts' practical requirements, was also to prove a mistake in the light of some surprising facts on sales trends which were to emerge shortly afterwards.

However, at the time the pursuit of the buck was paramount, and to this end BSA-Triumph also began planning to take over their own stateside distribution from BSA Inc at Nutley, New Jersey in the East and from Hap Alzina, the man who over two decades had done so much

for British motor cycles on the West Coast. The Group already owned the Triumph Corps of Baltimore, Bill Johnson's Triumph L.A., and BSA Inc. And they went on to buy out Hap Alzina, who retired in 1968, to form BSA Inc USA and administer it themselves under US management. The new operation comprised 1,600 outlets, against the Japanese who already were present in force with Honda controlling 2,000. The experienced expatriate Dennis McCormack, head of Triumph Baltimore since its foundation in 1951, was passed over, and the presidency of the new company went to Peter Thornton. The whole operation was set up in a lavish new headquarters in Verona, New Jersey. There was much sloganising — 'The Power of British Engineering, the Glory of American Styling' — but on the ground the dealers were struggling with a lack of new models, quality problems, and the fact that the 1968 selling season had been missed.

At the time, this fact, which represented a watershed in the company's fortunes, was blamed on the upheavals due to computerisation. But in fact there had been many other factors, and most of them can be summarised as being the result of the New Breed. Their leader was the new managing director of the Group Motor cycle Division, Lionel Jofeh, of whose forthcoming appointment Eric Turner had informed Bert Hopwood late in 1966. At this point Ryerson says Hopwood 'preferred to bide his time'; but as only those involved would have known prior to the publication of Hopwood's memoirs, in fact he immediately resigned in disgust, exasperated by the incursion of yet another aircraft-oriented outsider to the industry (Jofeh had been Chairman and Managing Director of the Sperry Gyroscope Co.), and by the passing over of experienced personnel such as himself, his co-director Charles Parker and the Small Heath works manager, Al Cave. Eric Turner tried to persuade him to stay, and told him that he was indispensable. However, the deciding factor, as far as Hopwood was concerned, was that there were several years to run until his contract expired, and his solicitor had advised him not to break it.

There may be an element of hindsight in what follows, but Hopwood's account has proved trustworthy in other respects, and of his initial encounter with Jofeh, he has this to say: 'From my first meeting with our new managing director I had some doubts as to our prospects.' Jofeh, he says, made it no secret that he knew all the answers and felt himself word perfect at an early stage in a strange industry. Ryerson quotes other colleagues who characterised Jofeh as 'vain, and

Face of the future. Lionel Jofeh, new BSA managing director for 1967.

cold; a man who wouldn't listen, who worked everything out on a slide-rule by himself.' To try and be fair, Hopwood himself speaks prior to Jofeh's arrival of 'two or three complacent top executives who preached the futility of taking on the Japanese'. Jofeh was hired in part as a new broom to sweep away that attitude, and by 1967 he was badly needed at BSA. Not only were the Japanese rising meteorically, but only a short time after the expensive installation of computers, the profits from the 1967 selling season, a £½ million growth in turnover, were neatly and completely consumed by the effects of the economic restrictions of a UK credit squeeze. Home sales were running at half the previous year's levels, and there were cuts in the Small Heath workforce, with 110 men being asked to accept voluntary redundancy.

Jofeh and his managerial team were not dismayed. Indeed, soon afterwards one of them told Jeff Smith, after he had presented a comparison report rating the 250 cc C25 Barracuda unfavourably against the Suzuki 6, that 'We have the Japs beaten for performance, quality and price, and next year we shall butcher them in the market-place!'. The New Breed regarded themselves, in Hopwood's words, as 'some sort of academic mission into the primitive backwoods of two-wheeled philosophy.' By July 1967 the sales staff had been reorganised, and despite the year's setbacks money seemed to be no object. Jofeh's bearers for this mission were more accountants, a bigger marketing team, more management consultants and a fresh round of market researchers. The latter forecast a slump in US demand for motor cycles. Production was to some extent adjusted accordingly, and when the opposite happened this was one cause of the missed 1968 season. In fact there was a boom, especially in the major Group market, the larger capacities. By 1969 motor cycle imports into America totalled 638,763 machines, and from 1970 to 1971 this figure had increased to over one million — however by that time 85 per cent of bikes sold were Japanese.

What now followed Jofeh's February 1967 arrival at Small Heath resembled a silent Charlie Chaplin film, with Charlie struggling with increasing frenzy to master the inexorable cogs of some infernal machine that grinds on faster and faster, regardless of his desperation. More and more high level, high salary jobs with cars were created. Meetings, including those at which decisions were to be made, grew bigger and eventually so large that only the BSA showroom at the end of Armoury Road was big enough to hold them, and inevitably in such conditions, few decisions were made. 'We were re-organised, co-ordinated, charted and "paperised" to such a degree that our offices simply were not big enough,' Hopwood recalls. Paperwork grew to such a scale that reading it was impossible. Some of it took the form of 'handsome textbooks with which we were issued and from which we gathered we were all now one big happy family'.

This was somewhat ironic, as under Jofeh, the BSA-Triumph balance once more swung the other way and the boot was on the other foot and determinedly thrust into Triumph's face. Harry Sturgeon had once again stimulated some road-racing effort there, and in 1966 and 1967 500 cc Triumphs won at Daytona. 'Jofeh literally hated the Triumph successes,' said designer Doug Hele, Jofeh's bitterness presumably increased by the fact that BSA had also unsuccessfully contested both events. Both Jofeh and Eric Turner openly advocated badge engineering, and the former 'seemed quite determined to make Triumph the underdog,' wrote Hopwood. He recounts how on one occasion, Jofeh, in a speech to the Meriden workforce made it clear that 'any person found promoting or favouring, in any way, the Triumph brand of racing machinery . . . would "get his cards".' The year was 1970 when the Tridents and Rocket III triples were teamed together, and the fact that the occasion at which the threat was delivered was the works Christmas lunch gives some indication of the new managing director's unique way with people.

Hopwood was appalled by what was developing and angry at how the late Harry Sturgeon's promises about the promotion of BSA's own young talent had been broken by the introduction of more aircraft executives. He was also anxious to defend the island of sanity he and Hele had established in the development department of Meriden and which had led by the late '60s to the truly legendary years of the 650 cc Bonneville and the 500 cc Daytona twins and to most of the development of the 750 triple. There can be little doubt that the tactics involved were occasionally rough, for the fate of the Ariel works and marque was a recent enough memory to mean both sides felt that not just their projects but their survival might be at stake. Clive Stokes, ex-NVT experimental department engineer, was to speak of 'Triumph's policy of destruction and board room sabotage'. Certainly Hopwood talks of putting his point of view forcefully to Jofeh at every possible occasion, which with Hopwood still general manager at Meriden, can't have helped the BSA-Triumph situation.

Expense and delay were the keywords of the period. Jofeh's mission control was the Research and Development Centre at Umberslade Hall, purchased by Eric Turner in 1967. In a sense this was both the realisation and the perversion of one of Hopwood's convictions. From his experience of being wrenched off plans for new product to deal with the latest crisis on the line, he felt sure that forward product design should be a separate function removed from the day to day activities of the factory. This Umberslade appeared to achieve by removing the design and development staff from all three factories. But as so often seems to happen in cases where bureaucrats' dreams of centralisation are indulged (witness the merging of county councils, or the DVLC at Swansea), an apparent economy measure proved extremely expensive. The hall was a handsome country house with parklands and peacocks on the lawn, situated near Henley-in-Arden and Solihull, midway between the Meriden, Small Heath and Redditch factories. But the building conversion necessary was not fully completed until the end of 1968, and thereafter the establishment was run with a staff of 300 at an estimated cost of around £1,500,000 a year.

As already mentioned, it didn't put a stop to inter-factory rivalry, and in addition to this, the competition staffs of the various factories stayed

Peacocks on the lawn, but winter is coming. Umberslade Hall, BSA R & D centre, early in 1969.

where they were, which explains how the racing versions of the 750 triples came to have their frames designed not at Umberslade, but by the small independent frame builder, Rob North. This was a Triumph initiative. No road racing department had been set up at Small Heath in 1967, and in October, ex-racer Alan Shepherd, who had been there for over a year, quit, talking of management refusal to follow his suggestions for making the big twins more competitive. Though there was some factory support in 1968, it was sporadic and far from whole-hearted. Paul Smart was hired to contest the production TT and the race chief was Tony Smith, who raced a lightened and polished stock B40 in a scrambles frame which was justified as part of the scrambles programme as well as 650s. He was responsible for a lot of development work on the twins, and on a Spitfire he was to take third place in the 1968 750 cc class of the Production TT. But in August 1969 the contractions of finance were to leave him without a works machine, and he stopped riding his own BSA machines in favour of Yamahas, as the BSAs were prepared by others and as he put it: 'silly things happened', such as the time when his fairing dropped off on to the front wheel at 130 mph. In April 1970 BSA temporarily pulled out of British production racing to concentrate, as we shall see, on the US.

Above *BSA race chief Tony Smith's personal B40 racer, 1967.*
Below *Trials Bantam might-have-been. Bushman in feet-up trim prepared by the dealers Comerfords in 1967.*

In fact BSA's only other sporting effort by the end of 1967 was the scrambles team, as the factory trials support had ceased in October and the works riders been let go, despite a 175 cc Bantam's creditable second place in the Scottish that year. Although the sale of trials irons in kit-form had eaten into the market for these machines, BSA's decision was much criticised at a time when British-type trials were catching on in the States and where trail bike sales were already booming. For a minimal outlay on trials, prestige could have been gained and useful development for trail machines carried out. It was an early evidence of the lack of specialist knowledge at management level. As well as the trials effort, the sale of the highly successful Victor Mk II 441 cc scrambler was halted at the same time, and when racing ace Giacomo Agostini wanted to buy one in November he was unable to do so. Though the roadster Victor and a US-oriented export-only Enduro version were still sold, and the factory effort and successes continued, they were conceding victory in the battle for over-the-counter superiority to the foreign two-stroke CZ and Husqvarnas, despite the BSA's competitive price, and the development work being carried out by Cheney, Heanes, Winwood and others to successfully keep the Victor in the picture. In November another nail was hammered into the four-stroke coffin by sales manager John Hickson who refused to supply any further engines to specials builders and in particular to Rickman, whose lightweight Victor-engined Metisse enduros were seen as a sales competitor to BSA's own Enduro. With the scramblers, presumably the intention was to replace the Victor 441 cc with the upcoming 500 cc works model, but a production version of this did not become available until 1971. So while Jeff Smith and his team-mates were to keep the BSA name prominent, no sales benefit could be derived from their successes. The reasons for these cuts were undoubtedly a combination of the first financial pinch of 1967, and the prevailing philosophy of slimming down the range. However in the light of the continuing production of the roadster Victor and the lavish expenditure in other directions, these appear to have been false economies.

When it came to the appointment of a director and chief engineer for Umberslade Hall, yet again experienced men in the company were passed over. One, George Todd, the two-stroke expert, after being appointed deputy development manager, resigned in July 1967 to set up his own renowned Bantam-tuning outfit. Doug Hele would have been another choice, but in the event in 1968 the appointment went to Mike Nedham, who came to the Group from Rolls Royce Aero Division, but was not without motor cycling roots. He worked at the Scott factory in Shipley in the 1930s, had been a regular scrambler, and organised grass-track events.

This at least was a healthy sign, for many of the New Breed not only lacked experience of the motor cycle industry, but also disliked and even despised the machines they were responsible for producing and selling. The most telling anecdote on this theme is recounted by Ryerson, and concerns Wilf Harrison, a lifetime BSA man and motor cyclist, who since 1950 had worked his way up from the Service Department until in 1966 he wa appointed export manager, which permitted him to take his meals in the Senior Management Dining Room. He used to ride his bike to work, and one day arrived at the factory, climbed off, went straight in for a meal, and was seen to do so by Lionel Jofeh. Later he was summoned and told by Jofeh: 'I would rather you didn't come to the Senior Management Dining Room in motor cycle attire'. This from the managing director of the BSA Motor Cycles Division. Possibly it was old-fashioned but practical riding gear which gave offence, for in 1969 BSA announced the marketing of 'stylish colourful riding kit in collaboration with a leading fashion designer'.

But motor cycle man though he may have been, Mike Nedham's work was hamstrung by the way Umberslade was organised with, as Hopwood puts it, 'design and development personnel scattered in a bureaucracy which was quite unmanageable', with 'creative design being carried out with low levels of experience and expertise', and a Department of Technical Services which he characterised as 'a free-ranging discussion group' producing no results. It was this absence of tangible results as the years passed which led to Umberslade being tagged Slumberglades. In a 1969 interview Nedham himself described his and the establishment's concern as 'measuring experiments accurately . . . using computer-aided design methods . . . understanding the fundamentals of stability . . . [and] building up an accurate bank of knowledge to help future design.' When queried on whether aeroengineering was a suitable background from which to come to the motor cycle industry, Nedham replied that 'in the effective relating of engineering to manufacturing and marketing', they were the same in principle. In principle perhaps, but in practice the time-scale for producing new aircraft models was at least double that for new motor cycles. Hopwood, who had

completely redesigned the early A7 twin into the A10 in three weeks and seen prototypes built and tested, problems ironed out and production start in November of the same year, now had to watch as his and Hele's current hope, five years after its conception, was still further delayed by Umberslade.

This was the 750 cc triple, 'by now being minced about by huge committees, becoming a target for testing their skills' as Hopwood put it. The styling of both BSA and Triumph models was transformed, and one remembers the first impression of the triple, particularly the BSA, causing some puzzlement, with contradictions between the cow-horn bars, futuristic ray-gun silencers and the tilted engine, set against the slab-sided tank and rather substantial side-panels and the front hub which seemed so large in the current BSA forks. It was, as they say, neither mickling nor muckling. In consequence, it was late in 1968 before the first triples were released in the United States, and despite in near-standard form setting several records at Daytona (though with no race wins) in early 1969, they had no time to carve out a niche for themselves before the arrival for the '69 selling season of Honda's ohc 750-4, with the fifth gear, disc brake, reliable switchgear and electric starting that the triples still lacked. The presence of the hot 500 cc Kawasaki Mach-III triple didn't help either. Even on their own considerable merits the triples did not sell as well as expected, and as Hopwood points out, only began to do so after 1971 when the Trident was restyled to resemble a more conventional Triumph. Hele and Hopwood's prototypes had been styled that way before Umberslade took over.

By the beginning of 1969 sales success for the triple was badly needed. Not only was this the first new model from BSA for nearly seven years, but 1968 had been a disaster. Initially the expansion embodied by the foundation of Umberslade and of BSA Inc USA, and the New Breed's big plans, had inspired confidence. Group shares rose from £1.20 to £2.35. But then the 1968 selling season had been substantially lost. Overall profits dropped to £2,058,957 after tax, partly due to stocks brought back from America and sold at a discount, causing losses of £729,000 (though during 1967 the pound had been devalued and this, by affecting dollar earnings, reduced the loss to £403,151). The main reasons, namely, the on-going chaos situation at the factory, should be emerging by now but in addition, a large part was played by the computer. As Ryerson points out, it was only as good as the men who programmed it, and their lack of organisation drastically affected supplies of both complete machines and of spares.

For, as Hopwood explains, in previous days there had been a comparatively simple and flexible system of incorporating modifications into the flow of production, with the whole production unit as well as the engineering director being alerted immediately modifications were decided on, thus avoiding over-stocking of parts, delays and obsolescence. However, with the coming of the New Breed, 'Value Engineering' was the in-phrase, and in practical terms this meant that changes were the responsibility of a committee numbering some 20 people, the majority of whom were out of touch with the production side. As Hopwood explains, the engine modification system 'broke down entirely . . . [and] ceased to function'. The computer itself was not infallible and caused one of the few strikes at Small Heath by failing to produce the wages on time. For an example of 'Value Engineering', one need look no further than the way in which the 1969 range included a partial changeover from BSF and CE1 thread forms to Unified Thread on all bolts, studs and components, as had been done for the Rocket III. This was long overdue—on the 1960 C15, for instance, there had been no less than six different thread-forms. However, the way in which it was carried out defeated the object. Although started in 1969, the changeover was never fully completed, with the result that replacing nuts and bolts on A65s can still yield irritating uncatalogued surprises. Ordering spares under those circumstances must have been a nightmare for dealers.

Hopwood further asserts that 'the computerised recording system in the spares department' was so unreliable as to be useless,

and that as a consequence, dealers bedevilled by unreliable machines were now also unable to obtain spares for them, or only the wrong spares. An especially bad state of affairs when one considers that spares are the most profitable side of any vehicle industry. As a consequence, 'pirate' or 'pattern' spares proliferated to fill the gap. The vast majority of these were inferior to the factory items and of course they brought no income to the company, so both cash-flow and reputation suffered further.

Another big bite was taken out of the Group's earnings as a direct result of the new organisation in the United States. As will be recalled, the new BSA Inc USA was BSA-owned, and administered by the company itself under US management. Unfortunately for them, as Dave Minton points out, this meant that after-sales service and guarantee claims were now billed direct to BSA in Britain. With the current standard of Group reliability (remember Minton's estimate of 60 per cent of A65s receiving more than one guaranteed servicing) it was very costly. Combined with the stocks discounted or returned, this meant that of just over £2 million profit, £1,018,267 was not from America at all but from the UK and other markets. So with 70 per cent of production going to America, and less than two years after the merging of the ranges, the decision to concentrate on the States was beginning to cause problems. More were to follow.

The results of what Eric Turner at the 1968 AGM admitted were 'disappointing' figures and 'an expectedly frustrating year' were not long coming. BSA shares in 1969 slumped spectacularly from a £2.35 high to a mere 30p (though the Alfred Herbert share fiasco mentioned earlier had a large hand in this). The tooling-up for the 750 triple, the expense of Umberslade, the drop in profits from America due to both the new organisation and the fall in bike sales (the 1969 season had been partially missed, and Japanese

Spaceship, or Brumagem dray? 1969 Rocket III, with styling 'minced about by huge committees' at Umberslade.

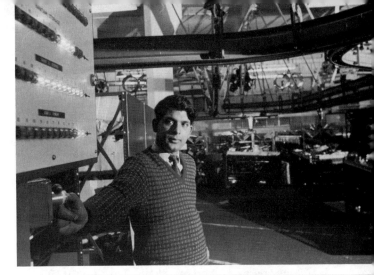

Right *Most Modern Plant in Europe III. Containers recalled from assembly to the marshalling stores were on tracks, but the system went off the rails.*
Below right *The picture that says it all. 1968, and a unit single sinks emblematically into the quicksands, along with the company. Even the model is disappearing, and the dog's called it a day.*

output that year leapt to 3 million) — all these were factors, as were wages. Not just the New Breed's salaries, but those of the men on the Small Heath shop-floor, which was looking sideways at Meriden. There the workforce, encouraged by Harry Sturgeon's reckless open-handedness in the days of the export boom (which will be dealt with in the Triumph section of a later volume) and by the trade union militancy of the Coventry area (Dennis Poore was later to speak of 'the notorious electricians of Chrysler' much as the Pope might regard a marauding band of incubi) had resulted, as Hopwood writes, in 'the Triumph wage structure [being taken] way out and beyond the very high Coventry wage rate'.

With all these factors now at work, the situation deteriorated rapidly. Despite only a small drop in turnover, profits for 1969 fell dramatically to just £588,501, and on July 30 1969 Jofeh was forced to announce 30 per cent redundancies at Small Heath which involved a total of 1,100 men leaving the company. He attributed this to a credit squeeze in the USA which meant that US dealers had run down their stocks, though he claimed retail sales were higher for the first six months of the year than the equivalent figures for 1968. When the drop in profits was announced, Eric Turner blamed high interest rates both in Britain and the States, increased manufacturing costs, and foreign competition. He also blamed the weather.

The New Breed were running scared by now, and their panic produced some bizarre manifestations. Moto-cross champion Jeff Smith, returning from a lecture tour of America, reported that one complaint he had heard concerned BSA oil leaks. According to Smith, he was promptly 'bawled at by one of the managers that, "our engines do not leak and cannot leak because the finish is too good" and that "something happens to them on the Atlantic"'! In fact, work was in hand to improve oil tightness and reliability of the models, especially the BSA twins. Some of this involved adopting Triumph components such as the internals of the front fork and the clutch thrust-rod for the twins, and some, like the replacement of the notoriously weak oil pump with a race-proved item, represented good sense.

But the twin's cylinder-block modifications, and work on machining the flywheel and crankshaft, and strengthening the con-rods, were expensive in the extreme, failed to cure the principal problem of vibration and came too late to revive the fortunes of the A-range which was suffering badly by comparison with the near-perfected Bonneville and Norton's Commando, let alone the Japanese.

There was a reason for the work, though. For chairman Eric Turner had decided, and the decision was formally taken early in 1969, to launch a 'new range' of machines. However, Hopwood's genuinely revolutionary modular range had not been considered a serious possibility, at the level where decisions were made, since Harry Sturgeon's death, even if the Group's economic straits had allowed it. Turner's range was to consist of new cycle-parts only and really comprised various versions of the B25 and A65 range machines fitted into new frames and forks. They had to do something, and the 'Glory of American Styling' plus strengthened engines was one way to go.

However, there was an exception, one genuinely new model. Following his return from America early in 1966, it will be recalled that the chairman had commissioned Edward Turner to produce an ohc 350. Though working on the project in a freelance capacity, Edward Turner, as Hopwood reveals, also had the help of several of designers who had been loaned to him. By 1968 he had come up with a 350 cc four-stroke parallel twin with a 180° crank-throw, a design which was notable for its lightness, and incorporated ohc drive by a train of gears — but which in Hopwood's view 'ignored many engineering fundamentals and was very unreliable'. Meriden's designer Brian Jones confirms this. 'The engine and gearbox centres were too close together so there was not enough volume in the crankcases, and therefore the oil couldn't drain down and the temperature ran very high.' And according to another ex-Triumph man, Les Williams, one reason for this, ironically in view of the BSA-Group's current profligacy, lay in Turner's old-fashioned cost-consciousness which had been a prime ingredient of Triumph's success. Turner's 350, says Williams, was 'definitely built down to a price', and was 'just too spindly' for a 350.

Unwisely, however, Jofeh had previewed a prototype to several American dealers, who were now eager for a machine in this small but popular capacity. Hopwood was accordingly asked to put it into production but refused, because in his view the design and development personnel whom he needed to do so were scattered hopelessly in an unwieldy bureaucracy, and also because with over 30 years experience of working with Edward Turner, he knew whoever went to work on it would be accused of delaying and altering a sound design. When Hopwood eventually agreed to help, his suspicions were confirmed with Edward Turner raging in a widely-circulated letter that 'Hopwood would delay production for one or two years if I know my man'. This was in 1968, and production was in fact delayed, because when in October of that year Hopwood ordered the tests which he considered necessary, they rapidly resulted in two crankshaft breakages and a failure of the valve-drive gears within 1,500 miles, an engine that used four pints of oil in 100 miles

and had to be rebuilt four times in 2,400, with frame and forks that were 'positively dangerous'. Hopwood goes on to describe a skimped crankshaft with unduly small flywheels and gearing that was unreliable and noisy. He later wrote, 'a complete redesign was necessary which had little in common with the original' — though this design is usually described as Edward Turner's swan-song.

Whether the redesign was completely satisfactory is also debatable. It featured final drive on the right, and chain-drive to the camshafts at a right-angle which Bob Currie described as awkward, and which a brief road-test confirmed was still noisy. The cycle parts however were excellent, being the forks and brakes from the new range and a splayed twin down-tube frame which earned high praise as part of a prototype housing a 500 cc Triumph twin. Despite numerous hurried or awkward features — these can be found fully described in the chapter devoted to the Bandit/Fury in Roy Bacon's *BSA Twins and Triples* — with the benefit of five gears and an optional electric starter, the little bike, as Bacon writes, was felt to have tremendous potential.

Of the 13 models which were displayed at the BSA 1971-range launch, there was one other all-new design, though it had already hit the streets in June 1970. This was the Ariel-3, a sort of moped tricycle powered by a bought-in Dutch Ankha engine. It has since become a sort of legendary joke, and it is as well to note, as Minton points out, that the idea, aimed at commuters and shoppers, was offered by its designer to other factories including Raleigh and Honda, and that BSA actually had to bid to get it. However, it was taken seriously enough, and not just at Small Heath. It's also instructive that after three years' stagnation there was a flood of buyers for the trike in the summer of 1973 when the Arabs first stepped on the oil pipeline and that Honda have produced their own version in the '80s.

A market did clearly exist, but one thing, simple as it may seem, had been bodged. Hopwood confirms that a consultant named Donald Barstow had pointed out a fundamental fault in the trike's basic geometry which caused riding instability. Unfortunately, this did not make itself evident at the maximum speeds at which the official testers ran it, but at the 25–30 mph cruising speeds at which its intended users would potter along. It was in this range that it was prone to wobbling and also engine seizure. It was also, in Hopwood's opinion, a victim of Umberslade Hall's stylists. As released it was certainly a bizarre conveyance

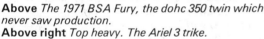

Above *The 1971 BSA Fury, the dohc 350 twin which never saw production.*
Above right *Top heavy. The Ariel 3 trike.*

with its rider seated in splendid isolation on a section which could bank into bends, while the two-wheeled rear part stayed put. It did not sell, and the failure was a costly one. Minton speaks of a total order for 30,000 of the Dutch engines which sold complete on the Continent for £12 and states that only 10,000 trikes were delivered to dealers, whose attitude, in view of the vehicle's oddity and of BSA's current reputation and past lightweight failures, was lukewarm. Minton reckons at least 20,000 of the engines were sold off at knock-down prices, Ryerson puts the figure at 50,000, and where Minton estimated the costs and eventual losses at about £½ million, the true estimate is probably closer to £1 million. The vehicle was produced in the period 1969–70 when the company's total profit, it will be remembered, was only just over £½ million.

During 1969 share prices had wavered upwards to 50p. The main effort continued to be the new range, which was Umberslade's responsibility, and by late 1969 Jofeh was worried enough about

the way the design centre was being run to swallow his pride and ask Hopwood to install himself at Umberslade and straighten out the situation there. For Hopwood had been confining himself to his office at Meriden since late 1968, as Jofeh's habit of continually by-passing him by direct instructions to his subordinates had led to as he put it, 'such violent differences between the managing director and myself that I found it most difficult to continue'. He had also washed his hands of the design and development centre. In the meantime, several of the boffins at Umberslade had been exploring in many interesting directions. AMC's Jack Williams, the racing singles wizard, was at work there for a while, design work on a Wankel engine continued and there was collaboration on a 250 cc water-cooled two-stroke twin created by an engineering team under Dr Gordon Blair with the aid of a computer at Queen's University, Belfast.

But when Hopwood reluctantly agreed to look into the situation at Umberslade at the end of 1969, he reported 'poor organisation and poor manpower', and quickly got to the nitty-gritty. He said that if there was no change, and quickly, 'our 1971 model year will be a disaster . . . Never have

I personally experienced such a mass production release of parts for new models, many of which have not been given an assembly check, let alone any sort of test'. He urged reorganisation into 'teams, each one nursing a product to the production stage', with experienced men in charge. After he had made his report, he, Nedham and Jofeh met, and the two seemed to agree to his proposals. But when nothing had been done by January 1970, Hopwood resigned, sickened by the fact that after nearly three years and with 300 staff, BSA was to come up with such a nondescript 'tarted' range as he put it. He still feels this was what really broke the company. He relinquished his executive role but remained available for part-time consultancy and 'to assist the racing effort'.

As far as racing was concerned, the idea was to concentrate on America, and was a matter of some urgency, as management had only given the go-ahead for participation at the February 1970 Daytona 200 race three months before the event. Despite the short amount of time allowed for the design, manufacture and shipping of the racers to America, the year was to be a triumphant vindication for the speed and strength of the triples. Housed in Rob North duplex loop triangular frames with triangular forks, five-speed Quaife gearboxes but with engines near to standard, bar fine tuning of camshafts, pistons and carburettors, the BSAs and Triumphs were piloted by American aces including Gene Romero and Dick Mann, and British past master Mike Hailwood. Though a Honda 750-4 won, Romero took second place at Daytona, and a string of wins from then on gave BSA/Triumph the first five places in the American racing championship series for that year. The wailing triples represented a spectacular come-back for the long-discounted British as a force in road-racing.

Sadly, like the moto-cross successes, (Jeff Smith was awarded his MBE early in 1970) none of this was exploited by the factory. The management never replied to Hopwood's March 1970 enquiry about marketing a Daytona replica, though he claims such a machine could have been produced as cheaply as or cheaper than the stock Rocket III, and it certainly would have made a real flagship for the 1971 range. It would have coincided with an even more spectacular year of success where, in fairytale fashion, Tridents such as Slippery Sam and the red-and-white faired BSAs, their frames modified and their engines further improved by Hele, now pushing out 84 bhp and ultra-reliable with it, took 1—2—3 at Daytona for 1971. Dick Mann was AMA Grand National

champion by the end of the year, while in England, riders like Ray Pickrell and Percy Tait won every major production and endurance race, the Isle of Man production TT for the second year running, the first ever Formula 750, the Bol d'Or and the Mallory Park race of the year with Derbyshire man, John Cooper, on a BSA beating Agostini, Sheene, Hailwood and all. Yet little sales mileage was made out of a race effort, which in America alone had cost $1,000,000, and whose American side had involved expenses such as renting an entire floor of the big Plaza hotel on the beach front at Daytona for the races. Since the departments of the giant enterprise no longer related properly to each other, efforts and success in one area brought little benefit to another.

The year of 1970 saw the roller-coaster moving faster and faster. Overall motor cycle sales in America, contrary to the consultant's prediction, had doubled, reaching 638,763 for the 1969—70 period. All records for exports of British motor cycles were broken for the first half of 1970 with machines to the value of £10 million being exported, but again against the predicted trend, only £2¾ million worth of that total went to the USA and Canada, partly because of the failure to foresee the boom which meant that the Group was unable to meet the dealers' demand for big bikes there. Of the rest, an unexpectedly large proportion went to meet demand in Europe. The Group's turnover increased by 11 per cent to £27,155,000 and shares edged up 70p, yet when it was declared, the profit was down to £352,194 after tax. It was a time of industrial unrest, and Eric Turner claimed that dock strikes, and strikes by component suppliers, had led to the loss of overseas sales of between 2 —3,000 machines.

The real villains were most likely the dangers already mentioned by Ryerson—the failure to restrain growth so as to husband cash flow from the limited and only partially exploited selling season, the diminished returns of that selling period from the States under the new management arrangements, and general extravagance, as well as the expense of producing the Ariel-3, tooling up for the Fury/Bandit and the new range, and keeping Umberslade going.

Turner was still expansive and optimistic, at least in public, and talked of a massive re-planning of Armoury Road for 1970 to achieve a production target of 100,000 machines a year. However, his optimism was possibly partly because the true situation was being kept from him by Jofeh. The latter's inflexibility seems to have led to his inability to contemplate failure. He simply ignored reports and failed in his turn to pass them on. Ryerson writes of tales of 'statements to the board by Jofeh that the machines would be ready on time whereas, it is stated with great firmness, there was no possibility of this happening, and Jofeh had been told so without a doubt'.

What was going on is best illustrated by the case of the notorious P39 oil-bearing frame for the twins. Hopwood doubted the necessity for producing it at all and pointed out that the recently developed Triumph frame could have been employed discreetly on both ranges. The oil-bearing concept, with a massive hollow frame spine acting as a reservoir for the lubricant and therefore dispensing with a conventional separate oil tank, was scarcely new, the use of it for the works moto-cross singles having already been mentioned. However, Rickman were marketing a version with excellent handling and of a similar frame and previously some police forces had been removing the engines from their Triumphs and slotting them into the Rickman product. One plus-point in the oil-bearing arrangement was thought to be weight-saving, but dry weight of a 1969 A65 Lightning was 390 lb, whereas for a 1972 Lightning with the new frame a weight of 383 lb was claimed — scarcely a substantial saving.

Umberslade Hall made what Hopwood called 'heavy weather' of the facelift of both frame and forks. Doug Hele, speaking to Ronnie Mutch in a *Penthouse* article on the collapse of the industry, is quoted as saying that the forks 'weren't supposed to be for any constructive improvement in the bike's handling — they were the first cast forks the bike had had — they were thought to be smart-looking and modern'. However, the piece goes on to say that when a prototype Triumph Bonneville fitted with them was taken to MIRA for testing and the rider applied the front brake at high speed, the forks snapped clean through. They must have gone back and got it right, for the production version on both BSA and Triumph, said to be derived from BSA moto-cross experience, never gave any trouble. The P39 frame too handled well, but caused trouble in other areas. Its eventual seat height was an excessive 33 ins for the BSA and 34½ ins for the Triumph once their 650 twin motor had been shoe-horned in, and even the BSA was at least an inch too tall for comfort, for all but the loftiest rider. This applied just as much in the United States, where an ex-factory tester Dave Vaughn put it, 'apparently the human race . . . are the same size as the midget British.' Ryerson writes that the fault went undetected because the bike wasn't 'handed over to some of the very expert

motor cyclists with which Small Heath abounded' for their opinion, but as Bob Currie was quick to point out, this did in fact happen, and sidecar ace Peter Brown was only one among several testers who unanimously condemned the frame in reports which the hierarchy completely ignored.

However, it was not just a matter of an uncomfortable and impractical design. In the hysterical atmosphere of the second half of 1970 the things that Hopwood had warned of in his report of the previous year came to pass. Parts released 'without an assembly check, let alone any sort of test' included major components, and in John Nelson's book *Bonnie* we learn first of the failure of the frame drawings to appear from Umberslade until November 1970, and then the failure of the frame and the 650 cc Triumph engine to marry satisfactorily, leading to a complete halt in production for several weeks in the last months of 1970.

Once again the company's parts were out of step with one another, and by then the publicity juggernaut for the range had been launched on its inexorable way. Indeed throughout 1970 the unprecedented step of buying advertising space in the national press had been taken to keep the BSA name in the public eye. Dealers were primed, and during November the range was launched at a two-day event costing £15,000 at the Royal Lancaster Hotel, and then the Hilton, London, with a flourish of trumpets and entertainment in the shape of Dave Allen and the Young

Tall trouble. An A65 Thunderbolt for 1971 in the P39 oil-bearing frame — an inch too high, and half a year too late.

Generation dancers. Styling is of course a matter of taste, but men of the '60s can still see the appeal of those naked fork stanchions, high and wide bars and minimal tanks. Some touches, like the false louvres on the twins' side-panels, were genuinely stylish, and the powerful new conical hub front brakes were admirable. However, the paint schemes for the twins were indifferent and the silencers used for the singles, together with the impractical light-coloured frames, were inexcusable. But it was all rather academic, as due to the disruption of production for the reasons already outlined, together with the tardiness of delivery and high cost by suppliers of components such as the electrics, the whole range substantially missed the 1971 selling season, dribbling onto the market late in the summer.

The facts could no longer be concealed, as the cash crisis had reached hair-raising proportions. In May, a £1,000,000 loss was privately predicted. In June, Peter Thornton, the BSA Inc USA President, resigned, and veteran Dennis McCormack returned to handle the US operation until Felix Kalinski took over in April 1972. Despite another increase in turnover, by the end of July there was no profit, but a £3,300,000 loss was being publicly predicted, and BSA shares dropped to 18½p. At that time the closure of the famous BSA Competition Shop was announced. Lionel Jofeh as managing director was the obvious candidate as sacrificial victim for all this. He left the company on July 8, it was later announced 'by mutual agreement', a relative term, as he was awarded a £35,518 golden handshake the following December to avoid 'a long and disagreeable' law-suit. Back in July an interim report on the crisis which had been submitted by Cooper's, the British consultants, was quoted to explain why the Group's 7,000 workforce was being put under warning of redundancy.

The report said that the problems were due to the previous year's (ie 1970–71) substantial trading losses, and the need to increase prices because of the rising cost of material, components and production in the current economic slump, all of which would reduce demand and lead to cuts in production. It was also due to trying to do too much, delays in the design of new models, and so a low volume of output before the peak selling season. The report had also blamed component shortages and defects, strikes, particularly at Meriden, and the inability to recruit necessary additional labour. The latter failure makes a telling contrast with the re-mustering of the skilled armaments workforce by the company at the outbreak of World War II, but the personal, family-firm touch had inevitably been one of the casualties of the '60s and of the New Breed's approach.

Behind the boardroom doors all this had been known since at least March. It was realised that the dohc twin would not be ready until late 1972, which killed any credibility it may have had with dealers. According to Doug Hele, the tooling for the bikes was scrapped on Jofeh's orders although it was not until November that the 350s were announced as cancelled 'from the immediate programme'. Just 22 pre-production bikes had been built at an estimated cost of over £1 million. An equally desperate sell-off of assets rapidly followed, including the remaining holdings in Alfred Herbert, and SMC and other machine-tool concerns. And since 80 per cent of the company output was now motor cycles, they and related assets went too. The Redditch factory was sold off for the site value, Umberslade's staff was pared down prior to its sale the following year, and the machines themselves were discounted, or like the Ariel-3, sold off entirely in job lots. Some 11,000 bikes were discounted in the States for 1971, and machines to the value of £100,000 again for 1972. In Britain the twins were reduced in price by £84 to £499. In January 1972 the ban on the sale of engines to specials builders was lifted and scrambler John Banks continued to compaign quite successfully on a Ken Heanes-framed B50-based machine; and by the end of that year BSA spares were being sold off cheaply in bulk, to the disgust of regular dealers who had already bought them at official prices. One beneficiary was Alan Clews of Bolton, who bought the entire residue of the Small Heath Competition shop, plus a batch of GP B50s, machine tools and 100 tons of engine spares for the singles. This led to the founding of his company, CCM, which during the '70s produced moto-crossers with heavily-modified B50 engines, thus keeping both his company and the four-stroke thumper tradition alive in a lean time.

It was the sale of the century, only justified by the extreme financial straits which BSA was in from July 1971. American banks had been involved in underwriting the company's operations there, and at the same time they pulled out, America was experiencing her own financial contractions. This was the year when Nixon devalued the dollar, with recessionary effects, and it was no time to be involved in the fortunes of a foreign company, several of whose dealers had already gone bankrupt.

Caught in the crunch. The dohc 350 Fury, scrapped during 1971.

The ultimate development of BSA's singles, CCM's 600 cc moto-cross thumper.

In fact, 1971 marked a watershed in the US motor cycle market—for so long the goose that had laid the golden eggs for the British industry. However, the down-turn was far from final, and marked by several fluctuations. Demand had levelled off in 1971, and by the end of that year there were signs of a slump, with overstuffed Japanese warehouses leading to heavy price-cutting. The then BSA Group Marketing Director, Ken Chambers, attributed this fall-off to the hard-sell mentality, with a lack of service and warranty back-up, scaring off buyers. However, 1973 saw British exports up again, and Hopwood asserts that *demand* was reaching record levels both in the USA and the rest of the world, though Ryerson quotes the Boston Consulting Group's 1975 report which spoke of a down-turn in all US categories in 1973. Then despite an artificial bulge, a 65 per cent rise in the first quarter of 1974 due to the energy crisis, there was a slump of sorts for the year as a whole, though big bike registrations were down only 7 per cent on 1973, and by 1975 they were back to the 1973 level. The picture, in fact, was never as clear cut as the Boston Group's report made out. Changing fashions and Japanese pressure including deliberate undercutting, which could in some terms be countered by skilful marketing, were as much factors as any final downturn in the market itself. If any final conclusion suggests itself from the conflicting statistics, it is just that for BSA to have relied so heavily on any one

market with its fickleness and fluctuations was unwise. Indeed, as late as 1977, the sudden strength of the pound against the dollar dealt the Meriden Triumph co-operative a near death blow in lost export revenue, as 90 per cent of their products were then going to the States.

Back at home in 1971 strong medicine was the order of the day and the biggest sell-off of all time was agreed on. By July 28 the board decided, and in October it was announced publicly, that Small Heath was to cease motor cycle assembly, and that both BSA and Triumph models were to be built at Meriden. Privately it had already been decided that the BSA name would come off the larger machines, which would be marketed as Triumphs. The BSA forge was closed, as forgings could be bought in. The unions at Small Heath reacted immediately and there was talk of factory occupation and a work-in although in the meantime production continued unabated. The chairman, Eric Turner, seemed unable to come to terms with the gravity of the situation and take decisive action which led to tangible and unfortunate results. Owing to the lateness of their release, the tall P39-framed machines had not yet flooded the market, and their faults were far from being impossible to rectify. Hopwood writes that he and Hele had engineered a prototype to correct the fault only weeks after Jofeh had departed, and he claims that the modifications to the BSA and Triumph twins could have been accomplished by

September in two weeks without delaying production.

Hopwood and Dennis McCormack put the case for pressing ahead immediately with the modifications to Eric Turner at 'one of the customary huge meetings', but Turner turned them down. So, wrote Hopwood, it was not until April 1972 that most of the problems had been eliminated, without, incidentally, any indication to the dealers of the improvements made — the Group was now desperate, and warehouse stocks of 11,000 of the existing machines had to be shifted any way they could. The failure to implement the improvements probably goes a long way to explaining the £1,150,000 loss made by the company up to January 1972, and this was Turner's direct responsibility.

The improvements were, in fact, very effective. A 1972 A65 Lightning tested by *Bike* magazine's Mark Williams, who has never been afraid to criticise when he felt it justified, said: 'the machine looks lower and it is . . . the shape of the [new, steel, four-gallon] tank is a distinct aesthetic improvement over the tall '71 machine . . . vibration is definitely down on the '71 range . . . [perhaps] due to the mill being held in a lower, more compact frame'. On steering and handling: 'the BSA is so clearly a viceless machine in practically any situation . . . more so [reported his fellow road-tester who had owned a 1970 A65 model] than earlier Lightnings which held road with greater reluctance than the new 'uns.' In fact the whole truncated range had now come right; the Rocket III with its race-proved engine, the two roadster A65s and the B50 thumper which once you could kick-start its 10:1 compression ratio motor, was a strong and reliable machine, as shown by the 1971 24 hour production racing successes (outright wins at Barcelona and Zolder, first in the 500 cc class at the Bol d'Or) of dealers' Mead and Tompkinson's B50, which they recently revealed differed from standard only in the matter of a hot cam, a bigger carburettor and some polishing and porting. But it was too late, as the majority of the market were off in other directions.

Nevertheless, thousands of these bikes were built. It was as if the mechanism of production were running out of control. Ryerson writes that 'bad programming [of the computer] resulted in it calling in supplies irrespective of the actual levels of production, leading to a huge imbalance of stocks', and hence incidentally some of the bargain sell-offs later. Some 6,286 BSA motor cycles were produced between August and October, then another thousand or so between

Lord Shawcross's arrival in November and the following April. By that time the workforce had been trimmed to 1,500, but work went on at Small Heath throughout 1972, mostly on components such as Rocket III/Trident engines, all of which were built at Small Heath for assembly at Meriden. *Motor Cycle Weekly* referred to the last complete BSAs being built at Small Heath in December of 1972, a batch of A65s. Many of the twins were registered for 1973 and 1974 as stocks slowly sold off.

Lord Shawcross took over as chairman from Eric Turner in November 1971, and spelt out the problems and some of the solutions at the Group's AGM in December. Shawcross had been on the board since 1968; he was a powerful and respected financier, a director of Shell Oil, and not without motor cycle connections, having chaired a number of inquiries into ACU disputes. When he said he was more concerned with the industry and the loss of thousands of jobs than with BSA as such, he was believed. He made it clear, however, that he was taking over in a caretaker capacity in order to see the Group out of its present troubles. In simplified form, the year's trading losses finally emerged as being over £2¾ million but this was just the tip of the iceberg. A further £1¼ million was expected for 1972 due to the scrapping of various models, and a further £4¼ million to cover the cost of the previous year's 'rationalisation'. After the withdrawal of the US banks, the Group had been taken on in its entirety by Barclays with a loan of £10 million, although another £5 million was necessary to meet production for 1972, which meant total borrowings approaching £22 million. This was the ultimate outcome of the financial over-extension pointed out by Ryerson.

To cover this, Shawcross outlined a financial reorganisation involving the disposal of most of the remaining BSA subsidiaries, 3,000 redundancies, shifting the motor cycle assembly to Meriden and the selling-off of 75 per cent of the Small Heath site, everything in fact, except for the general engineering production and the firearms side. This sale did not take place during his period of office. Shawcross appointed a new board, including a new chief executive, Brian Eustace, from the GKN group, and Bert Hopwood as an executive director with responsibility for troubleshooting in the motor cycle division. Up until then, Hopwood had been working on particular problems at Umberslade with Mike Nedham, who left the company early in 1972.

The consultants, Cooper's, had made a report in October emphasising that with motor cycles comprising 80 per cent of the Group's business, the new board ought to recognise that BSA would henceforth be primarily a motor cycle company and believe that it could make and sell motor cycles profitably. (It was this report incidentally which, speaking of the previous dislocation, made the oft-quoted admission that 'It would be idle to deny that errors of management contributed to this situation'.) The new emphasis on motor cycles was reflected in another board appointment, that of Dick Fenton, a big London dealer whose empire included British specialist dealers Harvey Owen and Owen Bros. He however was not an executive director. There were few of the latter, in fact, as Shawcross had understandably been disillusioned by the performance of their predecessors. However, an unhappy side-effect of this policy was that a managing director of the motor cycle division was never appointed, at a time when co-ordination of Small Heath and Meriden, with one making components for the other, was more vital than ever for the Group's survival, and Brian Eustace, the new chief executive, Hopwood felt, was rightly too busy with his overall responsibility for the whole BSA complex to oversee this area.

Shawcross' efforts to save the Group were doomed to failure, and most of the details of the period that followed will be found in the Triumph and Norton sections of a later volume. However, it is worth recording the bare outlines of the new management's efforts, as against great odds, they came tantalisingly close to saving both the industry as a major force, and the BSA name. For despite the losses and prevailing chaos, Hopwood kept his eyes on the fact that only competitive new products would provide a long-term solution to the Group's problems.

So at the same time as fielding the myriad problems 'rationalisation' had brought about, and putting together an improved 1973 range of what he thought of as 'the last major effort on basically ageing designs', Hopwood, drawing on development work done in his own time over a long period, was able to present to the board in March 1972 a detailed breakdown of a new modular range of machines, from a basic 200 cc ohc single multiplying up to a 1,000 cc five-cylinder V-engined superbike. The guidelines were to be as follows: a complete range, made by modern techniques, technically advanced enough to be produced for six years without major changes, with minimal assembly problems and low maintenance requirements.

They were to be far from drawing-board dreams — rig-testing of various features such as the ohc arrangements already built into a test

Trident, and a Bonneville converted to try out the new rear suspension system, was already taking place in 1972 and early '73, and by the spring of that year they were ready to build engine prototypes. But finance for the new range was the priority, and in June 1972 the Department of Trade and Industry was approached with regard to an interest-free loan of £5 million to help the ailing Group launch it. While State aid to the once-proud industry was to be regretted, one can only note the comparatively insignificant amount involved by comparison with both the Group's profits in the good years and its potential, and with the sums which were to be poured into other, sometimes far less hopeful enterprises — Concorde, British Leyland, British Airways and so on.

However, by then the Group's financial status, despite all their efforts, still looked shaky. True, the months of March and April had shown a total trading profit of nearly half a million pounds. But this had been in spite of continuing industrial disputes, mainly at the over-manned Meriden plant with its militant union representatives, and the US selling season had been substantially lost again to the Group, though in nowhere near as disastrous a fashion as the previous year. For 1972 losses were down to £465,000, and that was after £674,000 in interest charges including an increase in bank rates, and a £300,000 loss, due to devaluation of the dollar, had been absorbed.

By November 1972 the Department of Trade and Industry told Lord Shawcross that money, up to £20 million in fact, would be forthcoming, but only if the BSA Group and their principal competitors, Dennis Poore's Norton-Villiers, were to merge. There was nothing else on offer, and Shawcross doubted that Barclays would continue to underwrite the unprofitable Group for much longer. There was also growing criticism in the financial press, including pronouncements from Edward Turner, at what was seen as Shawcross 'dragging his feet' in accepting a viable plan for a unified industry. This was despite the new board's performance, for as Shawcross pointed out later, by April 1973 he had reduced the sum owed to his creditors to half of what he had inherited in July 1971.

Hopwood feels that as far back as the Group's original approach in summer 1972, the then Conservative government had decided not to help BSA. Possibly there had been hints or guesses from the government that Poore, a right-wing Tory himself, might attempt the closure of the troublesome Meriden factory, part of the by now notoriously militant Coventry area hot-spot of industrial unrest. Certainly Hopwood found the civil servants of the Department of Trade and Industry, in their representative Laurie Tindale, uninterested in his new and revitalised range, or indeed in anything but the immediate future. And certainly the recent failure of the Turner board, and the continuing unprofitability, must have put them off BSA.

But what was being ignored was that the Group's motor cycles outsold Nortons nine to one, and that Poore's company, which they proposed as the new 'Active Ingredient', had lost ground during the 1972–73 trading year, with profits falling by £236,000 for the first half alone. By leaving Shawcross and the Group no alternatives, Poore and his men cleared the way for large scale asset-stripping by Manganeze Bronze Holdings, Norton-Villiers' parent company. However, this would not be the first time that MBH had benefited from the contraction of the British motor cycle industry. In April 1973, following an article in *Motor Cycle Weekly* suggesting the benefits to BSA shareholders of

the merger, a letter from Norman Vanhouse, BSA-Triumph's Sales Executive, argued otherwise, pointing out that Poore had acquired the Woolwich-based AMC in 1966 *after* the official receiver had been called in to wind up the company. MBH had acquired the managing rights to the AMC names, machine tools and drawings from the official receiver, and AMC shareholders had not benefited from the deal at all.

This letter had been provoked by the latest turn of events in the early spring of 1973. The merger had looked inevitable, and in strictly secret negotiations between BSA and Norton the following terms had been hammered out. BSA was to acquire Norton-Villiers, with the Department of Trade and Industry insisting on Dennis Poore as chairman of the newly-formed company but with Lord Shawcross as deputy chairman. MBH in turn were to acquire BSA's non-motor cycle holdings. The equity, or ordinary share capital, of the new motor cycle company was to be divided equally between the shareholders and MBH. At this point, the morning of March 14, the very day when a draft circular to the shareholders had been printed ready for distribution, what is known on the Stock Exchange as a 'bear raid' was staged on BSA shares. That is to say, a broker named Ralph Clarke, acting on instructions from a client, sold BSA shares which he did not in fact possess, the object of the exercise being to lower the shares' price so that he could then actually buy the shares, and meet his commitment before Settlement Day which came around monthly or fortnightly. Hopwood believes that a leak from the secret negotiations had taken place.

At any rate, in this case the ploy was all too successful. With the existing uncertainty about BSA's performance, a wave of selling followed and the Group's shares plummetted from 18½p to 4¾p by 1.45 pm, at which time on Lord Shawcross' request their quotation was suspended. Shawcross, who was also Chairman of the City Takeover Board at the time, asked the Stock Exchange Council to investigate the wave of selling immediately. By the following September the trigger for the sales had been traced back to Clarke who was banned from the exchange for two years for 'discreditable conduct', as it was said that he had tried to mislead the investigators. He never disclosed his client's name.

It was disaster. Shawcross was left with the

Happier days, 20 years before, when the A10 was new, the helmet law undreamt of, and the slogan true.

options of calling in the Official Receiver or accepting a revised offer from Poore and the Department of Trade and Industry. Under this arrangement the new company, Norton-Villiers-Triumph (NVT) was to consist of an issue of stock worth approximately £4,800,000 from the money loaned by the DTI, and owned by the latter. About three-quarters of these shares were redeemable preference stock ie they had no entitlement to dividend for the first three years, but the company was committed to repaying the investors and the government at a later date. The other quarter was convertible redeemable preference stock, as the above but giving the investors/government the option to switch them to ordinary shares. Of the rest, £1,372,000 more convertible redeemable stock was to be MBH owned, as was £2,006,236 of ordinary shares at 10p each. The present BSA shareholders owned just £2,006,236 of the ordinary NVT shares, which they were offered in exchange for the BSA shares, one for one. They could also acquire 10 ordinary NVT shares for every £3 nominal of A and B cumulative preference stock of BSA. It was a fair distance from the original 50/50 BSA/MBH split.

The government, it will be noted, were supplying just £5 million, a quarter of the sum previously mentioned and a third of the minimum amount which experts considered necessary to launch the new company successfully. Even so, the decision to grant the money was criticised in the House by the then shadow Minister, none other than Tony Wedgwood-Benn, who flailed the government in office for spending such a sum on 'a lame duck'. This was somewhat ironic, in view of his role just over a year later, while in office, in providing a similar sum for the setting up of the Meriden co-operative.

But what really hurt the BSA board was another condition of the deal—namely, that in addition to £2 million from MBH for their share in the new company, the BSA non-motor cycle holdings were to be sold off to MBH for a further £3½ million. They consisted of Carbodies, the makers of London taxi cabs; the BSA Metal Components Division; BSA Guns; Birtley Ltd, a general engineering and building products firm; and BSA Heating, the central heating firm in which they had a substantial holding. According to Hopwood these firms between them achieved a profit of £576,000 for the seven months ending at February 1973. He and other board members therefore felt their value to be around twice what was offered,

Trouble for Dennis Poore's NVT—1973, and the Meriden sit-in gets under way.

and that the £3½ million was inadequate to put it mildly.

It can be argued that since Poore was taking on a company that was £11½ million in the red (and was hailed as a brave man for doing so), this cheap acquisition could be viewed as a legitimate way of boosting the fledgling new company's assets and thus its chances of success. However in December 1974, when NVT's fortunes were already flagging heavily to the tune of £3½ –5½ million losses, according to interpretation, MBH were showing a profit of £670,000. When auditors inherited from BSA, whom Poore was trying to sack, attempted to insist that the MBH figures were included with NVT's, the latter's managing director, Hugh Palin, explained that NVT were not part of the MBH group, and that investment was simply held in it—if NVT went broke, he reassured, it wouldn't affect the MBH share-holders. So the non-motor cycle acquisitions from BSA were pure profit for MBH only.

In April 1973 though the BSA Board felt the offer to be inadequate, following the shares

BSA 500

Oh, the great days in the distance departed—when happiness was still 100 per cent BSA.

and eventually whole machines, did not resume again until April 1974. Later that year the 1,200 Small Heath men had it explained to them by Hugh Palin that the Meriden co-op deal with cash from the government would mean a big cut-back for them, and they gave Tony Benn a rough ride when in November 1974 he came to explain himself to them; though they withdrew their objections to Meriden by December.

Whether it was he or their own management who should have been heckled, they were right in perceiving it as an either/or situation, as there was only limited government cash available for the industry. By the end of 1975 NVT were on the rocks, and on December 24 the last motor cycle of all was finally assembled at Small Heath. It was a Triumph Trident T160; around 5,000 of these late model triples were made there, and the 'Small Heath' Tridents were much sought after among the knowledgeable for their superior standards of assembly. This one was in Cardinal police trim for export to Saudi-Arabia (and probable eventual re-importation back to England as a 'classic'). The T160s had their engines inclined forward in the manner of BSA's Rocket III, and it was appropriate that the few remaining Small Heath workers adorned it, temporarily, with BSA badges, for old times' sake. Most of the factory was demolished during 1977.

But the sense of continuity of those Small Heath men does them credit. It is the writer's belief that a similar sense among the decision-makers could have saved the industry in however contracted a form, until better times arrived. Despite the outdated models, poor quality control, over-reliance on the US market and absence of a complete range, the Great British public knew little and cared less about the board-room upheavals. But the decades of reliable workmanship for which BSA had previously been so famous had planted the name indelibly in the national consciousness, and any industrialist unable to exploit that needed his personal balance-sheet looking into.

This account may seem to some to have been over-reliant on the version of events provided by Hopwood—a man of whom it has been said that he never even rode a motor cycle, though he has aches and pains to prove the contrary. I do so because in my own experience he delivered the goods, as the designer of the A10 and the Dominator, the strongest and most satisfying parallel twins—though that is just an opinion,

collapse they had no option but to accept it, and this was made public immediately ('Poore Takes Triumph!' said the *Motor Cycle Weekly* headline for March 21). The board kept trying for a better offer for the non-motor cycle interests right up until August, by which time most BSA shareholders had accepted, and Shawcross bowed out. Hopwood, unimpressed by Poore's lack of forward planning—he had rejected the new range straight away—and wary at his mention of a possible closure of Meriden, the consequences of which Hopwood accurately predicted for the new Chairman, resigned on August 21. Doug Hele stayed on with NVT until 1975 when it went under. In October 1973 however, NVT's newly-imported managing director announced that 'the BSA name is now dead and no more road-going models will be built under that marque'.

Despite the fact that, as we have seen, this was contradicted five years later by the resurrection of the name, here the story must end. Small Heath lingered on through NVT's subsequent stormy two years. For with the curtain going up in September 1973 on that long-running evergreen favourite, the drama of the Meriden blockade and the foundation of the workers' co-operative there, Small Heath stayed open as part of Poore's 'two factory' plan, despite the fact that at the time of the take-over Poore had announced 'that work would be concentrated in Meriden, the more modern plant'. But production of Trident engines,

and a Triumph man will tell you a different story. Others have interpreted Hele and Hopwood's actions in the '60s in a different light. Clive Stokes, an ex-NVT employee, quoted in an article on the industry by Ronnie Mutch, spoke of 'Triumph's policy of destruction and board level sabotage', and it's claimed that they 'snapped up any good development that did emerge from [Umberslade] before the BSA factions realised what was going on.'

Certainly there will always be disagreement on the causes of the collapse. Interestingly, Dave Minton, writing in 1972, blames not a surplus but a lack of marketing specialists at high level. But this tendency to label engineers as poor businessmen calls to mind Hopwood writing with grim relish of 'the engineering profession as the usual scapegoat'.

For the outsider, at least, it's easier to understand Hopwood's belief that a strong product with development potential is the bottom line for an industry of this type.

Hopwood was a lonely man for long periods of time and became a stubborn one with a belief in his own infallibility that was not always justified (the BSA Dandy and the Norton Jubilee may be cases in point), but undoubtedly necessary armour against the extraordinary individuals and attitudes he continually encountered in his long odyssey through this most unusual field of endeavour.

It seems no exaggeration to say that, in both the long and short term, he could have saved the company. The 1973/74 range may not have been in the fashionable new capacity classes, but it was strong, and there was always an underestimated loyalty to the marque that seems likely to have permitted survival had continuity not been fatally broken. The modular range devised by Hopwood provided solutions to the problems of the future, which if not 100 per cent viable, would at least have given the Group a fighting chance, and were in tune with the best of BSA tradition.

The documents, plans and reports which Hopwood quotes show clearly that he possessed those solutions at the time and not just with hindsight.

BSA: The M20/M21/M33 singles

The sturdy basis of the BSA singles range were the 500 cc M20/600 cc M21 side-valves. They were the bottom end in terms of performance, being aimed during our period almost exclusively at the side-car man. (It must be remembered that as late as the boom year of 1957, one in three large capacity machines was pulling a chair.)

They were also the basis historically, having been designed in 1936 by Val Page, the great talent who had arrived that year at BSA from Ariel via Triumph, as part of a new range of singles. These, like all Page's work, were well thought-out and a big step forward for their day. Drawing on his experience with the Ariel Red Hunter range, they

Archetypal role for side-valves. The 1,000th RSO goes to the AA—the happy gent second from the left is BSA managing director, James Leek.

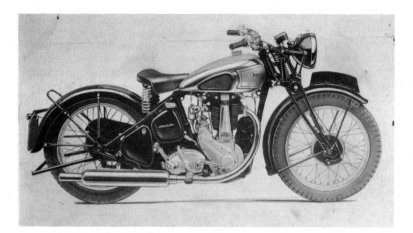

Rare early post-war M33, the ohv 500 cc engine in the side-valve's cycle parts. Early 1948, hence rigid rear end and girder forks.

introduced to BSA singles, dry sump lubrication and separate oil tanks, enclosed valve-springs and a bolted-up tubular frame.

The dimensions of the M20's engine remained the same (82 × 94 mm) from the start, but the similarly constructed M21 initially featured the old 'Sloper' model's bore and stroke (85 × 105 mm), only coming into line with the 500, and becoming one of the true long-strokes, with the 1938 change of dimensions to 82 x 112 mm. The single-port side-valve engines had aluminium crankcases and cast-iron cylinder heads and barrels, with the valve gear behind a plate emblazoned with the piled arms insignia. They featured steel connecting rods, roller big-end bearings and a built-up crankshaft. Electrics were supplied by a Lucas 6-volt, 60 watt Magdyno mounted behind the cylinder. The M20 had 3.25 X 19 in tyres front and rear, the M21 a 3.50 X 19 in rear cover. Both featured 7-in brakes front and rear which were found quite adequate for the day.

There followed the punishing trial by arms of World War II, where as already mentioned, large quantities of M20s formed the backbone of the British Army's two-wheeled equipment. And when the fighting stopped, it was the side-valve M-range's bottom end which was adopted for the post-war ohv B-range, so that all BSA singles were now distinguished by a kink in the right-hand bottom frame-rail to accommodate the bulge of their skew-driven double-gear oil pump. Twin engines, lacking this bulge, could therefore be dropped into singles frames easily enough, but not vice versa. The side-valves had moved from hand to four-speed foot gear-change for 1939. The 1945 (M20) and 1946 (M21) post-war civilian variants no longer featured tank-top instruments, and sported a new tool-box, unvalanced

mudguards and a rear carrier. In June 1948 both relinquished their girder forks and adopted the BSA telescopic fork in a suitably modified frame with a shortened down-tube. The new fork had also been designed by Val Page who was back with Ariel, now another part of the BSA empire.

For 1951 an alloy cylinder head was adopted for both. In that year also, a plunger frame became optional and for 1952 there was an optional dual-seat. (For details of the plunger-springing system, see the following section, the B31/32/33/34 Singles.) That was to be the limit of frame development, as since these bikes were aimed primarily at the ultra-conservative side-car market, it was never thought worthwhile to offer a swinging-arm version of either M20 or M21. However, plunger-sprung frames became standard from 1956 for the M33, another mount intended for side-car work. The M33 had been introduced for 1948, the first few with girder forks, and comprised the 500 cc B33 ohv engine in the M21's cycle parts. (For engine details and changes, see the B31/B33 section following.) While, like the whole M-range, it shared the B-range gearbox from the start, one detail in which it differed from the B33 was that it had a smaller oil capacity of 4, as opposed to 5 pints. Another variation involving the gearbox fitted to the M-range was that while, in common with the B-range, the primary chain was tensioned by drawing the box backwards, with the M-frame, the large nut on the front fixing bolt was inaccessibly located on the off-side and needed a long $\frac{5}{16}$ in W-box spanner to loosen it.

Fleet orders for the simple but stubborn side-valves continued, and it was this that kept production going after 1956 when the civilian M20 was dropped and the M21 became available for the public, with plunger springing now standard, to special order only. M21s replaced pre-war M20s for the AA, and were a familiar sight right up till 1968, painted yellow, fully equipped and pulling the AA patrolmens' side-cars, or RSOs (Road Service Outfits). The AA machines featured the tougher WD-type single spring clutch which had been replaced by the 6-spring type on civilian machines in 1946, plus heavier gauge wheel spokes and rims, purpose-built seats, tanks and rear mudguards, with the Magdynos from 1961 onwards supplemented by auxiliary alternators to power a two-way radio. Both M20 and M21 continued to form the largest element of the British (and other) Army's machines until as late as 1967 when they were replaced by BSA B40s. Their weight and low ground clearance (5½ inches) had not made

them a force's favourite. However, their long production run, combined with the 126,334 produced during the war—many were sold off as war surplus afterwards, either resprayed or still in their original khaki—has meant that most spares are still available and cheap for the 500s, though finding items for the 600 cc top ends can be a problem. As an example, complete new M20 engines could still be had for little over £140 in 1983 and at these prices represented a definite economy option for the British bike fanatic.

Interim M20. 1953, that year's tank, teleforks but still rigid rear end.

Semi-sophisticated side-valve. 1954 M20/M21; semi-nacelle, round tank badges, but still unsprung.

Plunger-sprung M33 for 1954.

Side-valve singles cannot normally be tuned, and their performance is not particularly exciting. Journalist Peter Watson owned a solo ex-WD M20, and writing in *Bike* magazine recommended the experience, in a back-handed way, to the novice: 'If you can learn to ride an ex-WD M20 fast (that's anything over 50 mph), nothing on two wheels will ever surprise or terrify you again'. He went on to ask: 'How can a frame that weighs so much, bend so easily?'. The usual side-valve habit of running hot is a constant feature, and pogoing along rutted city streets on a girder-forked ex-WD M20, with the exhaust pipe glowing cherry red, is one of my more lunatic neighbour's idea of high style.

Of course speed was never what the M-range aimed at. Though the M33 could just reach 80 mph, top whack solo for the M20 was around the mid-60s, a little higher for the 600 cc, and just over 50 mph with a chair attached. However, mpg figures for both were better than average for normally thirsty side-valve motors. Seventy mpg was recorded on test for a 1951 M20 solo (though around the mid-50s would probably be a more realistic expectation), and up to 50 mpg with a chair attached. And the great virtue of these heavy-flywheeled bikes was their immense pulling power from low speed. An idea of their tractability is given by the fact that although the final drive ratio on machines sold with side-car was lowered, they could cheerfully be driven with or without a side-car attached without changing the sprockets. Part of BSA's successful 1938 Maudes Trophy

bid had involved an M21 traversing London, twice, with its gearbox locked in top. Peter Watson went on to tell of driving his own solo machine through Lancaster and out to Morecambe while towing a friend's Morris Minor car. This is veritable ruggedness, and it explains why M20s and 21s, often the detritus of a departing British Army, can still be found chuffing around earning their living from Cairo to Manila, and from Athens to the Hindu Kush — though production of the last M21 occurred as long ago as 1963.

BSA: The M20/M21/M33 — dates and specifications
Production dates
M20 — 1937–55
M21 — 1937–63
M33 — 1948–57

Specifications
M20
Capacity, bore and stroke — 496 cc (82 mm × 94 mm)
Type of engine — sv single
Ignition — Magneto
Weight — (1951) 369 lb

M21
Capacity, bore and stroke — 591 cc (82 mm × 112 mm)
Type of engine — sv single
Ignition — Magneto
Weight — (1951) 370 lb

M33
Capacity, bore and stroke — 499 cc (85 mm × 88 mm)
Type of engine — ohv single
Ignition — Magneto
Weight — (1951) 372 lb (1957, plunger) 406 lb

BSA: M20/M21/M33 — annual development and modifications
1950
1 From mid-1949, new gearbox with enclosed clutch operating mechanism, and speedometer drive now taken from gearbox.
2 Rear wheel no longer QD type.
1951
For M20/21:
1 New alloy cylinder heads with larger fins and a phosphor-bronze insert for spark plug.
For M20/21/33:
2 Optional plunger springing available, initially for export only. Plunger frames featured QD rear hub.

Below left *1959 M21, surviving for fleet orders and smooth with it, courtesy of Motoplas fairings. But didn't it get awful hot in there?*

Right *Late M21 for 1961.*

1952
For M20/21/33:
1 Optional dual seats available.
2 From March: chromed petrol tanks and wheels discontinued.
3 New single-wing chrome and yellow tank badges.
4 Brake fulcrum pin and cam bearings stiffened.
5 Cylinder liners no longer fitted.

1953
For M20/21/33:
1 Chrome panelled petrol tanks and wheels re-introduced.
2 Redesigned number plate incorporating Lucas stop and tail light, blended into lines of mudguard by a steel fairing, with red reflector at bottom of the plate.
3 New adjustable headlamp/speedometer semi-cowling incorporating light switch and angled ammeter, and featuring underslung pilot lamp.
4 Redesigned tool-box shape for plunger-sprung machines.
For M33:
5 Con-rod shortened by $\frac{1}{2}$ in, and gudgeon pin placed lower in a split skirt piston.

1954
For M20/21/33:
1 Round plastic tank badges adopted.

1955
For M20/21/33:
1 Steering-head lock fitted.
2 Two-lobe engine-shaft shock absorber cam replaces four-lobe type.

3 Underslung pilot lamp discontinued.
4 Monobloc carburettors now fitted.

1956
For M21/33:
1 New 8 inch single-sided front brake, and valanced front mudguard to suit.
For M33:
2 Plunger springing now standard, as was dualseat.
For plunger M21/33:
3 Replacing the previous hole and tommy bar method of withdrawing rear wheel spindle, the spindle is now a bolt, removed with spanner. Four nuts secure light-alloy hub to boss of chain sprocket.

1958
For M21:
1 Previous semi-nacelle headlamp replaced by conventional headlamp.

1961
For M21:
1 Mid-year, auxiliary alternator fitted.

BSA: The B31/B32/B33/B34 singles
The 350 cc B31 and 500 cc B33 sprang from the same 1937 range of Val Page singles as the M20 and M21. The new model B31 was the first to resurface after the war and constituted the 'promise of good times to come' which had been the company's slogan while the fighting was on.
 Its link model with the pre-war range had been

the 350 cc B29 of 1940, an ohv single but with the side-valve M-range's bottom end, and a cast-iron barrel plus cylinder head with integral rocker boxes containing hairpin valve-springs. The latter had been the brainchild of Norton's Joe Craig while working briefly at BSA. For the post-war B31 they were replaced by double coil springs designed by another luminary, Triumph's Edward Turner, during a brief wartime sojourn at Small Heath.

So the ohv B-range adopted the M-range's proven bottom end, with its aluminium crankcase, bolted-up crankshaft and roller-bearing big end. The double-gear oil pump necessitating the kinked right-hand lower frame tube, the magdyno, the 7-inch brakes of new design for 1945, the four-speed foot-change gearbox, and the dry clutch—all the pre-war B-range's clutches had run in oil—were also in common with the side-valves.

But in one respect the B31 broke new ground from the start. It featured the BSA telescopic fork, another Val Page design, with external springs under the shrouds, and hydraulic bump stops, giving nearly 6 in of movement. But there was no hydraulic stop on the rebound stroke, and this caused a characteristic clang if the forks came to full extension. The fork was further modified by BSA designer Herbert Perkins and competition shop chief Bert Perrigo in late 1946, by the addition of a valve, another internal spring and a long tube with a series of metering cross holes, to improve the damping. This fork was a strong and more than adequate design; which was as well,

since the BSA Group continued to use it, in various forms, with few modifications until as late as 1963. By this time it had acquired external variations, on the C10, C11G, C12, the M-range, the B-range including the Gold Star, the A7 and A10 twins, as well as the S8 Sunbeam.

The new 1945 B31 engine was a carefully thought-out design, with its cast-iron head and barrel well-finned, as were the valve ports. The valves themselves were high quality items, with the inlet valve machined from a special nickel-steel alloy, and the exhaust valve of G2 austenitic nickel-chrome alloy. The valve and timing gear had been laid out with rigidity in mind, aiming, as writer Barry Ryerson points out, at mechanical silence.

This was also aided by a feature which had been introduced for 1939, the flat-base inverted-mushroom shaped tappets. The centre line of each cam and the axis of its tappet was offset by $\frac{1}{32}$ inch, so that the tappet would rotate while the engine was running and wear on the camshaft would be even. The cams themselves had been, and were to be, carefully developed, and were shaped to control the velocity and acceleration of the potentially noisy valve-gear. This was concealed behind a characteristic trapezoid push-rod tunnel, stamped with the piled arms and secured to the bottom of the rocket-box head by a castellated ring-nut. After a cover beneath the tunnel had been removed, adjustment of the valves was made at the tappets, again like the M-range.

With a compression ratio of 6.8:1, the 343 lb (dry weight) solid frame B31 produced 17 bhp and was good for over 70 mph and around 75 mpg. Its frame was a single down-tube cradle design similar to the M-range's but lighter, and at this time lacking the M-range's side-car fittings, as an earnest of sporting intentions. These were made metal in January 1946 with the introduction of the B32, a competition variant developed by Bert Perrigo in off-road trim (high-level exhaust, lower gearing, more ground clearance, as well as chromed mudguards). While at the beginning of 1947, there came a big brother for the B31, in the shape of the 499 cc B33, which was virtually a bored-out B31, but with 6.8:1 compression, raised gearing, bigger valves, a fatter rear tyre and heavier flywheels. All this produced a more useful power-to-weight ratio than the 350, with its near-identical cycle parts and bottom end. The B33 was capable of over 80 mph while still returning over 70 mpg. The B34 sporting variant followed.

These competition B32s and 34s were, of course, the models from which the illustrious Gold

Star was to spring, the link model being the B32 Special, a Clubman road racer introduced in 1949. The story will be found in detail in the next section ('The Gold Star'). It should be noted that all Gold Stars have the letters GS in the engine number, though not in the frame code.

As a further step towards the Gold Star the competition B32 acquired an alloy head and barrel as optional fittings for 1949, with the B34 following for 1950. But these engines retained the external pushrod tunnel, and it was not until 1952 that B32 and B34 joined the Gold Stars in featuring push-rods concealed within the barrel and head. The 1952 alloy-engined 500 cc variants were either sand or die-cast. This alloy engine, with separate magneto, became standard for 1954. But unlike the Gold Star with its pivoted-fork frame, they adopted a specially-assembled rigid version of the all-welded duplex frame then current. This was intended for Trials work. The position having reversed from the early days of the Gold Star's development, when in 1948, the popular sport was Trials, and the scrambles and racing Gold Star variants were lumbered with the Trials competition head casting with its unsuitably small valve head sizes. Now the Goldie was dominating the increasingly popular scrambles and road race meetings and the competition bikes were relegated to the waning Trials scene, where, with a swinging-arm frame introduced for 1957, the BSA aces kept them well in contention until the coming of the lighter and more suitable C15T in 1958.

Meanwhile, the roadster B31 and B33 workhorses were, together with the A7 and A10 twins, the backbone of the BSA range for the 1950s. Quantities of the 350s went to the Army and Police, and Peter Howdle estimates B31 production at around 8,000 a year during the '50s. As range leaders they were developed accordingly.

For 1948 the speedometer was moved from the tank-top to a bracket on the centre of the top fork yoke. 1949 saw improvement to the dynamo, and the existing rigid frame strengthened, with forged steel rear wheel lugs, as well as the BSA plunger-frame becoming an available option. This plunger system, as on the twins (and in scaled-down form on the lighter weight machines), consisted of a device connecting the rear wheel spindle to a pair of tubular sliders that moved up and down guide rods attached at each steel-bushed end to the frame. The sliders or plungers were controlled by a pair of coil springs per side, the stronger compression spring above the hub and the lower-rate rebound spring beneath, with the whole system enclosed in pairs of separate tubular boxes.

The only damping came from the grease in the boxes and, as Roy Bacon points out, any rust on the spring covers, as well as from the fit of the wheel hub to the frame, which could vary, with manufacturing tolerances, from machine to machine. The benefit for the manufacturer was that the arrangement could be produced cheaply and incorporated with very little modification to

Left *An ancestor. Pre-war M23 500 cc Silver Star of 1938.*

BSA COMPETITION Models

Right *Late competition cousin — 500 cc B34 for 1954.*

the existing frame jigs. For the rider it was a step in the right direction on the very much rougher roads of that time, though the system, particularly with the heavier machines, had to be regularly greased to ensure long life — every 1,000 miles was recommended — and care was to be taken if the machine was kept outside, as rain collected in the spring boxes and could weaken the springs or seize the guide rods. Plunger springing, especially if worn, could produce back-end weaving on bumpy surfaces at speeds above 60 mph, and it was also distrusted for some years by side-car men.

1949 was also the year when the B-range clutch, gearbox, tele front fork and hubs was shared with the M-range (from ZB-101 for the ohvs, ZM-101 for the side-valves). From then on for a time there was little significant development to the B-range. Volume production was king and the understressed engines, with their modest power output were long-lived and reliable, if a shade uninspiring.

So the big singles moved into the '50s, and weight rose dramatically from the 1951 rigid B31's 343 lb dry, to the 1954 plunger B33's 420 lb 'fully equipped' with oil but no fuel. The swinging-arm frame, which became available for the home market as an option for 1955 and which was standard for 1956, still weighed 410 lb dry, though this was reduced to a claimed 396 lb dry on the 1958 variant fitted with an alternator.

The post-war look consisted of matt silver panels lined in black and black-lined silver wheel centres. However, from 1948 there became available from the B32s as an option, handsome gold-lined green tank panels and wheel rim centres for the B31 (the B33 got the B34 equivalent which was Devon Red). Fully painted wheels, the result of chrome

restrictions, applied for 1952 only, after which chrome wheel rims were adopted for the whole range. However, for both roadster singles the prevailing colour was maroon, at that time the British industry's equivalent of Henry Ford's 'any colour you like as long as it's black'. This finish was alleviated by chromed tank panels and the new round red plastic piled arms tank badges (these were the smaller kind, the same as on the standard A7 and the sporting A10s—the Gold Star's larger round badge would fit only the A7 Shooting Star or the Rocket Gold Star). The roadsters stayed maroon until 1958, when almond green (B31) and grey (B33) finishes, still with the chrome tank panels, replaced the dark red.

Detail changes included improvements to the brakes for 1952, when an optional dual seat also became available. For 1953 both engines featured increased finning, and finned collars where the exhaust pipe joined the cylinder. The semi-cowling for the headlamp, speedometer and ammeter introduced on all the large roadsters was also adopted. Its only faults were an ammeter set at an awkward angle, and an unpopular under-slung pilot light. In addition the singles acquired the range's redesigned rear number plate, incorporating a Lucas stop and tail light. Furthermore, the 500 cc B33 came fitted with a new 8 in × 1.38 in front brake, as developed for the 1950 Gold Stars and featured on the twins.

Another 1953 internal change for the B33 must also be noted. To reduce piston slap, the con-rod was shortened by $\frac{1}{2}$ inch, and the gudgeon pin placed slightly lower in a split-skirt piston. Now while the bottom ends of B31 and B33 remained the same as each other, this means that for 1953 and later machines, should you wish to convert a 1953 or later machine from B31 350 to 500 cc capacity, you can use the B31 bottom end

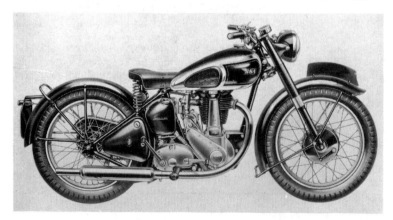

Handsome 350. Rigid B31 for 1952.

1953 B33. Plunger-springing and dual seat were still extra.

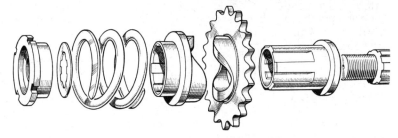

1955 mod. The two-lobe engine-shaft shock-absorber which replaced the previous four-lobe.

complete if you can find a pre-1953 piston. However, these pistons are no longer made, and if you want to use a new Hepolite piston you have to find and fit the later connecting rod. It should also be mentioned that earlier flywheels were heavier, and the later, lighter type give improved acceleration with little loss of pulling power. Another difference is that the B31 six-spring clutch then current had only three friction plates. The B33s featured two extra, but these will only go with the appropriate B33 clutch hub.

1954 saw several excellent new features for the roadster singles, with the introduction, as an option, of the new BSA duplex cradle all-welded frame with full swinging-arm rear suspension, though this was solely for export (and competition models) until 1955. The only drawback was the additional weight already mentioned. With this frame the gearbox developed from the A-range twins via the Gold Star was also adopted, with modified ratios, as well as a polished alloy primary chaincase replacing the previous pressed steel

item. For 1954, also with the new frame, had come the excellent Gold Star-derived single-bolt rubber-mounted fixing for restyled petrol tanks (4 gallons as standard, with a handsome 2 gallon option) with chrome side-panels, knee grips and the round badges already mentioned.

For 1955, with the frame adopted optionally at home (the rigid versions were dropped that year) came Amal Monobloc carburettors, as well as a redesigned engine-shaft shock absorber with two lobes instead of four. The new frame also carried a steering-head lock. The B31 acquired a new rear mudguard. For 1955 and 1956 only the manual advance-retard was reversed. This meant that the ignition was retarded when the cam return spring was compressed, ie when the lever was pushed forward instead of pulled towards the rider as was customary. For the remaining year it was fitted, the control reverted to 'normal'.

For 1956 roadsters, the swinging-arm frame became standard, as did the dual seat. Closer ratios were adopted for the B33's gearbox with a

64

third gear of 5.0:1; and both singles were fitted with sidecar lugs, to fill the gap created by the phasing out of the side-valve M-range that year. A further refinement was an optional four-section enclosure for the rear chain. Another distinctive feature of this major change year was the adoption, for both singles and twins, of the Ariel full-width hub with its 7 × 1.5 in brake front and rear, still featuring the excellent quick-detachable rear wheel in modified form, with a rubber plug fitted in the hub to give access to the taper-seated domed nuts on the driving studs. (The M33, and the side-valve M21 which survived for special order only, acquired the previous 8-inch front brake as well as the deeply valanced mudguard which the B-range retained.)

This 1956–57 Ariel brake had provision for adjustment not at the handlebars, but at the shoe fulcrum. As Peter Howdle points out in his *Best of British*, the brakes operated well enough in the dry—a mid-1956 B31 road test has the 420 lb machine stopping in 32 ft from 30 mph—but were not good in the wet, and when BSA for a period attempted a substitute of Ferodo 'green' racing-type linings, the results in wet conditions were even worse. A further drawback was that the rear brake was now cable-operated, with attendant sponginess, which meant that it was not adopted for the Gold Stars, as it was felt to be unsuitable for the Goldie's high speeds.

There were few further changes during the

company's 1957 period of retrenchment. For 1958 however, in line with their AMC heavyweight rivals but not their own twins, the BSA big singles acquires ac electrics, as well as slimmer Girling rear suspension units, and a clutch modified from 6 to 4 springs. The plates on this featured segments of Neolangite, a new friction material which was claimed to permit a higher oil level in the chaincase, but which in practice, did not eliminate a tendency for the BSA clutch to drag or slip. As with the twins, there was a change to a Triumph-type full-width cast-iron hub to replace the (also full-width) '56-on alloy Ariel type. This may have been rationalisation, but the new brakes and hubs were heavy, no more effective than their predecessors, and not well liked.

The change to ac electrics with a crankshaft-mounted alternator precluded the use of an engine-shaft shock-absorber, so the redesigned clutch assembly also incorporated a rubber-block vane-type shock-absorber. The rectifier and ignition coil were housed behind a tool-box cover which was now domed, and in place of the magdyno there was now a gear-driven contact-breaker. As already mentioned, it seems this conversion could equally have been applied to the A7/A10 twin range.

Further changes for 1958 included the welcome conversion from the previous $\frac{5}{8} \times \frac{1}{4}$ in rear chain to one of sturdier $\frac{5}{8} \times \frac{3}{8}$ in dimensions. There was also an equally welcome redesign of the

Workhorse on the way to work. 1956 B33 in swinging-arm frame with that year's Ariel-type brakes.

1958 B range's crankshaft-mounted alternator in detail.

previously awkward centre stand, which now featured roll-on feet and together with the A-range, a genuine one-piece headlamp nacelle. The petrol tanks were restyled, becoming deeper at the front so that their base-line was nearly level, and the tank side-panel chroming was extended round the upper curvature of the sides. As a result of the slimming down and removal of unnecessary clutter, these late BSA singles were some of the most handsome built.

However, September of that year saw the announcement of the new light 250 single, the C15. The writing was on the wall for the big bangers. There were no changes for 1959, and late in that year the B31 was discontinued. The 1960 B33 featured the new pear-shaped badges in line with most of the rest of the range, and like the twins, cam-action cable-adjusters abutting the handlebar pivot blocks for clutch and front brake levers, and a rear brake cam lever repositioned to provide increased initial pressure on the leading shoe. At the end of the year the 500 cc too was dropped from the range. Man-sized, economical (both of petrol and in terms of initial cost—in 1953 they were the lowest priced ohv singles on the market), with their many plus points for the rider such as their large fuel tanks and storage capacity and qd rear wheels, they were to be missed.

Their faults had rarely been fundamental. Awkward centre stands had been fitted up until 1958, and mild oil leaks had occurred which were to a certain extent masked by the black-painted heads and barrels. The occasional build-up of carbon on the B31's exhaust valve stem used to produce a characteristic squeak and the clutch was less than perfect. Added to that there was the rather loud exhaust note. One other potential source of trouble on pre-1958 machines was that the engine shaft shock-absorber lock-nut could come undone, resulting in excessive end-float and eventual disaster. One cure is to make up an alloy-bronze thrust washer and rivet it to the crankcase face. The alternator-electrics fitted from 1958 together with their AMC counterparts were desirable in some ways but featured a combined Lucas lights/ignition switch with a dubiously efficient emergency start position. The switch itself was also vulnerable in wet weather. Parts for it, such as the advance-retard assembly behind the contact-breaker, are difficult to come by.

But by and large they were very reliable, easy to start and good-handling at all available speeds, especially following the introduction of the swinging-arm frame. Prices are still reasonable, and an additional incentive for some is the possibility of tweaking by using Gold Star engine parts, though tuning an old iron engine with cams and compression ratios intended for an alloy one with its greater heat dissipation should obviously be avoided. Faithful plonking is more the B31/B33's line.

BSA: The B31/B32/B33/B34—dates and specifications
Production dates
B31—1945–59
B32—1946–57
B33—1947–60
B34—1947–57

Specifications
B31
Capacity, bore and stroke—348 cc (71 mm × 88 mm)
Type of engine—ohv single
Ignition—(1945–57) Magneto (1958–59) Coil
Weight—(1951, rigid) 343 lb (1956, s-arm) 410 lb

B32
As B31
Weight—(1951, rigid) 320 lb (1956, special rigid) 324 lb (1957, swinging-arm) 331 lb

B33
Capacity, bore and stroke—499 cc (85 mm × 88 mm)
Type of engine—ohv single
Ignition—(1946–57) Magneto (1958–60) Coil
Weight—(1951, rigid) 354 lb (1956, swinging-arm) 421 lb

B34
As B33
Weight—(1951, rigid iron engine) 330 lb (1956, special rigid) 329 lb (1957, swinging-arm) 336 lb.

BSA: The B31/B32/B33/B34—annual development and modification
1950
For B34 Competition:
1 Alloy head and barrel with separate pushrod-tunnel, optional extra, (as for B32 1949) saving 20 lb weight.

1951
For B32/B34 Competition:
1 Redesigned frame, with longer top tube, steeper fork angle.

1952
For B31/B33 roadster:
1 From March: chromed petrol tanks and wheels discontinued.

2 New single-wing chrome and yellow tank badges.

3 Brake fulcrum pin and cam bearing stiffened.

4 Dual seat available as option.

For B32/34 Competition:

5 Head and barrel redesigned again, sand cast with pushrod chambercast in roadster models.

1953

For B32/B33 roadster models:

1 Chrome panelled petrol tanks and wheels reintroduced.

2 Redesigned number-plate incorporating Lucas stop and tail light, blended into lines of mudguard by a steel fairing, with red reflector at bottom of the plate.

3 New adjustable headlamp-speedometer semi-cowling incorporating light switch and angled ammeter, and featuring underslung pilot lamp.

4 Redesigned tool-box shape for plunger-sprung machines.

5 Modified petrol tank mountings with a horizontal through-bolt at each end and slightly larger tank.

6 Increased engine finning, and finned collar where exhaust meets cylinder.

For B33 roadster model:

7 Con rod shortened by $\frac{1}{2}$ in and gudgeon pin placed lower in a split-skirt piston.

8 8 in front brake.

9 Deeply valanced front mudguard (as on twins).

1954

For B31/B33 roadster models:

1 For export only, new all-welded duplex cradle frame with pivoted-fork rear suspension, new gearbox with separate drain-plug, screw-out adjustment of primary chain, and modified ratios (1, 1.211, 1.759, 2.581 to 1), aluminium primary chaincase, modified head-steady stay, single-bolt petrol tank fixing with tanks enlarged to 4 gallons, still featuring chrome side-panels and kneegrips but now with round plastic piled-arms tank badges.

1958 B31 with that year's brakes, silencer and nacelle.

For B32/34 Competition:

2 Twin-front down tube frame as Gold Star but with rigid rear end.

3 Gearbox as above but ratios 1, 1.549, 2.339, 3.167 to 1.

1955

For B31/B33 roadster models:

1 As 1954 (1), for home market, as option.

2 Steering-head lock fitted.

3 Underslung pilot light discontinued.

For pivoted-fork machines:

4 Amal Monobloc Type 376 carburettors, with plastic pipes.

5 Redesigned engine-shaft shock-absorber with two lobes replacing previous four.

For B31 roadster model:

6 Redesigned rear mudguard.

7 Ignition advance-retard control lever operated by outward instead of customary inward movement to retard.

For B33 roadster model:

8 Rubber air cleaner connection to carburettor.

1956

For B31/B33 roadster models:

1 Swinging-arm frame etc, and dual seat becomes standard.

2 New Ariel-type full-width front and rear ribbed cast aluminium wheel hubs, webbed internally for rigidity, with centrally disposed 7 × 1.5 inch brakes adjusted at shoe fulcrum, not lever. Qd rear wheel modified, with rubber plug fitted to give access to four taper-seated domed nuts on the driving studs. Hole-and-tommybar rear wheel removal replaced by spindle which is a bolt.

3 4-piece rear-chain enclosure as option.

4 Front fork modified to take $\frac{3}{8}$ pint oil ($\frac{1}{4}$ pint previously).

1958 B33, showing alternator housing.

For B33 roadster model:
5 Closer gear ratios (overall 5.0, 6.0, 8.7, 12.9)

1957
For B32/B34 Competition models:
1 Duplex swinging-arm frame adopted, as Gold Star, with central oil tank.

1958
For B31/B33 roadster models:
1 Lighting and ignition now by Lucas 60 watt AC unit, with crankshaft mounted alternator, causing engine-shaft shock-absorber to be replaced by rubber-block vane-type incorporated in clutch assembly. Gear-driven contact-breaker with automatic advance-retard.
2 4-spring, 4-plate clutch with Neolangite segments, new friction material permitting higher oil level in chaincase. Clutch springs now have lock nuts.
3 Tool-box now houses rectifier and coil. Box is domed to suit, oiltank domed to match.
4 Sidecar attachment points fitted.
5 Redesigned roll-on centre stand.
6 $\frac{5}{8} \times \frac{3}{8}$ in rear chain replaces previous $\frac{5}{8} \times \frac{1}{4}$ in.
7 New full-width cast-iron Triumph-type wheel hubs front and rear, with 7×1.12 in brakes, plates enamelled black with polished rim bands. Front brake torque arm replaced by a slotted boss on the shoe plates which engages with a lug projecting from the inner face of the front fork leg. Front fork legs now have end caps, replacing previous pull-out spindle. Rear brake cable-operated.
8 Complete head-lamp nacelle replaces previous semi-cowling. Houses speedometer, ammeter and combined lights/ignition.
9 Petrol tank redesigned, deeper at the front, with base line more level, and tank side-panel chrome extended round the upper curvature of the tank side.

10 Horn now housed in new flat upper fork shroud beneath nacelle.
11 External rocker box oil-feed pipes deleted.

1959
No changes

1960
For B33 roadster models:
1 Rear-brake cam lever repositioned to provide increased initial pressure in the leading shoe.
2 New tank with pear-shaped plastic badges.
3 Handlebar adjusters provided at levers for clutch, front brake.

BSA: The C10/C11/C12 singles
The four-stroke tiddlers of the range, the side-valve C10 and ohv C11 in our period derived from pre-war models. These had been introduced with the C10 for January 1938, the C11 following for 1939.

Almost immediately post-war, when they were reintroduced in April 1946, both adopted versions of the BSA telescopic forks, with shrouded springs and hydraulic damping, as well as foot gearchange for both as standard. Most also featured a separate oil tank—previously this had been combined with the fuel tank and as late as 1949 some C11s retained this arrangement. This is the first example of many, many anomalies that will be encountered on the C series which were very much built down to a price—often with whatever BSA had to hand at the time. They were certainly cheap—the C10L at £144 was the second cheapest 250 in the land after the infamous Brockhouse Indian Brave, while the C12 was the cheapest ohv 250 of its day at just £160.

Both had featured coil ignition from the start, and while not exactly microweights (dry weight of a 1951 C10 was 270 lb), or exciting performers, they were 'proper bikes' in respect of fittings and feel, fairly reliable in a soft-tuned way, and economical to buy and run—the 1951 C11 would return an average of at least 80 mpg, and the figure at a constant 40 mph, the likely average commuting speed rose, to 94 mpg.

The two early machines shared similar cycle parts with the exception of their wheels, which were 3.00 × 19 in for the side-valve, 3.00 × 20 in for the ohv C11. Initially both heads and barrels were iron, but in a bid to counter overheating the C10 (along with the larger side-valve models) acquired an alloy head for 1951. The dry sump lubrication system with its skew-driven double-gear oil pump was similar to the B-range, the pump being mounted in the same position within the right half of the crankcase. Both the 63 mm × 80 mm engines featured roller bearing big-ends, and a built-up crankshaft running in a plain timing-side bush and a drive-side ball-race bearing. A pressed-steel primary chaincase cover was not one of the design's blessings. The coil electrics (at first) involved points in a car-type housing set at an angle forward of the cylinder, with automatic advance-retard. The rest of the system consisted of a dynamo set to the rear on the timing side, and chain-driven from the camshaft.

The frame of both bikes was initially rigid, a brazed-up, single down-tube, diamond-shaped item. The forks have already been mentioned, and brakes were 5½ in front and rear, the front in particular sometimes proving less than satisfactory. The separate three-speed gearbox, initially all that was available, was again not ideal, with widely-spaced ratios and a rather high bottom gear, which meant clutch-slipping on hill starts. The C11's valve-gear featured a cross-over layout for the push-rods, which were operated by a single camshaft with cranked cam followers; this cross-over arrangement had first been seen on a 1935 Francis-Barnett model, the Stag. Valves were of austenitic steel, with two concentric springs for each valve, and with the rockers spring-loaded endwise to prevent play and rattle. Compression ratios were a lowly 5.0:1 for the C10, 6.5:1 for the C11, and this meant no valve-lifter was needed. As there was no air-lever and, with the coil ignition, no advance-retard, the handlebars of each were notably uncluttered.

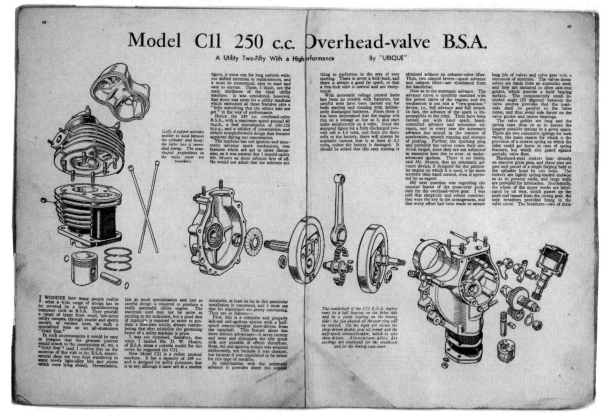

Below left *C11 engine internals, 1949.*

Right *Plunger C11 De Luxe for 1952.*

Below right *1954 C10L side-valve.*

There had been a De Luxe C11 available from 1948 on, but this merely featured a petrol tank and wheels in an alternative blue and chrome finish. For 1951, however, there was progress, with a four-speed gearbox, of similar design internally to the B-range, as well as a plunger-sprung frame, both being offered, though initially for export only. So for 1952, De Luxe models of both C10 and C11 became those with both plunger rear springing and four-speed box, chrome finishes having been dropped for that year. But all possible combinations were also available, including three-speed plunger and four-speed rigid. For 1953 chrome was back, dual seats were an optional extra, and speedometers were moved from the top of the two and a half gallon petrol tank, which they had occupied since 1946, to the headlamp shell where the ammeter was already located. For 1953 also the C11's 3×20 in wheels were reduced to a standard 3×19 in, bringing the diameter in line with both the C10 and the current Bantam.

For 1953 and 1954 there were more substantial changes. The C10L and C11G were introduced, with crankshaft-driven alternator electrics behind a chaincase modified to suit, and solid-state rectifier. However, some C10Ls (L was for Lightened) had C10 dynamo engines in the new frame, and the earliest alternator models had direct lighting. On most the dynamo was replaced by a 50-watt Wipac generator housed within the primary chaincase for the C10L, and the Lucas equivalent for the C11G. Their methods of adjustment differed, but only slightly. The ignition cam and auto-advance unit were keyed directly on to the end of the camshaft, with the points now housed behind a small cap on the timing side. Initially an extractor bolt was necessary to free the auto-advance mechanism from the camshaft, but

250 c.c. S.V. Model C 10 L   £95, plus £19. tax.

Engine: 63 mm. x 80 mm. 249 c.c. side valve; dry sump lubrication; oil tank 4 pints; A.C. generator supplying current through a metal rectifier to 9 amp.-hr. battery; coil ignition with contact breaker incorporating auto-advance built into timing gear; Amal carburetter. Primary chain drive in oil bath; clutch with built-in rubber cush drive; 3-speed gearbox with foot change, ratios 6.6, 9.8, 14.5. Welded tubular frame with plunger rear suspension; petrol tank 2½ gallons; brakes 5½ in. front, 5 in. rear; Dunlop 2.75 x 19 tyres. Cowl mounted headlamp; stop & tail lamp and electric horn; metal toolbox with kit; tyre inflator; licence holder. Finish: duo-tone green; bright parts including wheel rims chromium plated.

during mid-1954, a central bolt which itself acted as an extractor was introduced. There was an oil seal incorporated into the timing cover, and extreme care had to be exercised when replacing the cover, as damage to the seal allowed leakage of oil on to the contact-breakers, and all kinds of grief subsequently. (Later models had a hole drilled in the points cover to drain any oil off.) Further engine changes included a crankcase breather revised from the previous disc valve to a timed port linked to drillways in the drive-side mainshaft, as well as a three-vane shock-absorber in the clutch centre replacing the previous cam-lobe on the crankshaft.

Frame-wise the C10L featured an all-welded lightweight steel tube frame similar to that being

Above *1954 C11G, bicycle pump and all.*

Below *But does she cook as good as she looks? 1954 hype for the new C11G.*

used on the new Bantam Major. In fact it was identical to the Bantam frame, with gearbox plates crudely welded onto the bottom of the lower frame tube and with undamped teleforks to suit, incorporating gaiter seals and different front wheel spindle for the Bantam-type hubs. These hubs, used at the rear also, meant a reduction of brake diameter and width from 5.5×1 in to 5.0×0.62 in. In practice neither the 5 bhp Bantam's frame or wheels were to prove equal to the larger capacity 8 bhp engine, which tended to destroy wheel spokes and break frames. Both C10L and C11G adopted headlamp semi-cowls, in line with the larger machines, and the C11G featured a pressed-steel fairing between engine and gearbox, which was to continue on the later C12.

The spring-frame was now standard for the C10L, optional for the C11G, and the four-speed box now available only for the C11G. For 1955 there were complications due to simplifying the range, which meant that plunger springing became standard for both, though as writer Roy Bacon notes, 'a few C11G may have been built with rigid frames for that year', and also some very late C11Gs had swinging-arm frames, though they retained their single-sided hubs. Again only the C11G could be had with the four-speed box. The ohv model also acquired a deeper valanced front mudguard and a 7-in front brake with a strengthened spindle, no longer featuring a split-bush, or, like the previous year, adjustable cup-and-cone wheel bearings, and now with a hole for a tommy-bar replacing the previous hexagon-headed spindle bolt. Amal Monobloc carburettors were introduced as for the rest of the range. New camshafts with profiles to improve mechanical quietness, interchangeable with the old, were also adopted.

1956 saw the demise of the C11G in favour of a newcomer, the C12 (not to be confused with the 1940 C12, 350 cc side-valve). Internally this one was so similar to its predecessors that the engine numbers continued as C11G, but it incorporated a new gearbox, 'the light four-speed', with needle roller layshaft bearings, which was also adopted for the C10L. However, some C12s were fitted with the earlier A/B/M series box, with wider gearbox plates to suit. Weighing in at 312 lb dry, the C12 also featured increased output from the crankshaft-driver alternator, and external pipes to lubricate the valve-gear, with revised rocker-gear to suit. (Later C11Gs had already featured this positive lubrication, but as an optional extra.)

This revised engine was housed in a new single down-tube diamond-type frame, but this time

Rarity—C12 in police trim, 1957.

with pivoted-fork rear suspension and non-adjustable damper units—a *Motor Cycling* road test found them soft enough to induce pitching at top speed, which was still around 65 mph. BSA had clearly bodged the rear suspension, as one of its characteristics illustrated. At the rear of the gearbox plates, just one stud supported the frame and stand. This tended to wear the plates and the result was more often than not a 'hinge effect' which was alarming on corners but quite easily cured once detected. Otherwise the handling was good, and the machine was much more manoeuvrable than many of its competitors in the 250 class, such as the Francis Barnett or Panther.

The front forks were also revised, and incorporated full-width hubs with the same size brakes as before. Though early C12s had saddles only, dual seat was soon standard. Not so for the C10L, though it acquired the stronger frame, forks and hub (though not the larger brakes, and wheel size stayed at 2.75 × 19 in), as well as increased finning on the head and barrel. The C12 featured a combined headlamp/ignition switch mounted on the right-hand side-panel behind the oil tank, whereas the C10L now carried separate ignition and lighting switches on the headlamp.

And that was really all for the early C-range. 1957 saw little development in any of the current BSA models, and none for these lightweights. Side-valves were patently on the wane, and though it was the most pleasant British 250 of that type, the C10L was dropped in October 1957, and

the C12 went the following year, to make way for the Triumph-derived C15.

While scarcely road-burners, BSA had patently given some thought to what constituted a 'utility' bike, as commuter machines were then known. Cheapness, reasonable reliability with a minimum of attention, ease of starting and maintenance were the goals, and by and large these were achieved with the C-range for the 12 post-war years. Top speed on a C11 tested in 1951 was 64 mph, with 55 mph cruising, adequate enough for its intended purpose, with the miserly petrol consumption already mentioned. The C12, though heavier, differed little in performance with the C10 predictably slower at 56 mph top in a 1953 road test. The four-speed gearbox was a welcome addition for all, as was the dual seat since the C10/C11s saddles had been found by some to be too far forward for comfort. The brakes, whether 5 in or 7 in front, were a distinct weak spot.

The 'big bike' scale and fittings, while heavy, did provide effective mudguarding, useful storage space and a comfortable riding position (footrests, though not hand controls, were adjustable), with stability on poor surfaces and in cross-winds, though this applied less for the C10L with its Bantam cycle parts. Handling and roadholding were well up to performance, with the low ground clearance (about 5 in) due to the position of the centre stand on all three models being a limiting factor.

Several BSA Owners Club folk keep a C10 or C11 for their good looks and soft, chuffing character or in the case of the C12, their good brakes (when fitted with modern linings) and exemplary handling for a utility machine. But like so many coil-ignition Brits at the time and since, the lightweights were often let down by their electrics, with bob-weight pins that fell off, starter plate pins that snapped in half and advance-retard mechanisms that disintegrated. *Bike's* Royce Creasy wrote of a second-hand C11G he owned in the early '60s that 'it may have been the nastiest thing BSA ever made'. The difference of opinion is probably decided by whether, like greatness, you were born to one of the utility mounts, achieved one, or had it thrust by circumstances upon you.

BSA: The C10/C11/C12 singles — dates and specifications
Production dates
C10 — 1938–53
C10L — 1953–57
C11 — 1939–54
C11G — 1954–55
C12 — 1956–58

Specifications
C10/C10L
Capacity, bore and stroke — 249 cc (63 mm × 80 mm)
Type — sv single
Ignition — Coil
Weight — C10 (1951) 270 lb, C10L (1954) 256 lb

C11/C11G
Capacity, bore and stroke — 249 cc (63 mm × 80 mm)
Type — ohv single
Ignition — Coil
Weight — C11 (1951) 284 lb, C11G rigid (1954) 301 lb, C11G spring-frame (1954) 316 lb

C12
As C11
Weight — (1957) 312 lb.

BSA: The C10/C11/C12 singles — annual development and modifications
1950
No changes

1951
For C10:
1 Alloy cylinder head.

For C11:
2 Increased finning on cylinder barrel.
For C10, C11:
3 Optional plunger-sprung rear suspension.
4 Optional 4-speed gearbox.
5 Screw-in horn button repositioned on top of front brake pivot block.

1952
For C10, C11:
1 Chrome petrol tanks discontinued.
2 Sleeve gear oil seal for four-speed gearbox.

1953
For C10, C11:
1 Chrome side-panels on petrol tanks reintroduced with winged BSA motif tank badge.
2 Dual seats optional extras.
3 Speedometer moved from tank top to headlamp shell.
4 Headlamp features underslung pilot light.
5 Redesigned number plate incorporating Lucas 525 Diacon stop and tail light blended into lines of mudguard by a steel fairing, with red reflector at bottom of plate.
For C11:
6 19 in wheels replace previous 20 in.

1954
1 C10L and C11G replace C10 and C11. Both with crankshaft driven alternators. C10L with Wipac 50-watt generator, C11G with Lucas equivalent. Crankcase breathing modified from disc valve to a timed port linked to drillways in drive side mainshaft. Three-vane shock-absorber in clutch centre replaced previous cam-lobe shock-absorber on crankshaft.
2 Headlamp semi-cowl adopted.
3 Pressed steel fairing between engine and gearbox.*For C10L:*
4 New all-welded lightweight steel frame and revised telescopic forks, spindle, hubs and brakes as on D3 Bantam Major, plus plunger rear suspension standard and three-speed box only.
Mid-1954, for C10L, C11G:
5 Central bolt acting as extractor introduced for freeing auto-advance mechanism from camshaft.

1955
For C10L, C11G:
1 Bar a few rigid C11Gs, plunger springing now standard.
2 Amal Monobloc (Type 375/4) carburettors introduced, with plastic fuel pipes (though some

1958, the last C12.

later C12s were to retain the previous remote float carbs).

3 Camshafts with quietening ramps, interchangeable with previous, introduced.

4 Chromed seam strips for petrol tanks.

5 Small round petrol tank badges adopted.

6 Pillion footrests type altered.

7 Optional air cleaners; circlip-retained corrugated wire and gauze type replace previous centre-screw-retained zig-zag felt type.

8 Underslung pilot light discontinued.

For C11G:

8 Deeper valanced rear mudguard.

10 7 inch front brake with strengthened spindle, full-width hub, no longer featuring split bush or adjustable cup and cone bearings. Tommy-bar hole replaces previous hexagon spindle-headed bolt. Adjustable fulcrum pin in each brake to equalise shoe pressure.

11 Steering head lock fitted.

1956

1 C12 replaces C11G. Modified lubrication to valve rockers. Increased output from generator. New diamond-type frame with pivoted-fork rear suspension featuring non-adjustable units. (BC11G engines fitted to C12s have larger crankcases than the earlier engines.) Combined lights/ignition switch on right-hand side panel. Semi-cowled headlamp. Dual seat only. Larger round plastic tank badges, on slightly larger ($2\frac{3}{4}$ gallons from $2\frac{1}{2}$ gallons) petrol tank.

For C12, C10L:

2 New four-speed gearbox with operating lever now enclosed within box, as only option.

3 Telescopic front forks with hydraulic damping.

4 Optional, wire-and-fabric 'Pancake' type air cleaners modified.

For C10L:

5 Increased finning on head and barrel.

6 Separate lighting and ignition switches in headlamp.

7 Oil filter body now of C12 type, no longer also retaining the banjo union of oil supply pipe.

Late 1956, for C12:

8 From Frame No. 29-4560, strength of springs in rear suspension units increased 25 per cent.

1957

For C12:

1 From Engine No C11G-34426, change in strength of bob-weight springs on advance-retard mechanism.

BSA: The Gold Star singles

The BSA catalogue puts it severely. 'The Clubman's model Gold Star has been developed for competitions in road and short circuit events, and its specification is such that it is neither intended nor suitable for road use as a touring motor cycle.'

So classic or not, what is this section doing in a book of roadster models? Well, the dictum above came from a 1961 catalogue, and by that stage the roadster Gold Star variety had been dropped—this had happened for 1957—and strenuous efforts were being made to kill off the Goldie by the BSA Group management. So the catalogue omits to mention that, though race-bred, the big single had been available in touring as well as Clubman's, road racing, trials and scrambles trim.

And if further justification is needed for including the handsome and well-loved Goldie, it can be found in the way which the machine, production-based, passed many benefits arising from its development on to the rest of the range. These had included the swinging-arm frame, the single-bolt tank fixing and two enlarged front brakes.

Both the 350 cc B32GS and 500 cc B34GS were well suited by their history to double up as competition machines and sporting roadster. The

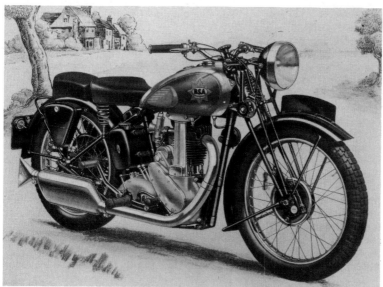

Left *Ancestor I: 1937 M23 Empire Star, basis of the Gold Star.*

Below left *Ancestor II: the 1937 Gold Star engine.*

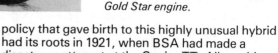

policy that gave birth to this highly unusual hybrid had its roots in 1921, when BSA had made a disastrous attempt at the Senior TT. All machines entered had failed to finish, and thereafter the company had sworn off any involvement with road racing.

However, by 1937, while still chary of an official factory racing programme, they wanted to build a machine that private owners could buy and race for themselves. And this was to be the area of motor cycle sport which the Clubman's TT races on the Isle of Man were to be introduced, ten years later in 1947, especially to cater for, with amateur riders from ACU-affiliated clubs mounted on commercially available machines, with permitted variations which changed from time to time.

In 1937 the M23 Empire Star, a touring 500 cc ohv single, was chosen as the basis of this effort; it was one of that range of singles designed by Val Page which was to form the basis of both the post-war B- and M-range. The 'Star' system had originated earlier, incidentally, with a tuned and bench-tested special version of a previous BSA classic, the 500 cc 'Sloper', the special Sloper being marketed as the Red Star. Now the M23 was developed by David Munro as a sportster, and in June 1937 was fettled and tuned so as to win a Brooklands Gold Star, which were awarded for a race lap speed of the famous pre-war Surrey circuit of 100 mph or more.

The machine, ridden by Wal Handley, which achieved this, with a fastest lap speed of 107.57 mph, was methanol-fuelled and featured a 13:1

compression ratio. But in 1938 a replica, also Val Page-designed, was marketed under the name of the M24 Gold Star. As well as recalling the feat at Brooklands, the name signified that each machine bearing it had been individually built out of selected parts, tuned and dynamometer-tested, with crankcases as well as valve ports, con-rods and flywheels all polished. This was to continue to apply to all Gold Stars (except 1970–72 B25 and B50 models, a completely different design derived from the C15 unit 250 cc single, which revived unjustifiably and most insensitively, the Gold Star name alone).

The 1938 machine featured a magnesium alloy gearbox shell and an aluminium-alloy head and barrel, the use of alloy being previously unknown in a mass-production motor cycle. But true to the guidelines laid down by the management — that the sports bike for economy's sake should resemble the production roadsters in as many respects as possible — its frame and girder forks were those of the standard tourers, and though it featured a lighter high-tensile steel frame together with a 20 in WMI front wheel, handling was not up to the 90 mph available performance.

Immediately after the war, the pre-war iron-engined tourer returned in the guise of the 350 cc B31, and in 1946, the B32, also iron-engined, for trials work. Their 500 cc equivalents, the B33 and B34, appeared in 1947, and after an initial girder-forked batch of B31s, all these singles featured the post-war BSA telescopic fork (for details, see The B31/B33 singles, page 60). And it was trials, in fact, which led to the next important stage in the Goldie's development, and ultimately, the development of the whole BSA range. Trials, and to a lesser extent, scrambles were very popular immediately post-war, being suited to the rough-and-ready machines and the low-octane fuel available — and they were not included in BSA's antipathy to racing. The sport, after all, had developed from pre-war road runs called 'reliability trials' which then adopted off-road 'rough sections' to keep things interesting, and testing their products in those punishing conditions had contributed much to BSA's reputation for rugged and reliable machines.

In 1946 BSA's competition manager Bert Perrigo, who was master-minding the B31's development into the competition B32, hired Bill Nicholson, winner of the recent Cotswold scramble, to develop and ride the works competition machinery. Nicholson was friendly with fellow Irishman Rex McCandless, who with his brother Cromie, was experimenting on a revolutionary new pivoted-fork rear suspension system. Although Velocette had developed a similar layout for the pre-war ohc Mark VII series of over-the-counter racers, their version had employed expensive oil-damped and air-sprung legs, while McCandless was simply adding springs to car-type damper units.

Nicholson proved himself as versatile as the machine he was helping to develop, for in 1947, in addition to his off-road successes, it was he who rode the link model with the pre-war alloy-engined M24 Gold Stars in its first road race. Although that year saw the first Clubman's TT, the race in question was the Manx GP, and the machine basically a version of the 1940 B29 Silver Sports iron-engined 350 cc, but now with light-alloy head and barrel, and Electron magnesium alloy crank-cases. Like the B29, it featured integral rocker boxes, and the hairpin valve springs originally designed by Norton's Joe Craig during a brief stop at Small Heath.

With suitably modified valve and ignition timing and bumped-up compression ratio, this experimental engine was housed in a frame which featured Feridax-McCandless pivoted-fork rear suspension. It circulated respectably until Nicholson miscalculated his pit-stop and ran out of fuel, and that was the hybrid 350's last race outing. However, in late 1948, a machine with coil springs replacing the hairpins but otherwise a substantially similar alloy engine, and, alone of all the singles, plunger springing as standard, went on the market for 1949 as the B32 Gold Star. For a short time it still featured the enlarged rocker boxes, despite their being unnecessary with the demise of the hairpin springs. A more serious limitation was the cylinder head's restricted valve angles. These were all common to the whole range, and though the racing version had the inlet valve machined out to 1 in diameter, and sported an Amal 10 TT carburettor, the engine's development was limited for a time by the need to keep in line with cooking production machinery.

Since trials were king and sales there greatest, racing had to take a back seat temporarily. But despite the restrictions, these first 350 cc Gold Stars, the ZB32s, shortly followed by ZB34 big brothers, offered an impressive variety of options. There was a range of four cams, three different sets of gear ratios (standard, scrambles and racing), four different compression ratios for instance (6.5:1 touring, 7.5:1 racing on Pool fuel, 9:1 on petrol/benzole, and 12.5:1 on alcohol for the 350), conventional, straight-through or megaphone silencers, and 3 or 2 gallon steel petrol tanks, as well as different wheel sizes for different jobs. 43-tooth clutch and 42-tooth rear wheel

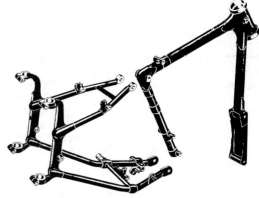

sprockets were standard, with a 44-tooth clutch sprocket as an option from 1954 and there were engine sprockets available from 15 to 21 teeth, and gearbox sprockets of 16 or 19 teeth. It all amounted to the road rider's, and especially the Club rider's, dream — to drive your stock machine to competition events, transform it at minimum effort and expense into a purpose-built mount, and then blow the (preferably exotic) opposition into the weeds. At that stage of the various games involved, though not of GP racing, this was still a real possibility, and it was helped by the BSA's strength and versatility, by points like the good accessibility to the timing case for valve timing, by the way in which modified parts were introduced quickly by the factory to help riders with problem areas, and by the genuinely economical purchase price and running-costs, which was one positive result of the management's cautious approach—a 1954 500 cc Gold Star set you back £239.14s, against £366. 0s. 0d. for a 350 cc AJS 7R racer.

The decision to exploit the racing potential of the engine was taken after a 350 cc Gold Star ridden by Harold Clark had won the 1949 Junior Clubman's TT, a feat they were to repeat every year until 1956. Now the development department could put their full resources into finding more horses from the big singles with no sacrifice of reliability, in contrast to their previous necessarily unofficial approach. Bill Nicholson said later that the bike 'wasn't really designed — it just happened.' But while this may have been true of its origins, and in some cases the cycle parts — as we shall see with the continuing story of Nicholson's work on a new frame — another story emerges from the book *Goldie* — a tale of prolonged, continuous application and craftsmanship on the part of engineering experts and the steady overcoming of problems in many areas of the machine.

Above left *Post-war 350 Goldie — B32 GS for 1950.*
Above *First post-war plunger frame.*

The author of *Goldie* felt that, as well as wanting to steer clear of the factory politics involved, this high point of Small Heath's efforts had been essentially a team effort, and so in the main declines to name those involved — himself included, preferring the pseudonym 'A. Golland'. But journalist Bob Currie had identified him as Arthur Lupton, the man once responsible for BSA factory service sheets and manuals, and his detailed and absorbing 'development history', while occasionally irritatingly vague on dates, redresses potential gaps in knowledge caused by subsequent events such as the demolition men at Small Heath burning ten tons of BSA technical literature before anyone could stop them.

Other names prominent in Gold Star development at one time or another were ex-Rudge man, Roland Pike, who, as race shop chief, master-minded the late DB and DBD versions; camshaft wizard Jack H. Amott; Bert Hopwood, who worked on the engines extensively, revising cylinder head design, modifying cam forms, and introducing the eccentric spindle tappet adjustment, all of which resulted, as intended, in the successful 500s for Daytona in 1954; as well as factory tuning experts like Cyril Halliburn, and Hopwood's cohort Doug Hele who collaborated with Bill Nicholson to produce a camshaft for the 500 cc scrambler which went into Johnny Draper's bike and boosted its power, according to Nicholson, to 43.6 bhp. But the development department drew on many skills and talents, such as the factory gear-cutting and pipe-bending facilities, as well as the work needed on valves and valve-springs and the special form-grinding which the manufacture of those valves involved. The Goldie was indeed a team effort of which the whole factory could be proud.

The 500 cc B34GS had appeared for 1950 after a successful prior appearance, for works versions, in the 1949 ISDT. It, and the 350, featured a new 8 in front brake, which was later to be adopted by the twins. Its engine had the same 88 mm stroke as the 350, with an 85 mm bore — the pre-war 500 by contrast had featured a long stroke of 94 mm. The 350 and 500 Goldies at this stage could be tuned to develop 24 and 33 bhp respectively. And for 1952 came important developments on the heads and barrels; or rather, in late 1951 for the 500 cc, which at that point adopted a cylinder head altered to feature separate bolted on rocker boxes, despite fears (later proved unfounded) from the development men about possible loss of rigidity from the new arrangement.

The change was to keep in line with production requirements, and for the same reason the metal of the head and barrels, both more deeply finned now, changed from sand-cast to die-cast, the external clue on this being that the new push-rod tunnels had the piled arms insignia on them in relief rather than engraved. The 350 adopted these features from April 1952. At the same time, as for the 500, the valve angles of the head were reduced, and were no longer symmetrical. This meant that the downdraught angle of the inlet port could be increased to 15°, and a flatter type of hemispherical combustion chamber used. The inlet port was reshaped for a venturi (fireman's nozzle) effect. All these changes were undertaken with a view to more efficient gas flow and cylinder filling. The exhaust valve material was altered to the superior alloy steel Nimonic 80, though this

was an in fact misguided attempt to solve the problem of the valve collapsing slightly after prolonged heavy throttle openings, making for a difficult re-start. The actual problem was that the exhaust valve head, in the constant quest for weight-saving, had been made a little too thin, and redesign of valves and cotters, at the same time as an increase in size for both valves, was to solve the difficulty. So much so that it was later found the exhaust valve size could be reduced, twice, without further trouble.

The other big change to the 350 engine, which was still the main focus for development at this time, was that the con-rod was shortened half an inch to reduce engine height, the external clue being one less fin on the barrel, now nine-fin, though internally there was no alteration to the stroke. The changes in the head had meant a redesigned, lighter piston, with a scoop cut from the shorter skirt to clear the flywheels at BDC, now giving a standard compression of 8:1 for the Clubman's B32. The cams were redesigned to give slow transition ramps and consequently greater tappet clearances. These machines, having won from 1949 to 1952, continued to dominate the Junior Clubman's TT both numerically and on the leader board. The Senior event proved more difficult to master, due to the Norton International and Triumph twin competition.

Clubman's TT victory, Junior 1st and 2nd, 1952. Eric Housley (left) and Bob McIntyre (right) in the saddle. Bert Perrigo and Sales Manager, S. F. Digby fourth and third from right.

Meanwhile the experiences of factory trials and scrambles ace Bill Nicholson bore fruit in the production models for 1953. From as early as 1949 he had used two-way damping on his front forks, and he had been dissatisfied with the frame on his competition machinery, basically the pre-war one, simply adapted to the post-war tele forks, which on full extension off-road still let the mudguard hit the front down tube and exhaust pipe. In an article in *Classic Bike*, Nicholson told how for 1950 he fitted a longer top tube which extended the head lug forward and allowed the front down tube to sweep back at a sharper angle. Quite possibly there was direct experience brought into play here, for in his piece in *The Book of the Gold Star*, Titch Allen writes of Nicholson finishing a Scott Trial with his wheelbase shortened $1\frac{1}{2}$ inches as the steering head had been forced back and the front down tubes bent back by continual bulldozing through thick mud — finding that it handled better that way they measured the steering head angle, which was 63°, and kept it like that from then on. If true, this was 'suck it and see' with a vengeance. Certainly Nicholson altered the trail from $2\frac{1}{2}$ to $4\frac{1}{2}$ in, which with only an inch longer wheelbase moved the weight distribution further back, gave better purchase to the rear wheel, and improved the handling.

As already mentioned, from the beginning Nicholson had been working closely with the McCandless brothers on their experimental pivoted-fork rear suspension with hydraulically damped suspension units. In fact he had already internally converted the plunger units, which factory policy obliged him to be seen to be using, to hydraulic damping. Now for 1951 he combined these various strands of development and built his own design frame. This was a duplex cradle-frame of all-welded construction, featuring the 63° head angle. The first version was a rigid one for trials,

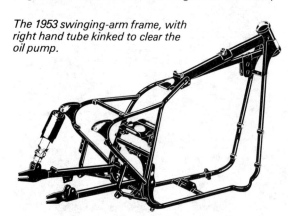

The 1953 swinging-arm frame, with right hand tube kinked to clear the oil pump.

and later in the year he added a privoted-fork rear end for scrambles. For his off-road purposes Nicholson had also reduced the weight, his own trials machine coming in at just 265 lb. The BSA versus AMC trials and scrambles battle was in full swing at that time, as well as a generation game, with older experts, like Nicholson and AMC's Hugh Viney, squaring up to the best of the rising generation which included Jeff Smith and Gordon Jackson. Nicholson's frame was effective, but it wasn't BSA production, and the Irishman had to fight hard to get his innovations accepted — which he eventually did by going to the top, in the shape of managing director James Leek (see page 13). The rigid version became the trials production model for 1952, by which time on the swinging-arm scrambles frame Nicholson had modified the Girling units to his own satisfaction, replacing the standard shim valves with orifice control. As he wrote later, 'BSA had exclusive use of these legs for two years, and Girling showed their appreciation with an annual cheque to me for several years after.'

Early versions of the frame, with the designs drawn up by Bernard Knight, had been pressed into service with the British Army team for the 1951 ISDT, which was led by Captain Eddie Dow, a name that will recur in the Gold Star story. And for 1953 the Goldie adopted the duplex swinging-arm frame as standard, as well as another piece of Nicholson work. This was the adaptation of the A7 twins' stronger gearbox for the big singles, which meant that primary chain adjustment was achieved by pivoting the newly designed shell of the box, rather than drawing it directly to the rear as previously.

Internally, some pinions were machined with internal dogs, while their mating gears were machined so that they telescoped inside, shortening, and hence stiffening and strengthening, the shafts. As the author of *Goldie* writes, 'the pinions were moved in pairs, selector forks being controlled by a camplate in turn operated by the new changing mechanism . . . Because the changes in direction of the (cam-tracks) were less severe and covered a larger area than the earlier type, wear was considerably reduced,' and gear engagement and retention improved. Four sets of ratios, trials, standard, scrambler and road racing, were offered. The clutch was also strengthened at the same time. An alloy primary chaincase replaced the old pressed steel item, and was both better looking and more effectively oil-tight. The 8 in front brake as standard with the 7 in brake continuing on trials and scrambles models, a six-pint oil tank, swivel-

1953 Gold Star Scrambler.

GOLD STAR and COMPETITION MODELS

bolt mounted against vibration, with a matching redesigned tool-box and a dual seat as standard, were among the other modifications of what now added up to an even more handsome and effective sports motor cycle.

These were the BB-series machines, and that was virtually the final version of the Gold Star as far as the cycle parts went. The whole BSA range benefited from the improvements. The head angle, though listed in the data books as 61°, in fact became Nicholson's 63°, and after the frame had been strengthened early on with a wrap-around gusset at the steering-head, production versions of it with minor modifications were adopted by the cooking roadster singles for 1954, and by the A7 optionally, and the A10 as standard, at the same time. And it really was substantially the same frame throughout the range—a BSA Owners Club member had had this spelt out for him in 1962 when he checked with the factory Service Department as to whether his Gold Star's frame was in fact made of Reynolds 531, the specially light and strong tubing; and they confirmed that it was not, and that apart from the lugs applicable to the type of competition the machine would be used for, the Gold Star specification was just as for the ordinary B31/B33.

Another difference in practice was that after the Clubman's exhaust/silencer changes for 1954, the crankcase or the lower frame tube could be grounded when cornering hard, because everything was tucked away so neatly. Steering and handling were adequate rather than

outstanding, but at the time, with Triumphs still hinged in the middle, AMC hindered by jampot rear suspension units until 1958, and the Norton Featherbed frame and Roadholder forks restricted to their top twins for the time being, the new arrangements for all the twins and big singles gave BSA a very convincing edge in the marketplace.

Back in the early '50s, the already-mentioned Army ISDT teamster Captain Eddie Dow, after taking Golds in that event for 1951 and 1952, like Nicholson proved to be as versatile as his mount. Buying a 500 privately, Dow rode it to considerable effect in the 1953 Senior Clubman's race, breaking Geoff Duke's lap record for the course before breaking quite a lot else besides when he crashed at Laurel Bank and wound up in hospital for three months. Whether it was due to Dow's performance or his blind faith, the company then decided to abandon the successful 350 which had spearheaded their development so far, and concentrate on the 500, with ex-Rudge tuner Roland Pike and Bert Hopwood masterminding the effort (though there was also to be a Cyril Halliburn-designed under-the-counter factory DBD32 with an oversquare engine capable of revving to 8,000 rpm).

The result, by April 1954, were the distinctively square-finned CB32s and CB34s, which had been redesigned to give 30 and 38 bhp at 6,800 and 6,600 rpm respectively in road racing trim. equating to top speeds in that form of 102 mph + for the 350 and over 110 for the 500. This was the start of the run of truly classic (and now highly

BSA GOLD STAR Models

Left *1954 square-finned CB32.*

Right *1954 CB engine.*

valued) Gold Star machines. The CB engines at that time were introduced for the Clubman's and Racing versions of the bike, and BBs being retained for the touring, trials and scrambles version until well into 1955.

The CB engine, with its massive square finning, had a redesigned head and barrel. Head gaskets of the Plexal-peelable type now gave fine adjustment of the thickness of the gasket, and hence reduced the gap between barrel liner spigot and head and helped eliminate the problem of blown gaskets. On both 350 and 500 the con-rod was shortened, and on the 1954 500 oval flywheels were employed to permit the piston skirt to clear the flywheel at BDC. The crankpin was now of EN36, and a mechanically timed crankcase breather, as on the Twins, was adopted. The method of cylinder head attachment was modified, with a fifth through-bolt, of the type that screwed into the crankcase, but located inaccessibly inside the pushrod tunnel, replacing one of the bolts previously securing the head directly to the barrel. The valve gear was lightened by the use of eccentric rocker spindles for adjustment purposes, eliminating the previous 'nut-and-bolt' valve clearance adjustment system in the push-rod tower. Valve tips were stellited, and a Nimonic 80 exhaust valve fitted. The pistons were modified, and standard compression ratios increased to 9:1 for the 350, 8.75:1 for the 500. The CB32's bottom end was strengthened, coming into line with the larger drive side main roller bearing as previously used on the ZB and BB 34 500s (though not their trials versions) and with

its lubrication modified. In the gearbox, the bearings at both ends of the layshaft were changed from plain bushes to Torrington needle rollers, boxes so modified having a 'T' included in the prefix to their number. The Girling rear suspension units were reduced in diameter to so-called 'slimlines', for all but the Scrambles models which adopted them the following year.

For the first time an Amal GP carb was offered, as well as alloy wheel rims. Further optional extras were 'clip-on' handlebars, stubby grips bolting directly on to the fork stanchions so that normal bars could easily be removed and refitted. These were a diabolical strain on the wrist for prolonged road riding, as they were only one inch higher than the 31 in seat height, but just the thing for the sporting Clubman, in combination with rear-set brackets giving adjustability to the footrests. These brackets are prized items today, as without them the pillion mountings have to be cut away and a mounting plate welded to the main frame cradle, playing havoc with a bike's originality.

The result of the CB's appearance was a clean-up in both Junior and Senior Clubman's TT races, a double 1—2—3 win for 1954. It was a vindication for the team and for James Leek, who had encouraged the search for power while retaining the push-rod design. And a rebuke for his principal competitors the AMC group, who had taken over Norton the previous year in time to see the ohc Internationals, genuinely race-bred, but unlike the full-race Manx still eligible for the Clubman's, blown away.

It happened again in 1955, when Eddie Dow

took first in the Senior during the only year in which the race was run over the shorter (10.8 mile) Clypse course. This was only fair, and Dow could now retire and set up shop in Banbury as *the* Gold Star specialist, where he was responsible for several improvements, including one to the front end, the Superleggera fork, with a special yoke, long bushes and a ball-valve to give two-way damping, which reduced fork travel and was to be featured on most racing Gold Stars. There was also a much-pirated float bowl extension, as well as definitive versions of the famous swept-back exhaust and 'twittering' silencer, so called because of the distinctive metallic chirping sound it produced when the engine was on the over-run.

1955 had seen both the BB and CB models marketed for the touring and Scrambles versions, with the CB variants for Clubmans and road racing, and the DB32 and DB34 also introduced for the Clubman's and racing models. The 500 DB engine reverted to round flywheels, necessarily smaller than the previous ones, which it had been found uneconomical to produce, but with the same results being obtained by shortening the piston skirt again. In quest of greater rigidity, for the DB32 the thickness of the cylinder barrel liner was increased from 3 mm to $\frac{1}{4}$ in, and this meant that, for the 350 only, it could now register direct into the crankcase mouth and became the barrel's major component, with the finned aluminium shell for cooling only. The fifth head to barrel through-bolt, introduced the previous year, was dropped after being thought too inaccessible, and the former arrangements returned to. Pressure feed of oil to the big end was achieved by reversing the previous system, which had featured a nozzle or quill, embedded in the crankshaft. The nozzle was now an extension to the mainshaft and registered in a garter seal in the timing cover through from the main oil supply at pressure.

Externally the main changes for the Clubman were a new exhaust and silencer, with the exhaust length shortened by sweeping the revised pipe back across the cylinder, and the silencer internals in two parts—a megaphone shape followed by a small expansion chamber, and then a short straight—through absorption silencer. The rounded shoulders at the front of the silencer were reduced to a conical shape to avoid fouling on corners. Also the carburettor, a $1\frac{3}{8}$ in Amal GP for the 1954 DB34 Clubmans, with a $1\frac{3}{16}$ GP for the DB32, had its float-chamber support changed to a vertical mounting. A Monobloc carb was adopted by the scrambles model, and clip-on handlebars became standard for the Clubmans. Late in 1955 the rear brake drum was changed to the 'Alfin'

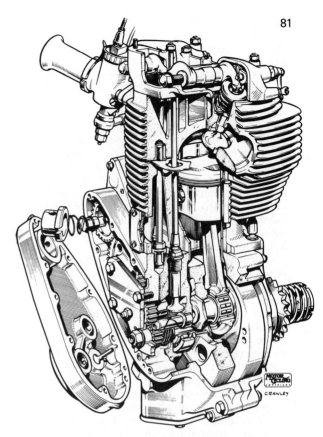

type, a finned light alloy casting bonded into position, ventilated, as the front brake had been since 1950, by six holes in the backplate, which were blanked off by detachable plugs. Both a speedometer and a rev counter were now fitted—previously it had been either/or.

The 1955 DBs were to be the limit of development for the 350, and the next year saw what was virtually the ultimate version of the 500, the DBD 34. The AMC bosses were now complaining about the pace of race development on the Gold Star engine, and they were not alone in feeling that the Clubman's TT, with an overwhelming majority of the riders Gold Star-mounted, was becoming farcical, or as Titch Allen put it, 'a BSA benefit'. However, why a factory should be penalised for coming up with a successful sports production machine at a reasonable price is a mystery. There were, after all, other reasons for the Clubmans to search for extra horses—the special rigid-frame Goldies had done well at Daytona in 1954, and the US market demanded more power.

So what proved to be the apotheosis of the Goldie emerged for 1956; the Clubman's or racing DBD34 500 cc (the DB34 was retained for touring and scrambles, and the DB32 unchanged). The ACU, under pressure of other business and perhaps growing tired of the 'benefit', had banished the race to the week after the International event, and new regulations had also made silencers obligatory. However, Roland Pike had developed, from the previous year's combination of silencer and megaphone, a variation known as the 'twittering' silencer on account of a characteristic metallic chirping sound on the over-run, compounded of the extractor action of the silencer plus a large degree of valve overlap. Both 500 and 350 Clubmans were fitted with this. The same regulations meant that the Clubman versions had to fit lighting, including a generator, which came in the form of a Lucas Magdyno and accumulator equipment plus a 7 inch headlamp (racing and scrambles versions retained a dynamo-less magneto). Power for the racing DBD34 was up to 42 bhp at 7,000 rpm, so the introduction as an optional extra of a full-width hub 190 mm front brake, with linings 2 in wide, was timely, though its action was sometimes criticised as spongy. It consisted of an alloy hub bolted to a cast-iron drum, but with the shoes on an alloy backplate. The standard 8 inch front brake was also modified, small cast fins being fitted. The clutch friction material was strengthened, and in the gearbox, needle-rollers were added to the mainshaft sleeve-gear as well as the layshaft, hence creating the famous RRT2 gearbox — RR for extra close ratio, T for Torrington needle-rollers, 2 for the two times they were used as well as indicating a higher first gear than the RRT box.

With the Mountain circuit restored, Gold Stars took first and second in the 1956 Senior Clubman's, and the victor, farmer Bernard Codd, went on to win the Junior too. However, that was the end of the Clubman's races on the Isle of Man; 1957 being the year of the TT Jubilee, the organisers shifted the Clubman's off the island to become just another national race. This was far from the end for the Goldie in terms of racing, however, and by the late '50s they had set lap records at almost every British short circuit. But at National and International level its real background had been trials and then scrambles, where at home, on the Continent and in the USA, Gold Stars continued to be successful for several years. Their strength and reliability compensated for heavy weight and an engine designed for other things, although works rider John Avery compared the late trials and scrambles motors unfavourably with their AMC heavyweight counterparts in terms of low down punch, recalling how the DB

series would pop and bang low down and had to be revved constantly to keep up. Nevertheless, they were winners.

But development really stopped in 1956, which left the bike with its fundamental Achilles heel, the built-up flywheel assembly, a basically pre-war design, with the mainshaft pressed into the wheels and secured by rivets, each of which was a potential point of stress concentration. Its timing-side main bearing was a notorious weak spot, as were the con-rods, where adherence to production requirements meant that, although they were polished and crack-tested, only one central rib was used to stiffen the big-end eye. The crankshaft limitations might have been by-passed by the adoption of features developed by Roland Pike and found on the Geoff Monty racing GMS 250 and on the Taylor-Dow special racer, namely an outside flywheel with a one-piece crank and car-type big-end. However, Roland Pike departed to SU Carburettors in 1956, and development thereafter was stifled. As already mentioned (see page 24), David Munro stated that this was due to Edward Turner, Triumph's presiding genius, who felt the Goldie represented a threat to his Tiger 100 sports twins.

For 1957, the touring versions had been dropped, but both the DBD34 and the DB32 had been available in scrambles as well as racing and Clubman's versions. But at the end of the year the 350 was deleted from the catalogue, and the 500 was officially available in Clubman's or scrambles versions only. (From 1955 to their demise at the end of 1957, the competition or trials versions had been simply alloy-engined B32 and B34s, equipped with the BB-type engines, and not Gold Stars as such.)

Despite management disfavour, the Goldie's popularity ensured its survival for several years. Some American dealers, it was said, refused to order their quota of BSA twins unless a batch of Gold Stars were also supplied. Even the banished 350 crept back, as the 1959 catalogue included for Gold Stars '350 cc engine optional to order', and although this was blanked out in the subsequent year, the 350 cc DB32 was still available if one made a point of ordering it. This situation continued until production of both Goldies was finally ceased for 1963, though a trickle of machines to special order continued into 1964.

Their basis, the cooking B31/B33 singles, had gone in 1960 and 1961 respectively, and there were problems with Lucas about the supply of magdynos. It was also argued that, in a large concern like BSA, a couple of thousand machines a year, which being hand-made and bench-tested,

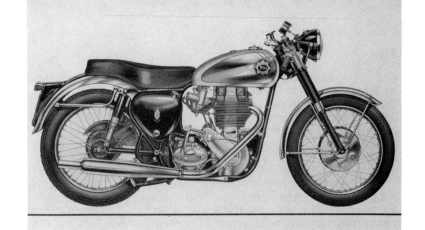

Ultimate: the street-legal Clubman's DBD34, for 1957.

Keeping the (US) customers happy. The DBD34 in Western USA export road trim.

Far out. Gold Star 500 cc Catalina scrambler.

BSA GOLD STARS
500 c.c. O.H.V. Custom Alloy engines

CATALINA SCRAMBLER 500 c.c. O.H.V. Alloy Single

The Gold Star in complete scrambles trim! Has scrambles gearbox, engine under-shield, sports tires, racing oil tank, special engine set-up now with full-race cams, reverse cone megaphone and larger carburetor for more horsepower output. World's most successful 500 c.c. Scrambler!

GOLD STAR Road Racer
500 c.c. O.H.V. Alloy Single

BSA Custom Gold Stars are representative of some of the finest engineering available in the motorcycle market today. With engines individually built to the most exacting racing standards and equipment tailored for the specific function whether it be the speedway, scrambles course or road racing, each BSA Gold Star represents the maximum form of development. Consistent winners in competition events, both at home and abroad, the words "BSA Gold Star" have become traditional over the years as emblematic of the finest in competition motorcycles.

tied up the most expert fitters and mechanics, and were just not worth it—although this ignored the prestige attached to the name as a whole by the production of a competitive machine of real excellence, as well as the fact that up till then the Gold Star had been one of the few racing machines ever to make a profit for its manufacturers. Ironically the Japanese, labouring in the '50s under far greater disadvantages, could still manage to build a replica Gold Star. Several thousand were produced by the Showa-Hosk company up to 1958, and not content with the revered basic design, their engineers experimented with different alloys for head and cylinders, and even an ohc conversion. Showa-Hosk were shortly afterwards absorbed by Yamaha, and one cannot imagine all that Gold Star data being ignored when the Japanese giant spearheaded the revival of big four-stroke singles with their XT500.

What remains of the Gold Stars themselves can be confusing. As we have seen, there was a genuine touring version up to the end of 1956. With the stock compression of 7.5:1 (for the BB34—7.25:1 for the CB), these were said to be easy-starting and docile mounts. But wasn't it missing the point of the Goldie to settle for a performance not far from the iron-engined B33? Possibly, but as we have seen Gold Stars were fairly easy to convert from one role to another (with some exceptions such as the original 7 inch rear brake, which did not permit the use of detachable rear sprockets). On the tourer vibration was down, petrol consumption up from the mid-40s to the mid-60s and with a normal ratio gearbox the bike was a good deal more tractable in traffic. So the tourer made sense for the road.

And you did still get a lot for your money. There was the expensive bit for BSA, the hand assembly by experts involving careful component selection and matching, especially of the big end—crankpin, rollers and con rod. The alloy head and barrel themselves meant a saving of some 20 lb weight over the iron engine. Then there were of course all the options available, which unlike the iron engine, the Goldie would be sure to be capable of exploiting. And there were ball as well as roller bearings on the drive side, and for 1954 the timing side housing was reinforced with strengthening ribs, though as we have seen this was never wholly adequate for racing stresses.

The crankcase itself was stiffened, both with additional internal ribs and by an increase in the width of the external ribs. The pistons differed in design from stock, and were machined to a high standard, the skirt being machined on an industrial diamond, and the crown turned to a high finish and then polished. The surface-finish of the barrels was also subject to considerable care. Stellite tips were brazed on to the valve stems, which were of improved nickle-chrome material, and from quite early on, the valve springs were of specially selected and ground material; later they were of chrome-vanadium alloy steel, which was itself then uprated. The valve gear employed lightened push-rods of duralumin and rocker barrels of reduced diameter, and the 1954-on modifications to the valve-operating mechanism has already been mentioned. Although once again racing stresses sometimes revealed flaws, the con-rods were polished and submitted to magnetic crack testing both to ensure a sound roller track, and to prevent something they were prone to, disintegration just below the small end. Even the suspect crankshaft got the treatment, employing crankpin nuts of larger than standard thread diameter, with their faces ground true with the threads. They were later made of case-hardened 50-ton steel with a 5% nickel content. The flywheels were balanced, and their rims and faces polished. For the racing versions, the braking surfaces were lightly machined in situ after the wheel was built to ensure perfectly concentric drums. It was quite a package, and most of it applied to every Gold Star made.

But the Clubman's is what the Goldie is really all about. Despite the factory denial cited at the beginning of this section, Vic Willoughby while testing the machines that won the 1955 TT, wrote that they were 'tractable enough for fast touring on public roads, though naturally, they are not as docile as might be desired for heavier traffic conditions'. So they do have a place in this book of roadsters, and certainly plenty of Gold Stars were, and are, run on the road in Clubman's trim, and many roadsters, whether genuine Gold Star, competition B32/34s or cooking B31/33s, were superficially converted to Clubman's specification by cowboys, and fitted with clip-ons, rear-sets and sports silencers.

However, with the genuine Clubmans, many of the modifications aimed at racing make for an awkward time on the road. The legendary RRT2 gearbox, which gave the DB34 a capability of just under 60 mph in first gear, has been described as a 'five-speed box with no first', and this meant that the clutch has to be slipped up to 20–30 mph. The Goldie fanatic would reckon this was worth it to experience the apparently endless acceleration in the steep first gear, but another minus point in traffic was the difficulty in finding first again once

Right *Performer: Jeff Smith on the 1956 ISDT Gold Medal-winning mount.*

Below right *One-off. Only rigid-frame Gold Stars were for US Daytona 200 race.*

the clutch had warmed up. (The BSA clutch was never a strong point, and many prefer to substitute the more effective Triumph equivalent.)

Alloy racing wheel rims are liable to dent, and kick-starting from cold the high-compression motor with its massive GP carburettor (for tractability and economy, this is often now replaced by an Amal Concentric, which is said to transform the bike as a roadster) was a considerable knack, and if not mastered immediately, virtually impossible, as was restarting once warm (Goldies would bump-start beautifully, however). The full-throated exhaust note from the twittering silencer could prove an embarrassment, noise pollution in a big way. In fact the Goldie could be said to offer a total sensory experience, as enthusiasts maintain that near-magical properties reside in Castrol R, a vegetable-based oil with a distinctive aroma (and an impractically long warm-up period for everyday use).

The noise, the smell, the feel of the power delivery which is particular to big singles taken to its apotheosis, in conjunction with good brakes—particularly the earlier 8 in single-sided front brake, though ironically it is the much more variable 190 mm full-width which is always sought by restorers—and its excellent, if not effortless handling and steering—these explain the enduring appeal of the Gold Star, which was arguably also the best bike from the greatest British factory. But it is for the true believer only and for those prepared to labour long and constantly. Eddie Dow himself considered it was safer to think of the bike as a highly stressed racer when it came to maintenance and tuning, whether you looked on it as a road bike or a racer, and advocated replacement of the con-rod and big-end assembly every 50 racing hours, and the Nimonic 80 exhaust valves every 20—and considered correct engine-timing and carburation (and the clutch-slipping skills) essential if the magic was to work. But for both the enthusiast and motor cyclists everywhere, these machines must remain, in the words of the author of *Goldie*, 'the acme of production sports motor cycles'.

BSA: The Gold Star—dates and specifications

ZB 32 GS 350 cc — 1949–52
ZB 34 GS 500 cc — 1950–52
BB 32 GS 350 cc — 1953–55
BB 34 GS 500 cc — 1953–55
CB 32 GS 350 cc — April 1954–55
CB 34 GS 500 cc — April 1954–55
BB 34 GSD 500 CC (Daytona solid-frame racer) — 1954
DB 32 GS 350 cc — Mid-1955–57, then 1959–63 by special order only
DB 34 GS 500 cc — Mid-1955–56
DBD 34 GS 500 cc — Mid-1956–57, then 1958–63 Clubmans and Scrambles only.

(Over the entire production period there were some B32 and B34 engines produced with the prefix 'X' denoting experimental or prototype engines, or those issued to the Competition Department as part of the development programme.)

Specifications
ZB32/BB32/CB32/DB32:
Capacity, bore and stroke — 348 cc (71 mm × 88 mm)
Type of engine — ohv single
Ignition — Magneto
Weight — 305 lb dry (1951) 380 lb 'approximately' fully equipped *(Motor Cycling)* (1954 Clubmans)

ZB34/BB34/CB34/DB34/DBD34:
Capacity, bore and stroke — 499 cc (85 mm × 88 mm)
Type of engine — ohv single
Ignition — Magneto
Weight — 305 lb dry (1951) 383 lb fully equipped (1955 Clubmans)

BSA: The Gold Star—annual development and modifications
1950
For B32 GS and new B34 GS:
1 8 in diameter × $1\frac{3}{8}$ in width single-sided front brake, with cast iron drum mounted on pressed steel hub.

1951
1 Alloy wheel rims as optional extras.

1952
1 Petrol tanks fitted with a brace across the bottom to prevent the two halves flexing.
2 No chrome on petrol tanks, wheel rims, stays, primary chaincase, chainguard, brake backplates and handlebars; all matt silver.
3 Four gallon petrol tank an optional extra.
4 Height of (optional) dual seat lowered half an inch.
5 Eccentric pin adopted for rear brake pedal adjustment.
6 De-frothing tower added in oil tank.
7 Kickstart and rh footrest modified to increase clearance.
8 Crankcase webs enlarged, for stiffness.
For B34 GS:
9 Cylinder head modified. Head and barrel now die-cast not sand-cast as previously, and rocker-boxes now separate from head. Valve angles reduced (from $24\frac{1}{2}°$ to 33° 45 minutes for inlet, 20° to 33° for exhaust) and downdraught angle increased from 7° to 15°. Inlet port reshaped to give tapered venturi form.
10 Austenitic iron valve seat inserts changed from screw-in to shrunk-in type. Valve guides shorter than previously, made of Hidurel 5, and pressed in.
11 Upper part of pushrod tunnel now horizontally finned.
12 New cylinder head permits 8:1 cr pistons, lighter than previous, with crown less raised, reduced stiffening rib and thinned-down wall. Skirt length reduced by $\frac{1}{4}$ in, scoops added to clear flywheels at BDC. Piston compression rings changed from $\frac{3}{32}$ in-wide L-section to $\frac{1}{16}$ inch plain.
For B32 GS, April 1952 from engine No ZB 32GS 6001:
13 Changes 9, 10, 11, 12 as *for B34 GS*, and
14 Exhaust valve steel changed to superior alloy, Nimonic 80, and exhaust valve head size increased from 1.470 in diameter to 1.525 in. Underside of head now blended into the stem with a long taper portion, and 'tulip-head' of valve reduced to a small saucer.
15 Connecting rod shortened by $\frac{1}{2}$ in, dropping number of barrel fins from 10 to 9.
For B32 GS Clubman, from June 1952:
16 Inlet valve head diameter increased from 1.532 in to 1.600 in, and now with a thicker head tapering slightly to the normal diameter.

1953
1 BB versions introduced with swinging-arm frame and hydraulically-damped rear suspension by three-position 'fat' Girling units. All-welded duplex main frame, with welded into the radius in each of the twin seat pillars a steel gusset plate forming the anchorage for the rear fork pivot spindle.

2 Revised, single centre-bolt, rubber-padded petrol tank mounting. 4 gallon steel tank now standard (with 3, 2 gallon options), fitted with large, round, red background Gold Star plastic badges.

3 Oil-tank fixing bolts passed through and were located in rubber cups, and with one of the two securing bolts now of swivel type. Previous metal oil pipes with rubber connections changed to armoured flexible type.

4 Gearbox becomes modified A7-type, but pivot-mounted and remote from engine, with mountings above and below new gearbox shell. Some pinions now machined with internal dogs, and their mating gears machined so as to telescope inside, hence shortening and stiffening shafts. Pinions moved into pairs, with selector forks controlled by a camplate operated by the new changing mechanism, with changes in direction of cam-tracks less severe and covering a large area, so reducing wear and improving gear retention and engagement. Choice of 4 sets of ratios.

5 Polished cast-aluminium primary chaincase replaces previous pressed-steel type.

6 New $5\frac{1}{2}$ pint oil tank shaped to suit frame, and new toolbox on lh side to match.

7 Chrome restored to petrol tank panels, mudguards, stays, chainguard, wheel-rims, damper lower covers, fork spring covers, headlamp rim.

8 Ignition timing lever set up the reverse of 'normal' ie full advance given when the control cable was slack, ensuring that ignition remained at full advance if cable should break.

For Roadster, Clubmans:

9 Dual seat of new type, and now fitted as standard.

10 Redesigned new number plate incorporating Lucas stop-tail light blended into lines of mudguard by a steel fairing.

For Clubman's, Road-racing BB32:

11 $1\frac{3}{16}$ in diameter Amal GP carb as optional extra.

1954

For Clubman's, Road-racing B32 GS and B34 GS from April 1954:

1 CB engine is produced. Conrod shortened again. Massive finning on head and barrel. On cylinder head, inlet tract lengthened by $\frac{9}{16}$ in, increased in diameter, tapering for first 3 in of length from $1\frac{3}{32}$ in diameter to $1\frac{3}{16}$ in diameter. Venturi diameter also increased to 1.455 in diameter, but no change in valve size. Reduction in exhaust port throat diameter to $1\frac{3}{8}$ in and use of a smaller (1.470 for 350, 1.530 for 500) valve.

Sparking plug insert now omitted, to improve heat transfer from plug to head.

2 Material of valve spring collars changed from 40 ton steel to high-grade Duraluminum. Valve springs of similar size but heavier poundage and better quality wire. Cotter seating angle increased to 20° to prevent possibility of valve pulling through collar. Hardened steel bell-end in rocker-arm discarded, replaced by cup machined in the arm to accept rounded end of push-rod, for lightness. Rocker arm drilled to provide positive oil feed.

3 Tappet adjusting components at bottom of push-rods discarded. Spigoted sleeve in push-rod now fits directly into the hollow tappet. Tappet increased in diameter. Provision for adjustment of valve clearances made at rockers, by making their bearing diameters on the spindles eccentric by 0.030 in, giving adjustment of 0.060 in.

4 Cylinder head held down by fifth through-bolt attaching head to barrel, of type screwed into underside of head and attached to crankcase like the other four. New bolt located inside push-rod casing, replacing one of four previous 'independent' bolts securing head directly to barrel.

5 Changes to flywheel. Crankpin material now 5% nickel steel. Keyway locating driving side of crankpin in the flywheel discarded. Consequently alignment marks included, to avoid crankpin obscuring flywheel/crankpin oil feed holes. Also deleted was small oil bleed hole from gearside flywheel, as a potential originator of cracks between crankpin and mainshaft. Flywheels (already $7\frac{1}{2}$ in diameter, and narrower than standard singles) replaced by new type with refashioned bob-weights for increased strength, with central disc area of wheel reduced in proportion to decrease flexibility. Balance factor increased from 55 per cent to 58 per cent for 350, 65 per cent for oval flywheels.

On 500 cc:

6 Engine breathing changed to timed rotary arrangement located in timing cover and driven by magneto pinion. Spring-loaded against the cover, it was ported to breathe through ports in the cover into an outlet in the cover's underside, and also to drive the rev counter box.

For CB34 GS:

7 With shorter conrods flywheels become oval so that piston skirt can clear flywheels at BDC. Balance factor of these flywheels increased from 55 per cent to 65 per cent.

For CB32 GS:

8 Driveside flywheel altered to accommodate a larger mainshaft, standardising with the 500 cc

Love object. A beautifully restored DBD34.

and allowing a larger drive side main bearing, also as on 500 cc.

For CB32 GS and CB34 GS:

9 Bearings at both ends of the gearbox layshaft changed from plain bushes to needle rollers.
10 Clutch strengthened, and new insert material, Ferodo MZ 41, of woven fabric as previous but with inserts of zinc. Number of plates in clutch increased from four to five. Strength of the compression springs increased.

For Clubman's and road-racing variants:

11 Optional clip-on handlebars offered, bolted direct to fork stanchions so that normal bars could be removed/refitted.
12 For road racing Amal $1\frac{3}{32}$ for CB32, $1\frac{7}{32}$ for CB34, GP carburettor, with remote horizontally rubber mounted float chamber, fitted.

For all versions:

13 'Slimline' Girling rear suspension units introduced, their mounting bushes having detachable centre sleeves, and their rubber bushes concave in shape.

For all CB engines:

14 Copper asbestos gaskets replaced by Plexal-peelable cylinder head gaskets. Eventually standard on all Gold Stars.

1955

For Clubman's, Racing B32 GS and B34 GS:

1 DB 32 and DB 34 engines introduced. For DB 32, aluminium cylinder liner thickness increased, and liner now located directly on to crankcase mount at bottom, and carried cylinder head direct at top.
2 For both big-end cage dimensions slightly modified. Flywheel diameter reduced to 7 inch diameter and $1\frac{5}{16}$ in width. For 500 cc, flywheels revert from oval to circular dimensions and 58% balance factor. This was permitted by the diameter reduction, and by shortening the piston skirt by $\frac{3}{16}$ in. For both, valve pockets were modified to suit reduced valve head diameters. 'Slimmer' valve springs introduced, with insulating washer under exhaust only, and exhaust valve guides shortened at their lower ends. Smaller valve springs adopted, and thus top diameter of valve guides reduced. Exhaust valve size now 1.410 for 350, 1.520 for 500. 500's inlet valve size increased to 1.785. Standard compression was now 9:1 (350 cc), 8.75:1 (500 cc), with the piston crown height increased to raise compression, and twin supporting webs added between the gudgeon pin bosses and crown. Piston weight reverts to pre-1952. For 500, scraper ring changed from slotted to Wright two-piece type. For both, Witham valve springs fitted, smaller, but with wire ground and shot-peened, with steel washers and smaller alloy collars than previous.
3 Fifth head-to-barrel through-bolt (introduced for 1954) now deleted due to its inaccessibility, and previous arrangement returned to, ie, four through-bolts and four 'independent' bolts.
4 Pressure oil feed to big end bearing achieved by reversing previous system (of nozzle embedded in timing cover). Nozzle now part of mainshaft, with nozzle registering in a garter seal in the timing cover.
5 Aluminium finning introduced on the 7 in rear brake, which became a light alloy casting bonded into position.
6 Rear brake now features 6 cooling holes each drilled in back of drums, and blanked off by removable steel plugs, as on front since 1950.

For Clubman B32 GS, B34 GS:

7 Both speedometer and rev-counter fitted on fork crown.
8 Swept-back exhaust pipe and new silencer with front rounded shoulders cut back to give increased ground clearance, and two-part internals, a megaphone shape followed by a small expansion chamber, then a straight-through absorbtion silencer, all of which gave more noise and more power.

For Scramblers B32 GS, B34 GS:
9 Amal Monobloc carb introduced.
For all versions:
10 Girling rear suspension units' mountings now use a one-piece rubber bush with a steel sleeve bonded into it.

1956

1 DBD 34 engine introduced, with cylinder head modified to feature wider carburettor mounting centres permitting adoption of Amal $1\frac{1}{2}$ in GP carburettor as standard. Inlet valve head size slightly larger (at 1.850).
For Clubmans, Racing B32 GS and B34 GS:
2 Modified version of previous year's silencer, giving distinctive 'twittering' sound on the over-run.
3 RRT2 ultra-close-ratio gearbox, so designated because of introduction of a needle roller now featured in the sleeve gear, as well as at each end of layshaft, signified by the '2' next to the 'T' for Torrington needle-rollers.
4 New 190 mm front brake ($7\frac{1}{2}$ in × 2 in), lighter and smaller but with a larger frictional area, as option.
5 Clutch friction material on plates changed to Ferodo MS6, synthetic rubber impregnated with zinc plates.
6 5 gallon alloy petrol tank as option.
For Clubman's B32 GS and B34 GS:
7 Revised ACU regulations for I.O.M. Clubman's TT led to Clubmans machines being supplied with lighting equipment including a Lucas Magdyno and accumulator and a 7 inch headlamp.
For DBD 34, during 1956:
8 Inlet port dimensions reduced slightly to $1\frac{7}{16}$ in, since with $1\frac{1}{2}$ GP carburettor, the tiny lip so created was found to improve power marginally.

1958

For all B34 GS:
1 Heavier ($\frac{5}{8}$ × $\frac{3}{8}$ in) rear chain replaces previous $\frac{5}{8}$ × $\frac{1}{4}$ in. Sprocket went from 42 to 46 teeth.
2 Rear brake drum has three small fins machined integrally, and lightening holes deleted.

1959

For Scrambles B34 GS:
1 An oil tank housed centrally between the frame-loops with filler neck reached through the fore part of the seat offered as option.

1962

For Clubmans, Racing B34 GS:
1 Amal GP2 carburettor adopted.

BSA: The C15/B40/B44/C25/B25/B50 unit singles

Nowadays the C15 and its derivatives are frequently attacked for epitomising all that was bad, old-fashioned, undergunned and unreliable about British bikes. Before joining in the kicking, it may be as well to remember that like the Wild Bunch, the C15/C25/B25 'came too late and stayed too long'.

However, in late 1958 when it was announced, the new C15 Star 250 had a lot going for it. Some 30 lb lighter than its predecessor the C12, at 280 lb dry and with the seat height of 30 in which its 17 in wheels helped to achieve, it was in the tradition of the 1920s 'round tank' 250 model and quite manageable by learner lads and lasses alike.

The little bike was neat and uncluttered, the styling very BSA, with heavily valanced mudguards and cowled headlamp. The price was right at £172, compared with £196 9s 8d for the AMC 'lightweight' 250, which was actually 65 lb heavier, and £179 19s 6d for Royal Enfield's bottom of the range 250, the Clipper. It was economical too, returning 80–90 mpg on long runs. The specification was bang up to date — short-stroke unit construction engine, alternator electrics, full-width hubs for the 6 in cast iron brakes, etc.

Off-road sporting production versions, the 20 bhp C15T trials model and C15S scrambler, from works machinery masterminded by Bert Perrigo and campaigned and developed by Brian Martin and his men, were to follow shortly. They were substantially different from the roadsters — frames, forks, wheels, crankshaft assemblies, pistons, camshafts, cylinder heads, valves and gearbox clusters, as well as the inefficient energy transfer electrics which were to plague them until 1963, all were distinct. However, BSA had correctly anticipated that light-weights would be the future direction of development in these sports, and in the hands of the factory experts they enjoyed considerable success, which cast reflected glory on the cooking roadsters. In addition, with learners restricted to machines of 250 cc and under during 1960, it's little wonder that the C15 ended up being the only bike to make a profit for the factory during the '60s. As always, the man with overall responsibility for the engine design, Triumph's Edward Turner, had displayed a sure grasp of the market.

Of course, a bit later on, another sideways look at the opposition was not to be so flattering to the little BSA quarter litre. At the end of 1961 another 250, Honda's Dream, hit the Earl's Court Show.

With push-button starting, 180 degree crank throw giving excellent balance, an ohc engine producing 24 bhp and a maximum speed around 90 mph, against the current C15's 15 bhp and a top whack of about 75 mph. However, the price of the Honda at £249 against the then price of £168 for the simple Ceefer—yes, it had gone down since 1958, things like that sometimes happened in those days—meant they were scarcely in direct competition. In any case, there would always be a place for a simple four-stroke single.

However, the type of single engine BSA had plumped for was the problem. As mentioned, the designer was Triumph's Edward Turner, at that time head of the BSA automotive division which included both factories, and what he had done was to take the motor from his 199 cc Triumph Tiger Cub design which was itself derived from the 1953 149 cc Terrier, and blow the Cub's 63 mm × 64 mm dimensions up to 67 mm × 70 mm for the Star, giving 247 cc—though Small Heath were to erroneously claim this as 249 cc right up till 1971. The new engine was then set upright, not inclined forward like the Cub, though usefully one could still remove the alloy cylinder head while the engine was in the frame, hampered only by a couple of awkward cylinder head nuts hidden amongst the fins. The engine was offset substantially to the left in the tubular, brazed-lug construction single downtube cradle frame, which for that reason was asymmetrical, in plan.

1958 C15 250.

The unit itself included several unusual features for the time. The primary drive was taken from a sprocket cast integrally with the iron clutch drum. And in the kickstart mechanism, the kickstarter ratchet was incorporated within the bottom gear pinion, though this meant that the kickstart and right footrest were awkwardly close to one another. The plain big-end bearing, as found (and known for a proverbial weak point) on the Cub, gave rise to numerous problems, and likewise the plain bush for the timing-side main bearing.

Another problem inherited from the Cub concerned the points and condenser, which sat in a capped distributor tower located to the rear right of the cylinder. This could be rotated to set the coil ignition, but the clamp holding the distributor, which was identical to the Cub's clamp, was subject to wear and would then slip and alter the timing. (Wear to the drive, on the mainshaft worm gear and its mating gear on the distributor drive shaft, could also cause this, and these gears were modified early in 1960). The alternator's early-type shellac-covered coils could work loose and fail, while a further problem with the C15 and later the B40 was the ineffective Lucas alternator system with no regulator, which caused much trouble with overcharging in hot weather; for instance, touring abroad, you were wise to ride with your lights on to avoid overcharging and boiling the battery. BSA indeed advised topping up the Lucas ML9C (C15) and ML40 (B40) batteries every week.

Another unfortunate feature of the light engine was the fact that all the mating surfaces were thin, and even with careful tightening, these soon became less than oil tight, particularly at the head and crankcase joints and especially around the primary chaincase. The oil filtration system was crude by today's standards and regular oil changes together with thorough cleaning of the oil tank, pipes and filters as well as the sump filter and gauze were absolutely necessary. Otherwise particles in the oil would cause rapid engine wear—the alloy piston with its generous clearances was particularly prone to 'picking up'. The impurities would also spoil the seating of the one-way ball valves in the system, which could then lead to still more oil leaks. (A smear of Vaseline around them during assembly often helped them seat more securely.) Oil also tended to seep from the oil tank filler cap. The primary chaincase could also leak from the oil seal behind the clutch if, as happened after a while, a groove was worn in the fourth mainshaft gear bush by the clutch housing seal, or if it was disturbed. Oil then seeped out of the clutch housing and showered the rear wheel. The only remedy was to fit a new bush and seal. As if that wasn't enough, the first grommet through which the alternator wire passed was another potential trouble spot.

Below *Close-up of the 1959 C15 power unit.*
Below right *Jeff Smith quick to exploit the scrambles potential of a punchy new lightweight C15S.*

A less lethal, though awkward legacy from Triumph, were the early slotted rocker caps, though these were soon replaced with hexagon-headed ones. The nice idea of fluting the primary chaincase cover, a first for BSA and retained until the end of the series, was surely a Turner touch. Triumph, too, was the up-for-up change pattern in the four-speed unit gearbox—the gear-lever too was interchangeable with the Cub—this way of shifting was then unique to Meriden. The box worked well and smoothly when in good condition, but was liable to rapid wear on both the selectors and the dogs, after which gear-changes became clonky and false neutrals frequent—renewal of the cam-plate spring was a temporary cure for this. One harmless feature of the engine was the high-pitched whine made by the valve train, which did not indicate wear or maladjustment, but was simply a feature of the beast.

Another slight complication for the home mechanic was that this early version featured no less than six thread types on its nuts, bolts and studs. There was Whitworth (or BSW, British Standard Whitworth) a coarse strong thread with 20 threads per inch, useful for studs going into alloy); and BSF (British Standard Fine), introduced as part of a metal-saving programme during World War II and retained since. The heads of these were one size smaller than the equivalent Whitworth. And one is of course not surprised to find that spanner jaws marked, say, $\frac{5}{16}''$ W/$\frac{3}{8}''$ BSF, ie with the BSF larger, are not actually

inconsistent with this 'one size smaller' principle, because they are in fact nearly twice that size across the mouth, since the $\frac{5}{16}$ in and $\frac{3}{8}$ in refers to the diameter of the thread appropriate, according to system, to a bolt with a head that fits the spanner. Clear?

Then there was BA (British Association, for nearly everything below a quarter of an inch) B.S.Cy (or CEI, or Cycle Thread, with 26 threads per inch, often used to counter vibration, and they coincide with BSF at $\frac{1}{4}$ in); BSP (British Standard Pipe, used on petrol tank and oil tank unions); and finally BSA-thread (the company's own contribution, developed for sizes above $\frac{7}{16}$ of an inch). It sounds like a storeman's nightmare, and perhaps this was what Nora Docker had in mind with her comment to Sir Bernard about his 'wretched nuts and bolts'.

However, it would be wrong to over-emphasise the negative points about the C15 at this time. A *Motor Cycle* Reader's Report on the bike in the mid-'60s characterises the 250, like so many British bikes, as reliable if it didn't go wrong initially and once it had bedded in. There were some niggles, including rapid wear on the skimpy $\frac{1}{2} \times \frac{5}{16}$ in rear chain, which could need renewing after as little as 2,000 miles and was to linger on all the unit singles until the 1967 C25/B25. The rear suspension provided by non-adjustable Girling units was on the soft side for pillion work—one punter spoke of 'fowl handling' but that would surely have been more appropriate for a Bantam, and the two-way damped, long-travel front forks with their low spring rates were generally reckoned to be adequate.

Poor accessibility was also criticised; the outer timing cover plus the exhaust pipe had to come off to replace a clutch cable, and the tool-box fixing, with threaded pillars to be mated blind with loose captive bolts, was a torment for years to come. The horn was described as 'like a well-worn raspberry'. But the riding position was praised, as was the quality of the chrome and enamel, the smart pear-shaped acrylic badges shortly adopted by the whole range, the $2\frac{1}{2}$ gallon tank's single-bolt fixing, as well as the good acceleration in 2nd and 3rd gear and the ability to cruise all day at 50–55 mph. If the major problems were never entirely absent—particularly oil leaks, brittle piston rings, cylinder barrel wear, and the plain big end's (and sometimes the main bearing's) habit of letting go—at least, as with the Cub, they could be remedied fairly cheaply, and overall, the C15 gained the affection of the 16 to 21 year-old first time riders who made up the bulk of its owners.

A sports version followed in April 1961, dubbed the Sports Star SS80 in a cheeky (and inappropriate) allusion to a great pre-war Brough Superior. The idea was that it would, with a favourable wind, reach a top speed of over 80 mph, but the lack of adequate damping front and rear meant that it weaved mildly at those speeds. Also it was under-braked. Internally the compression had been raised from the C15's modest 7.25:1 to 8.75:1, and with sports cams, larger carburettor and inlet valve and heavy-duty valve springs, this gave a claimed output of 20 bhp. The fly-wheels were of forged steel as against the C15's cast iron, and the gear ratios closer. The plain big-end bearing was also replaced by a caged roller-bearing.

The little bike was smart, with round badges and chromed panels on a gold-lined black 3-gallon petrol tank, as well as plated fork crown pressings and a buffed timing side crankcase cover and

Sports C15—the 1961 SS80.

cylinder head fins. There were chrome mudguards as an option, though these were of the heavy full-valanced pattern until their 1964 replacement by blade types. Practical improvements included flat handlebars, which with clip-on control levers allowed a full range of adjustment, unlike the C15's Bantam-like welded-on type. And there was a slipper-type tensioner for the short, previously non-adjustable duplex primary chain; the tensioner was to be adopted by the B40 the following year, but not for the standard C15 until 1965. Owners came to know that they should not worry if it appeared to be worn, as it didn't work effectively until the chain *had* scored into it deeply. (The same applied to C15 friction clutch plates, which also always looked worn.)

The SS80's clutch hub was modified to include equal-thickness cush-drive rubbers, something the C15 also adopted. An impractically loud exhaust note probably delighted its trainee tearaway owners. But in general the decision to hot up the cooking roadster could only lead to grief in terms of overstressing already shaky areas like the mains and the electrics. It was made necessary though, as author Roy Bacon points out, by market forces at the time. The new legislation limiting learners to 250 cc meant that youngsters wanted the maximum performance from the capacity to which they were restricted, and ignored lower-powered but more reliable alternatives. So the race for more horses without a major re-tool was on.

For the qualified general road rider, a more promising variant was offered by the 350 cc B40, introduced late in 1960 for 1961. Bored out to oversquare dimensions (79 mm × 70 mm), with flat top pistons giving a compression ratio of 7:1, the valve angle slightly reduced and a valve-lifter

fitted, the motor differed from the 250 externally in featuring a fully cast-in pushrod tunnel, as opposed to the C15's short chromed tube between crankcase and cylinder head. The small-end eye was also wider for the 350. The B40 flywheels were heavier, being about $\frac{1}{8}$ in larger and the crankcase was enlarged, with thicker metal around the bearing housing and larger stiffening webs. A wider rear brake drum was necessary to line the chain up. The clutch, too, was strengthened by local thickening of the metal around the slots of the cast-iron clutch drum, to give extra rigidity. From the start it replaced the screw-driver slots on the C15's rocker covers with the hexagonal flats which the 250s also adopted.

The 3 gallon tank, as on the SS80, featured chromed tank panels and round tank badges consisting of a gilt star on a silver background with BSA initials overlaid in red, which echoed the small Star badge on the timing-side crankcase, a nice touch found on the whole series from the beginning until 1965. The B40's wheels were enlarged from 17 to 18 in, the frame was strengthened and a sturdier front fork, similar to the old B31's, housed a new and quite effective 7 inch front brake.

All this meant that the B40 was 20 lb heavier than the C15, but it remained 100 lb lighter than its 350 cc predecessor, the B31. And in fact its advantage over that machine as well as the AMC heavyweight 350s, was that it was not a scaled-down engine in ponderous cycle parts designed for a 500, but a true middleweight with a decent power-to-weight ratio. With an output of 21 bhp and a lowish top speed of just over 75 mph, but with high gearing genuinely able to cruise effortlessly at 60, it provided a pleasant, more

A step up and in the right direction — the 1961 B40 350 Star.

than adequate mid-range ride, with firmer though still non-adjustable rear suspension units which were found in test to eliminate the 250's problem with passengers (the 250's springs were also uprated in the middle of that year). B40 engines have proved perhaps the most popular and versatile of the series, early involvement in road-racing and scrambles progressing to grass-track, sand-racing, trail riding and currently pre-'65 four-stroke trials.

A sports version, the SS90, followed in May 1962, with an 8.75:1 compression ratio, larger inlet valve and carburettor, heavy duty valve springs, as well as raised gearing and a closer ratio box as on the scrambler. All this produced a claimed 24 bhp and a hoped-for 90 mph potential, though a June 1962 *Motor Cycle* road test produced only 82 mph — atrocious weather was blamed. The finish on the SS90 was flamboyant red, and otherwise much as the SS80. The year of 1962 also saw a remodelling of the rather short dual seat for the unit singles (and the Bantam Major), as well as two new Lucas alternators, both with output raised from 50 to 60 watts, but with a different output curve to match the different engine characteristics of the C15 and the B40 respec-tively. The ignition switch on both, still located under the seat, acquired a detachable key, and the C15's compression was raised to 7.5:1. Both B40s got the caged double-row roller bearing big-end as on the SS80, as well as a redesign for the 7 in front brake, with floating action of the shoes

giving a self-servo effect.

The AA replaced some of their M21s with B40s in 1962, as the Army were to do in 1967. The Civil Defence and its Auxiliary Fire Service also bought up several hundred 350s which were crated up, unused, only to be unpacked and sold when the organisation was run down in the early '70s. These machines provided some genuine low-mileage examples of the bike, and I was fortunate enough to own one for a while. It was quite a pleasant experience, though that front brake proved less than adequate for modern London traffic conditions on at least one memorable occasion.

The Army soldiered on with theirs until replace-ment with two-stroke Can-Am Bombardiers began during 1978. Ex-WD B40s are still being sold off at the time of writing, but are probably best avoided. While they employ a Scrambles-derived frame as well as the stronger 1966 scrambles-type bottom end, and the new two-way damped forks plus 12-volt electrics, they were fitted with trials pattern tyres not particularly suited to the road, and on early models a small Amal butterfly-valve carburettor fitted to ensure water-tightness, which to cut costs had been modified from the carburettor of a stationary engine. With dual seat, massive pannier frames and a fully enclosed rear chain, the WD B40 weighed in at 350 lb and most of them will have been well thrashed before they fall into civilian hands (some Army despatch riders I met spoke of going round the clock three or even four times not being unusual). They are only really to be recommended to kamikaze green lane riders with a thing about olive drab.

For the next couple of years there was little change for the unit roadster singles, but off-road versions of the bike prospered, as a result of developments from Brian Martin's comp shop, and from 1962-on also by Ernie Webster of the design department, leading to the emergence of a really exciting machine. Progressive boring and stroking of the engine produced first an unsuccessful 420 cc motor but eventually the alloy-engined 441 cc machine with which Jeffrey Victor 'Whizzo' Smith took the World Moto-cross championship in 1964 and again in 1965. Whether because of his success or his middle name, the new machine was called the Victor GP Scrambler. Among many modifications, it featured stub-toothed gearbox pinions, a strengthened crankcase to eliminate flexing, and stronger main bearings.

Meanwhile the roadsters were being developed too. In 1964 the C15 had finally adopted the caged roller big-end bearing as already featured on the

SS80 and B40s, as well as the 3 gallon petrol tank and a further raise in compression to 8:1. But for 1965 there were more fundamental changes denoted by C15F/B40F engine prefixes. A redesign of the contact-breaker location, introduced on the previous year's works trials and scrambles models, meant that on all the unit singles the distributor tower was no longer there, the points being housed in a sealed compartment in the right hand of the timing-side crankcase behind a chrome-plated cover, and the drive for the advance mechanism and cam now being taken from the camshaft.

There was also a redesign of the clutch-operating mechanism, with the introduction of a rack-and-pinion arrangement which gave a straight-line thrust on the clutch rod. The operating lever was mounted externally above the crankcase, which greatly simplified changing clutch cables. The C15 finally acquired the slipper primary chain tensioner as on the SS80. Inside the gearbox, the gearchange selector quadrant was also redesigned to provide more positive selection. The mainshaft and the layshaft were also redesigned and the kickstart mechanism revised. The new mainshaft carried a ratchet pinion housed in the outer compartment of the box, while the accompanying toothed quadrant was integral with the kickstarter spindle, of which the outer end now had an oil seal. The layshaft now ran in a needle roller-bearing in the hollow end of the starter spindle. Previous models could be converted to this, although changes to the crankcase were involved.

Together with the provision of a larger-bore

Left *Suede desert boots, string-back gloves — and a 1961 B40 as passport to international pleasure. Or at least the Grand Union Canal.*

WD B40 for 1967. Scrambler's frame and bottom end, two-way damped front forks, 12-volt electrics.

New 1965 C15. Points shifted to timing case, revised kickstart mechanism, generally a Good Thing.

crankpin oilway in an attempt to prolong big-end bearing life, and various other detail improvements, this represented a determined effort to solve some of the unit single's problems, and the C15s and B40s of 1965 and, as we shall see, particularly from mid-1966, represent the most desirable versions of the engine. (For though the UK civilian B40s had been dropped at the end of 1965, the WD type as well as some of the civilian-style Civil Defence batch were to make their appearance in 1967.) They were strengthened and improved in the light of off-road experience, but had not yet had their compression and output unwisely raised.

A production version of the 225 lb 441 cc Victor scrambler, with its oil-bearing Reynolds 531 frame, had become available for 1965, as well as a Victor Enduro trail version, with an 8:1 compression engine housed in the C15T frame. Both incorporated several developments eventually to be found on the roadsters, particularly the alloy barrel, still round finned, and Jeff Smith's own design of two-way-damped front fork, with a clack valve and scalloped restrictor at its lower end aimed at giving progressive resistance, as well as hydraulic prevention of the fork bottoming and topping. The back wheel also featured a genuine quickly-detachable single-sided hub as found on the previous big bangers. This front fork, sensibly gaitered, was immediately adopted by the BSA roadster twins.

Despite the demise of the UK civilian B40 for 1966, a roadster version of the Victor 440 did not appear until 1967, but in the meantime some of its benefits were transmitted to the rest of the range. In 1966 the SS80 was replaced by the C15 Sportsman, a similar machine (though close-ratio gears were no longer provided), but restyled, with a racing-type hump-ended dualseat and a separate chromed elongated headlamp shell replacing the old nacelle. Handlebars acquired a rearward sweep, and conspicuously silly side-panel transfers depicted a heroic jet-helmeted rocker clutching a trophy—which he had obviously nicked.

From July 1966, modifications were announced for both the Sportsman and the basic C15. Both engines of this series were identified by engine numbers including the letters 'C15G', and 'C15SG' respectively, with 'B40G' for the remaining export, WD and CD B40s being produced, which also benefited in this way. They adopted the Victor's bottom end, with its heftier main bearings (ball-bearings on the timing side and rollers on the drive side) accommodated in the stiffer Victor crankcase casting. There was also a new lubrication system with the oil pump now the same size as the 650's, and oil to the rear chain was metered from the primary chaincase. The gearbox was improved again, with needle-roller bearings now fitted at both ends of the layshaft, for the top gear only, though the C15G did not gain the Victor's stronger tooth form for the indirect gears. First, second and third gears were lowered, though top gear ratio remained the same and top end performance was unaltered. Some, but

Far left *1965 hot B40, the SS90, with cosmopolitan aspirations again.*

Left *New 1965 B40, best of the bunch.*

Right *1966 C15G Star*

not all, of this series also adopted the late C15T-type frame, no longer with bolted-on rear sub-frame, which came in for the 1967 C25 and will be found described below.

By 1967 the factory moto-cross team was waging the increasingly unequal battle to find a solution to the big four-stroke single's inability to rev. The fiasco of Jeff Smith's 1966 titanium-framed machine (see page 32) had at least resulted in a new long-stroke (83 × 93 mm) 494 cc engine. And that year the 441 cc Victor Roadster hit the streets, alongside a radical alternative, and soon to be a replacement for the C15. This was the C25 Barracuda, which featured all the Sportsman's improvements, plus a compression ratio revised to 9.5:1, and a one-piece forged-steel crankshaft with bolted-on flywheels like the 650's (crankshaft problems had been a continuous headache as the 250's power crept up). As its designation suggested, the C25's output was a claimed 25 bhp at 8,000 rpm.

The engine's appearance was distinctive, with the big new light-alloy head and Victor-type square-finned cylinder barrel with its integral pushrod tube. The redesigned head featured a change in the method of tappet adjustment from the traditional screw and locknut system, to rotary cam adjuster. This was not shared by the B44, or later the B50. Internally it sported hot Victor-type cams, large diameter inlet valve and heavy-duty valve springs. The con-rod was of forged Duralumin, but unfortunately the big-end had reverted to a plain type with thin-wall forged shell

bearings. Both C25 and B44 featured for the first time Amal Concentric carburettors at a steep down-draught angle, with pillbox-type air filters directly attached.

The much superior frame for both was still of single-down tube cradle type, similar to the export Victor Enduro and to the C15T before it. The rear sub-frame was no longer bolt-on and the swinging arm changed from the C15's phosphor-bronze bearings and bushes to rubber-bonded bushes, which, when the time came, were very hard to remove. And both machines had the Victor's two-way damped front fork internals (though without gaiters and with wheel attachment by fork clamps, not by a pull-out spindle), as well as single-sided 7 in brakes front and rear, the latter wheel being of the old quickly-detachable type. Styling included a new alloy rear light assembly, minimal blade mudguards and, like the Sportsman, a seat with a 'humpy rump' as one scribe put it, together with new shaped fibreglass oil tank cover and matching side-panel, plus an impractical 1¾ gallon two-tone fibreglass petrol tank with scalloped knee recesses and a hinged snap-filler cap.

The C25 with maximum revs at 8,250 could pull 55 mph in second and 72 in third, though it was slightly overgeared, and changing into top, even with the engine wound up, produced a drop in acceleration. Top speed was 86 mph, though staying there for long, even if the vibration allowed it, was not to be recommended. In common with the Victor Roadster, seat height at 31 in was somewhat excessive, and the take-up

of the clutch was rather short so the bike could be stalled rather easily. The brakes and lights (the headlamp was a shallower chromed shell, with the speedometer now separate on top of the fork crowns) were a genuine improvement, and at last there had been a slight enlargement on the rear chain, to $\frac{5}{8} \times \frac{1}{4}$ dimensions. But for the traditionally minded, the new 250 still vibrated, rattled and leaked oil just as its ancestors had. A new problem was to be the loosening of the main body of the alternator rotor on its central boss, which set up a hammering action that destroyed the rotor keyway and ultimately the crankshaft. Despite being explicable in terms of market pressures (see page 36) it was not a healthy

direction for the company or for riders, who also at £249 faced a price rise of £43 on the old C15, which was dropped in mid-year.

With one of the bewildering and alarming strokes which typified the new BSA management, 1967 also saw the production Victor GP Scrambler dropped in September, shortly after it had taken 1st and 3rd in the MX des Nations. But the Victor Enduro continued, for export only, and the engine of the new-for-1967 Victor Roadster resembled it in featuring an 8:1 compression from a cast in linered barrel, compared to the scrambler's chrome plated bore directly in the alloy cylinder. The Roadster's power output at 29 bhp was well down on the scrambler, which

Above *1966 C15 Sportsman. Note the transfer.*

Left *1967 C25 Barracuda. Fibreglass, high output, low life expectancy.*

since their bottom ends were identical gave the Roadster a reassuring edge of robustness, though ensuring its top speeded remained under 90 mph. In fact its performance closely resembled the 250s, but it achieved it with a lot less hysteria and over-revving—the C25 peaked at 8,250, against a recommended maximum of just 5,750 for the B44.

The Victor's seat height at 31 in was not ideal, and a high American-style handlebar (it became standard for the range for 1968) gave the best handling for the plot's set-up and power characteristics. Bottom end punch, steering and acceleration were superb. This was the essence of the Victor, wheelies, over-taking and storming up hills. Negative points for 1967 included the same dubious styling as the C25 with the $1\frac{3}{4}$ gallon fibreglass tank—red and white, the 250s being blue and white for export, orange and white for home—and go-faster racing transfers on the scalloped sidepanels. The front end was light, and accentuated by the high bars, this meant weaving at the highest speeds, at which point also the single-sided 7in front brake proved less than adequate. The exhaust note was either healthy or embarrassing depending on your levels of aggression, and the exhaust valve lifter that was fitted was, unlike the 250s, really necessary to the rather taxing starting process, which from cold wasn't helped by the absence of an air lever. Correct ignition timing settings were also vital for an easy start, and achieving these was helped by the provision, on both machines, of a pointer inside the chaincase and a marker on the rotor, which allowed the use of a strobe for timing. At about £30 dearer and 30 lb heavier than the C25, the Victor Roadster was definitely the more desirable machine.

1968 brought a change of name for both; the Victor Roadster became, as it had been all along in the States, the B44SS Shooting Star—a name revived from the sporting A7 500 cc twin of the '50s. In April the C25 Barracuda became the B25 Starfire, once again as it had been from the start in the US, where another Barracuda was already being marketed. The 1968 441 cc had fractionally lower gearing, as well as an 8 in front brake in a new full-width hub, and a new method of clamping the front wheel spindle in the fork ends with bolt-on caps, plus a revised oil feed to the valve gear.

Like the 250, it adopted the export styling now current throughout the range (the high bars, gaitered forks, and side reflectors under the fuel tank nose and on the side of the alloy tail-lamp

fitting), as well as a more practical toggle instead of the old rotary lighting swtich on top of the chrome headlamp. To begin with only the 441 cc featured the new tank badges, a three-dimensional ribbed moulding in anodised light alloy, though the same pear shape as the more attractive but fragile acrylic moulding it replaced. But in April when the 250 became the B25 it adopted the badge as well as a more sober paint job, all-blue tank and panels with black frame (which the B44 was to echo, in red, for 1969). The 1968 250 also then acquired a 7 in front brake with the full width hub, and the 441's front wheel clamping arrangement.

For 1969 most improvements applied to 250 and 441 cc alike, the minor exception being an oil pressure light in the headlamp which the 250 didn't acquire until 1970. The main changes included an excellent new 7 in twin leading-shoe front brake, which reduced its stopping distance from 30 mph to just 28 ft, a front brake cable including a switch to actuate the rear brake light, improved internals for the silencer, larger ($3\frac{1}{4}$ gallon) fuel tanks, made, like the side-panels, in steel as the law was to require, an improved dual seat with an aerated top, folding foot-rests, provision for a rev counter to match the speedometer, and a new wiring harness allowing conversion to capacitor ignition for off-road or competition. Also, as with all the big bikes, Triumph-type lower members were fitted for the front fork, together with Triumph two-way damping shuttle-valves for the lower end of the fork stanchions. This new and slightly shorter front fork went some way to curing the front end troubles at speed, and certainly improved the cornering. The company may have been going to the wall, but someone was trying, and the 1969-on B44s are the ones to go for.

Other features during the year were the beginnings of the changeover from the gloriously-mixed BSF, CEI, etc, thread forms to Unified Thread, which was the same as American National, for bolts, studs and screwed components, though the BSA manuals warned that: 'Suitable threads were not always available in the unified system, especially the large diameters with fine threads', and advised the checking of threads when replacing, especially in the case of captive nuts and similar items.

Another welcome measure was an increase in the width of crankcase and primary chaincase joint faces by 15 per cent, in an effort to combat oil leaks. For the B25 this involved an altered crankcase, outer and inner timing cover and cylinder barrel.

The standard B25's compression was raised to 10:1, but a sensibly detuned version with an 8.5:1 compression ratio and lower gearing was also introduced. This was the black-and-white finish Fleetstar, similar to the Starfire in most respects but returning to the more practical C15-type fully-valanced mudguards, and offered optionally equipped with BSA-subsidiary Motoplas accessories like leg-shields, crash-bars, panniers and a half-fairing—all BSA's now carried tubular connectors so that fairings could be fitted.

There was also an export-only semi-trail version of the 250 with chromed high-level exhaust and wire heat-shield to the left, plus wide bars, fat tyres (3.25 × 19 front, 4.00 × 18 rear) and a neat little 1¾ gallon polished alloy tank finished like the Victor GP—and Bob Currie has revealed that it was at his suggestion—in bright yellow at the front, which set off the red winged BSA transfer nicely. The dual purpose 441 cc Victor Enduro, also still export only, was renamed the Victor Special and now featured an 8 in SLS brake and a quickly-detachable 6 in headlamp. With their

lower gearing, these bikes were clear antecedents of the coming 1971 B25/B50 oil-in-frame dual purpose machines, and since then discerning owners of that range have chased examples of the exhaust and silencer from the Victor Special, or the 1968 Triumph 250 TR25W variant. (The 250 Triumphs, introduced for 1968 onwards, were badge-engineered Starfires with detail differences, which are discussed in the Triumph Singles section of a later volume.) Both of these machines featured chromed exhausts and silencers tucked in to the right of the machine, a neat and good-looking, if noisy, solution to the problem of high-level exhaust pipes.

1970 saw a further harbinger of the coming range with the works 499 cc (84 × 90 mm) MX Victor, a 38 bhp engine in an oil-bearing frame on which John Banks contested the World Moto-Cross championships. A production version was announced at the end of the year. Back on the street, both the B25 and B44 had their engine breathers modified, plus an improved method of locating the spring-carrying cups in the clutch

1968 B25 Starfire 250. New front brake, export styling.

1969 B25 Starfire.

Above right *Arm-wrencher. A 1969 B44 Shooting Star on test.*

pressure plate, and further modifications to the silencer. It became cigar-shaped, to reduce the decibels in view of the new MOT requirements. In common with the twins, improvements included a redesigned oil pump, modifications to the electrics, and a redesigned needle jet holder, needle jet and needle on the Amal Concentrics, improving the consumption figures which for the B44 had become rather high — 53 mpg at an average of 60 mph on a 1969 Shooting Star, and these were machines which could be cruised at a genuine 70 mph. Style-wise both B25 and B44 discarded the former oil-tank side-cover, the left-hand side-panel was reduced in size and the oil-tank filler cap finally repositioned to avoid the rider's leg.

Finally, vitally, the much-superior cast-iron three stud-fitting oil pump, as on the twins, replaced the previous distortion-prone alloy pump, and can be retro-fitted with a little work. The new models replacing the Starfire and the B44 were 'street scramblers' — that, rather than the previous 'Shooting Star' or the traditional 'Sports Special' or 'Super Sports' was what the SS suffix in the B25 SS and B50 SS 'Gold Stars' was about, and at that time in Britain the concept was not popular. Ironically so, since by the time of writing both the general idea of small mock-trial bikes for the street has been thoroughly accepted, courtesy of Messrs Honda and Suzuki, and also because of Yamaha's revival of the four-stroke 500 cc dual-purpose big single, with the other Orientals now following suit.

The use of the Gold Star name was a liberty which gave considerable offence to the traditionally minded. It may be noted however that owners of pukka 85 × 88 mm DBD 34 Gold Stars have been known to fit an oversize (84 mm + 0.40) B50 piston in their treasures, as these are nearly identical and save money on the normal DBD34 replacement. (Another piston dodge relating to the unit singles is the possibility of replacing a 250 piston with one from a Rocket III or Trident, though it is not known what compression this produces.)

Probably the use of the Gold Star name, while undeniably ill-calculated, was just a stab at some kind of continuity. For at the time the new B25 and B50 looked unfamiliar, as well as like mutton dressed as lamb. Despite the catalogue change from 249 to 247 cc, wasn't the 250's motor just the Starfire? (Yes, it was, and indeed any 1967-on 250 engine will slot into the new cycle parts with minimum work.) British attention lingered on the impractical dove-grey colour of the new frame rather than its excellent handling and

weight-saving design (the B25 SS at 290 lb was a fair improvement on the Trail version of the Starfire at 320 lb dry). The rationale behind the range was to offer road-going machines which could be adapted quickly for cross-country riding (here the weight-saving would be vital, although it was not sufficient to make the machines as they stood competitive in Enduros). But the great majority of British riders did not possess the opportunity to exploit the dual-purpose potential.

There were three versions of both the B50 500 cc machine (B50 SS, B50 T Trail and the MX scrambler), and the new B25 (B25 SS, the B25 FS Fleetstar still with 8.5:1 compression, and the B25T Trail), as well as two 250 Triumph equivalents (the TR25 Blazer SS and the TR 25 W Trail — later, in 1974, the last B50s, MX variants, would be marketed in the States as the Triumph TR5MX). All the motors except the Fleetstar were 10:1 compression jobs, and all featured the new oil-bearing frame. The 250 engine had strengthened con rods, a 5-plate clutch with the lip at the rear of its centre deleted, and a redesigned rocker box.

This was a version of the Mk IV BSA works moto-cross frame, and its main feature was a $2\frac{1}{4}$ inch × 14 gauge top tube, which together with the tank rail and the $1\frac{1}{2}$ inch × 11 gauge front down tube, served as a four-pint oil container (no oil was carried in the twin tube engine cradle or the rear subframe). A detachable oil filter with

At rest. A 1969 B44 Shooting Star.

gauze element was screwed into the base of the front down tube, and on the 250 in addition there was a further full-flow filter unit with replaceable element mounted behind the gearbox.

The B50 engine had been developed from the experience of road-racing and moto-cross — the MX version was virtually a replica of the bike ridden to victory by John Banks. It featured a needle-roller big-end bearing, and its redesigned crankshaft was supported on three main bearings; by ball and, inboard, roller bearings on the drive side and by roller bearings on the timing side. The 250's engine still had a plain big-end bearing and

thus its lubrication system differed, both in circulation flow and in the method of lubricating the primary chain. On the 500 this was managed not separately but via a flow from the mains, which on reaching its level then returned via a weir to the crankcase. Breathing was via the chaincase.

The trail versions differed from the SS machines by having a frame half an inch taller, no rev counter, a 6-inch SLS front brake, a high-mounted front mudguard and lower gearing (via a 16-tooth gearbox sprocket for the B25 T, 15-tooth for the B50 T as against 16-tooth for the 1971 B50 SS, 17-tooth for the B25 SS and 1972 B50 SS — all

Left *1970 Export B40 Rough Rider, based on the WD B40.*

Right *Active ingredient of the new oil-in-frame range. B50 MX Victor scrambler for 1971.*

shared a 52-tooth rear wheel sprocket until the 1972 B50 SS changed to 47 teeth in an effort to raise the always dual-purpose gearing which proved low for road use). Trail frames were black from the start and fitted with good spring-loaded footrests. Both features were adopted by all the singles in 1972.

On the street bikes as on the twins, a new 8 in twin leading shoe conical-hubbed light-alloy front brake was fitted, incorporating an air-scoop. Lockheed-designed, it provided car-type click-action adjustment of each shoe at the shoe pivots which could be reached with a screwdriver via a hole in the conical face of the hub which had to be unplugged. The action of the 'comical 'ub' as it was known in South London, was excellent, indeed sharp enough to merit caution, and stopped the B50 SS in 29 ft from 30 mph. The 7 in brake at the rear was also conical and of similar design, but the rear wheels were no longer quickly detachable. The swinging fork was now carried on needle roller bearings, and the whole fork could be moved back to adjust the rear chain, adjustment being regulated equally by pegged snail cams on each side of the fork.

The front fork, with damping now by clack valve not shuttle, featured not steel but light-alloy sliders, with four-stud-cap fixings for the wheel spindle, while the upper parts of the stanchions were gaiterless and exposed. The chrome headlamp was supported in spindly-looking shaped brackets of chromed steel rod supported in rubber mountings attached to the fork sliders. The steering head employed two Timken taper-roller bearings. The new forks with $6\frac{3}{4}$ in of travel gave a fine ride off-road as well as on, though with the machine's high handlebars, forward-located footrests and tall build (seat height was 32 in, though the narrow nose on the comfortable dual seat meant this didn't feel as awkwardly high as it might have), the steering could feel as if it was turning too far when cornering. As with a chopper or any of the US-styled bikes, you simply learned to take bends with less degree of lean than on a conventional roadster, and with that accepted handling and road-holding were excellent.

The electrics were also a departure. Grouped Lucas switches for the electrical system were incorporated in the handlebar lever pivot blocks, with dipswitch, horn and headlamp flasher on the left and the direction indicator switch on the right. Indicators were now fitted as standard, even on the trail bikes, just as sump-guard bash-plates were on the street versions. Unfortunately, the short dip and flasher levers were awkward to reach, and a thumb going for the indicators

tended to blip the throttle inadvertently as well.

The 12-volt electrical system featured a normal alternator and battery lighting set-up, but incorporated a capacitor as standard so that machines could be ridden with headlamp and battery removed. A grouped electrical pack, called the 'black box' and developed for the Army ISDT team, was carried beneath the fuel tank. It was a cast light-alloy container housing the ignition coils, capacitor, Zener diode, rectifier and direction indicator relay. On its side was a four-position ignition switch, with an interlocking ignition/lighting circuit that ensured the lights could not be tampered with while the machine was parked. A nine-pin plug and socket connection at the rear of the box enabled the headlamp, complete with indicators, main-beam, pilot and oil-pressure warning circuits, to be instantly detached.

Styling was distinctive. Dunlop K70 tyres, 3.25 front and a fat 3.50 at the rear, on 18 in rims, heightened the chopper image promoted by the tiny 1⅞ gallon angled and striped tank, steel for the SS, alloy for the Trail, which was handsome but quite impractical for the road. Not only was the range about 70 miles with a reserve of about five, but the thing was too narrow to get between the knees in the normal riding position. There was also an optional 3 gallon steel tank, a hump-backed item completely at odds with the overall street scrambler styling. A

BSA GOLD STAR 500 SS

Comical 'ubs, dove-grey frames, a certain flamboyance. 1971 oil-in-frame B50 SS 500 cc street scrambler.

further dubious feature was the very large capacity lozenge-shaped silencer, finished, like the exhaust pipe, in heat-resistant matt black paint, and unfortunately covered with a perforated stainless-steel leg-guard. It was mounted on the right at a steep angle with a horizontal tail pipe at the back, also covered by a piece of perforated steel-ware for the benefit of the passenger's knee. The muted and blurred bark it produced was not unpleasant, however.

Since BSA was now in its death-throes, although there had been evidence of the 250's potential—factory tester Dave Vaughan confirmed that a development version clocked 99.9 mph at MIRA—the B25 ceased to be catalogued for 1972, though some continued to be made that year. There was little development either on the B50, which was a pity. It was a strong motor, as demonstrated by Nigel Rollason and Clive Brown's 24-hour endurance race victories at Barcelona and in Holland on the little-modified Mead and Tompkinson B50 in 1971. The seat height and riding position made it less than ideal for touring, though certainly its power meant that it could handle two up at 70 mph with no problems, returning mpg figures in the high 50s under those conditions. Several BSA Owners Club members have praised its touring characteristics explaining that once a flat handlebar and the large tank have been fitted,

the gearing raised—a 47 tooth rear wheel sprocket coupled with a 16 or even a 19-tooth gearbox sprocket—take the top speed from around 80 to over 100 mph.

But features like the cam-and-peg rear chain adjustment (very necessary, since the rear chain was still the B25's less than adequate $\frac{5}{8} \times \frac{1}{4}$ in item, and stretched quickly), the blackbox electrics and the forward-tilted footrests showed that it really had been put together with off-road in mind, and in some ways the handling proved a more satisfying compromise than Yamaha's XT 500 was to provide off-road. After all, the B50's engine clatter, plus the vibration from such a powerful engine in a comparatively light frame, did make long-distance riding a bit of an ordeal anyway. However, I owned a B50, and for short haul, stop-and-go motoring, the engine's punchy power characteristics made for an inspiring, pant-kicking, arm-wrenching ride (the clutch take-up and transmission remained sharp). The bike was an instant rejuvenator, with the good times limited only by the difficulty of getting it going in the first place.

The B50, like the late versions of its great namesake the Gold Star, was a bitch to start. A 10:1 compression ratio made the use of the (awkwardly positioned) exhaust-valve lifter a must, and the downdraught Concentric permitted only the lightest tickling before flooding. The continued absence of an air-lever did not help cold starts either. As with the B44 and Starfire, correct ignition timing was vital—a situation complicated by the fact that a number of early flywheels had their timing marks in the wrong place and consequently needed to be set at 0.385 and not the normal 0.304 before TDC and hence could not be timed with a strobe light. (Another BSA wheeze on the early B50s was a dipstick for the engine oil which, if you filled it to the top mark, was actually over-filled. They'd done the same thing on the 1967 B44.)

Around 5,700 B50s were built in all, the last being produced during 1973, marking the end of a line going back to 1958. To sum up, whatever the purists may say, the unit singles were undoubtedly popular in their day, and continue to have their fans—in fact sometimes the remoter areas of Wales and Cornwall seem to be littered with non-runner C15s and Starfires and their disgruntled owners. Nice looks, light weight, good mpg, and an excellent interchangeability and spares situation, are all attractions—when they're going. There are a couple of firms specialising in servicing these bikes alone, as well as CCM of Bolton—whose gaffer Alan Clews designed and built his own moto-cross variants with heavily modified B50 engines. They kept a small corner of the sport open for four-strokes during the '70s, until their withdrawal in favour of own-brand two strokes during 1981. Clews had had the foresight to buy up the bulk of remaining BSA unit single motors and spares, and is consequently willing and able to supply engine spares for the post-1966 B25, B44 and B50s, as well as rebuild their motors to a high standard.

Making the best of one of the earlier 250s would probably involve converting it to 12-volt, changing the condensers to the big Triumph type mounted on a rubber-covered plate outside the engine, fitting the Lucas capacitor system, replacing the clutch push rod and the piston rings, sticking in the lowest compression piston you can find (or converting to a Fleetstar one if you have a Starfire), putting an Allen screw kit and a lot of tender loving care into assembly of the primary chaincase, and most importantly for any C25/B25, fitting the final B25SS con rod and the three stud cast iron oil pump.

But if you have any choice in the matter, with the 125 cc limit for learners about to come into force at the time of writing, there will soon no longer be any practical reason to opt for the generally less reliable and interesting 250 than, say, a '65–'67 B40, a '69-on B44, or even a B50 (but only if you can find one and you're feeling fit). But still — the cycle part goodies on the oil-in-frame B25s could make them a dangerously seductive prospect, and judicious de-tuning with a Fleetstar piston might produce something that combined fun and a reasonable life expectancy.

BSA: The C15/B40/B25/B44/B50 unit singles — dates and specifications
Production dates
C15 250 Star — 1958–67
C15 T Trials — 1959–65
C15 S Scrambler — 1959–65
C15 SS 80 Sports Star — 1961–65
B40 350 Star — 1961–65 (Civilian) 1967 (WD Military, CD)
B40 SS 90 Sports Star — 1962–65
B44 GP Scrambler — 1965–67
C15 Sportsman — 1966–67
C25 Barracuda — 1967
B25 S Starfire — 1968–70
B44 VE Victor Enduro Trail — 1966-68
B44 VR Victor Roadster — 1967
B44 SS Shooting Star — 1968-70
B25 FS Fleetstar — 1969–70
B44 VS Victor Special Trail — 1969–70
B25 SS Gold Star — 1971–2
B25 T Victor Trail — 1971–2
B25 FS Fleetstar (oil-in-frame) — 1971–2
B50 SS Gold Star — 1971–3
B50 T Victor Trail — 1971–3
B50 MX Victor Scrambler — 1971–3

Specifications
C15/C15T/C15S/C15 SS80/C15 Sportsman/C25/B25/B25SS
Capacity, bore and stroke — 247 cc (67 mm × 70 mm)
Type — ohv single
Ignition — Coil (C15T/C15S, energy transfer)
Weight — C15 (1959) 280 lb Sportsman (1965) 275 lb, C25 (1967) 315 lb, B25 S (1969) 302 lb, B25 SS (1971) 290 lb

B40/B40 SS 90
Capacity, bore and stroke — 343 cc (79 mm × 70 mm)
Type — ohv single
Ignition — Coil
Weight — B40 (1961) 300 lb SS90 (1962) 295 lb

B44/B44GP/B44 VE/B44 VS
Capacity, bore and stroke — 441 cc (79 mm × 90 mm)
Type — ohv single
Ignition — Coil (B44 GP/B44 VE energy transfer)
Weight — B44 (1967) 320 lb

B50 SS/B50 T/B50 MX
Capacity, bore and stroke — 499 cc (89 mm × 90 mm)
Type — ohv single
Ignition — Coil (B50 MX, energy transfer)
Weight — B50 SS (1971) 310 lb.

BSA: Roadster unit singles — annual development and modifications
1959
For late 1959 C15:
1 From engine No 9009, distributor drive shaft bush now locked into position by a grub screw.

1960
For C15:
1 Lucas 564 stop-tail lights fitted.

Early 1960
For C15:
2 From engine No 11715, mainshaft worm gear, and its mating gear on the distributor drive shaft

modified to reduce wear and hence variation in ignition timing. Only interchangeable with previous type as a pair.

1961
For C15, SS 80:
1 Hexagon-headed rocket caps replace previous slotted type.
2 Recommended total rear chain up and down movement increased from $\frac{5}{8}$ in to $1\frac{1}{8}$ in.

Mid-1961
For C15:
3 From engine No 24401, second piston compression ring changed to a type with a slight taper for better oil control. Interchangeable with previous.
4 From engine No 27665, an $\frac{1}{8}$ in washer fitted for oil tightness between the small cover plate of the gearbox camplate pivot and the gearchange pedal. Can be fitted to earlier models.

1962
For C15/SS80/B40/SS90 (introduced mid-May):
1 Detachable key for ignition switch, and new horn.
2 Restyled dual seat with narrower nose, abutting petrol tank more closely.
3 New alternators; for SS80/C15 Lucas 60 watt RM18, for B40/SS90 Lucas 60 watt RM 19.
4 New-pattern fuel tap with horizontal outlet used together with a modified carburettor banjo union, for B40/SS90.
5 Gearbox oil capacity increased from $\frac{1}{2}$ to $\frac{3}{4}$ pint, for this year only.
For SS80/B40/SS90:
6 Big end now caged, double-row roller bearing, with crankshaft and con rod to suit.
7 7 in front brake assembly redesigned, with ends of shoes remote from operating cam made flat so that they slide on fulcrum pin as well as pivoting on it, to achieve self-servo effect. To avoid over-fierce bite, leading edge of each friction surface chamfered back $1\frac{1}{4}$ in.
8 Slipper tensioner for duplex primary chain (as already on SS80) adopted.

Mid-1962
For all SS90 and B40:
9 From engine No 4331, correct setting for ignition timing changes from $\frac{1}{16}$ in (.0625) before TDC, to .0007 before TDC, both with ignition fully retarded.
For C15:
10 Compression ratio raised to 7.5:1.
11 Points gap increased from 0.012 to 0.015.

Mid-1962
For C15:
12 From engine No 31287, stronger springs in rear suspension units.

Late-1962
For C15 and SS80:
13 From C15 engine No 41775, SS80 3028, vanes of the clutch hub modified to accommodate equal-thickness cush-drive rubbers in place of the alternate thick and thin rubbers used previously. Interchangeable as a unit with previous.

1963
For SS80:
1 Pear-shaped petrol tank badges.

1964
For C15, SS80, B40 and SS90:
1 Smiths magnetic speedometers replace previous chronometric type.
For C15:
2 Big end caged roller-bearing, as already featured on other unit singles, adopted, and hence also crankshaft assembly and con rod.
3 3 gal petrol tank as on SS80/B40/SS90 adopted.
4 Compression ratio raised to 8:1.
For SS80 and SS90:
5 Optional chrome mudguards now of blade pattern.
For SS80:
6 Gearbox sprocket changed from 17 to 16 tooth lowering rear ratios from 5.985, 7.194, 9.917, 12.64 to 6.36, 7.64, 10.54, 13.43.

1965
For C15, SS80, B40 and SS90:
1 Engine redesign, with contact breaker tower eliminated and contact breaker now housed behind a chrome-plated cover in a sealed compartment in the timing case, and drive for it now taken from end of camshaft. Ignition timing by contact breaker adjustment which must now be made with timing fully advanced.
2 Gearbox redesign with clutch now operated by a rack-and-pinion affording a straight-line thrust on the clutch rod. Clutch control lever now mounted above and outside the timing-side crankcase. Mainshaft and layshaft redesigned. New mainshaft carries a ratchet pinion housed in the outer compartment of the box. The accompanying toothed quadrant integral with the kickstarter spindle, of which outer end has an oil seal. Layshaft now runs in a needle-roller

bearing in the hollow end of the kickstarter spindle, and is fitted with a loose thrust washer at its end. Gearchange selector quadrant redesigned to give more positive gear selection. Upper face of camplate now marked with T to assist correct assembly. Gearchange spring bolt replaced by pivot pin.

3 Larger bore crankpin oilway.

4 O-ring seals added to oil-pipe unions on crankcase.

5 Pear-shaped tank badges now provided with a separate rubber backing strip.

For SS80:

6 Chromed blade mudguards as standard.

For C15:

7 Slipper-tensioner for primary chain as already on rest of range.

1966

For C15

1 Chrome petrol tank side panels as standard, on tank now 2.6 gals.

2 New late C15T-type frame, with $\frac{1}{2}$ in greater ground clearance and seat height (now $5\frac{1}{2}$ in and $30\frac{1}{2}$ in) and $\frac{3}{10}$ in longer wheelbase (at 51.5 in).

For C15 Sportsman:

3 As SS80, but without close-ratio gearbox and with racing-type dual seat with humped rear, separate chrome-plated headlamp carried on brackets from fork shrouds, and new handlebars with rearward sweep replacing previous flat ones.

Mid-1966

For C15 and C15 Sportsman:

4 For C15G engines with prefix, C15SG for Sportsman, 441 Victor Enduro bottom end

adopted. Main bearings now ball on timing side, roller on drive, accommodated in Victor crankcase castings. New lubrication system no longer passes through previous plain timing-side bearing to big-end, but is now fed into right-hand end of crankshaft. Larger oil pump, now same size as twins. Cams and followers now lubricated by oil draining from the rocker box.

5 Gearbox also modified. Needle roller bearing fitted at both ends of layshaft. Top gear ratio still 5.98, but 3rd 8, 2nd 11.05, bottom 16.7 to 1.

6 Rear chain lubrication now by means of a metering needle incorporated in the primary chaincase.

7 Ball-ended control levers as standard.

1967

For C25 and B44 VR (for main engine and cycle changes from C15, see text):

1 Pointer fitted on inside of primary chaincase and marker on the rotor allows setting of ignition timing by strobelight. Correct setting is now 0.342 before TDC for C25/B25, 0.284 before TDC for B44 VR (later 0.304 for B50 SS), set with the engine running fast enough to be fully advanced.

Big Brother. 1967 441 cc Victor Roadster.

2 Rear suspension units now with chromed top covers and semi-exposed chrome springs.

3 New cast light alloy rear light units.

4 Rear chain enlarged from $\frac{1}{2}$ x $\frac{5}{16}$ in to $\frac{5}{8}$ x $\frac{1}{4}$ in.

5 Cushioned handlebar grips.

For C25:

6 A shim fitted to the gear side of the crankshaft to provide limited end-float (maximum permissible 0.002—0.006 in).

7 Small sealing rings, previously fitted on rocker spindles of C15, no longer fitted on C25.

1968

For B25S and B44 SS:

1 New front brakes in full-width hub, 8 in for B44, 7 in for B25. New method of clamping front wheel spindle in the fork-ends with bolt-on caps for B44 immediately, B25 from April.

2 Due to merging of US and British ranges, clip-less gaiter for front forks, high-rise handlebars, and side reflectors under nose and on side of tail light unit, now standard. No front registration plates – these must be fitted by a UK dealer.

3 35-amp fuse fitted in wiring feed-line adjacent to battery.

4 New anodised, three dimensional ribbed moulding, light alloy pear-shaped tank badges for B44 immediately, B25 from April.

5 Toggle light switch replaced previous switch replaces previous rotary one for B44 immediately, B25 from April.

6 Gearbox filler plug now provided with dipstick giving oil level.

For B44 SS:

7 Oil supply to valves mechanism has feed now taken directly from crankcase oil return union, not from return line as previous.

8 Gearing lowered from 5.056, 6.289, 8.321, 13.41 to 5.353, 6.659, 8.811, 14.20 by use of 17 not 18-tooth gearbox sprocket and 49 not 47-tooth rear wheel sprocket.

9 Exhaust valve lifter no longer fitted.

1969

For B25 S and B44 SS:

1 New slightly shorter fork giving half an inch less movement at 5 in, one inch longer wheelbase at 53 in, $\frac{1}{2}$ in less ground clearance at 7 in. Triumph-type lower members with different construction internally. Damping is now by a shuttle valve at the lower end of the fork stanchion together with a restrictor rod secured at the base of the sliding member.

2 Introduced during 1968, new type contact-breaker points, providing a fine adjustment facility when timing the ignition, by slackening two screws which retain the contact-breaker assembly, then turning a small eccentric screw at the bottom of the plate. New contact-breaker cover, previously steel but now a polished casting carrying sunken BSA lettering.

3 Previous $1\frac{3}{4}$ gallon petrol tanks and side-panels, all of fibreglass, replaced by steel $3\frac{1}{4}$ gallon tank and steel panels. Petrol tanks now fit twin taps, with left hand side stand-pipe lower to provide reserve supply.

4 Improved dual seat with perforated aerated top.

5 Majority but not all of thread forms on bolts, studs and screwed components converted from BSF, CEI, etc forms to Unified Form.

6 Stop-light switch fitted to front brake cable, actuating rear brake light.

7 Revised internals for silencers.

8 New 7 in twin-leading shoe front brake in full-width hub.

9 Width of crankcase and primary chaincase joint faces increased by 15 per cent.

10 New wiring harness, with provision for conversion to capacitor ignition.

11 Folding footrests, and foot-rest rubbers of more wear-resistant material bearing a revised BSA emblem in a rectangular panel.

12 Rev counter, and matching speedometer, fitted as option, driven from a worm on timing side of the crankcase through an aperture at front of timing chest.

13 Tubular connectors welded to steering-head gusset plates to allow fitting of fairing.

14 Fully exposed chromed rear suspension unit springs now give about $\frac{1}{2}$ in less movement at 2.56 in.

15 Grease nipple fitted in clutch cable casing, and an adjuster mid-way in the front brake cable run.

16 Concentric carburettors modified to dispense with detachable pilot jet.

17 Previous red warning light for headlamp full beam becomes blue or green.

For B44 SS:

18 Oil pressure warning light provided.

For B25 S:

19 Compression raised to 10:1.

20 B25 FS Fleetstar introduced. 8.5:1 compression ratio, 21 not 24 bhp, 52 not 49-tooth rear wheel sprocket giving 7.35 not 6.924 top gear ratio. Fully valanced mudguards, rear suspension unit with black-painted top covers and springs.

21 Con rod modified, bottom end thickened and little end bush deleted. Flywheels modified to provide clearance for this thicker rod.

22 Mid-year, from eng. no. BC12468, drive side main bearing, previously ball, changed to roller bearing. Method of crankshaft fixing therefore altered from previous fixing to drive side bearing when rotor nut tightened, to fixing to modified timing side shaft's ball bearing.

1969 B44 power unit close up – square fins, new dual seat, steel tank and badge.

1970

For B25 S, B25 FS, B44 SS:

1 Former oil tank side cover discarded, left-hand side panel reduced in size to match. Oil tank filler cap repositioned to avoid rider's leg.
2 Engine breathers modified to increase efficiency at high rpm.
3 Improved method of locating spring-carrying cups in clutch pressure plates.
4 Redesigned oil pump. Appearance similar, but driven spindle now spigots into top cover, driving spindle still spigoted to the scavenge gear, but the top/body sections of the casing are dowelled for more accurate location.
5 Redesigned silencers, cigar-shaped, with quieter internals.
6 Front fork stanchions now of a hard chrome-plated micro-finish to increase oil seal life.
7 Wiring harness now includes provision for indicator warning lights.
8 New design Lucas coils.
9 All ht leads have inbuilt suppression to prevent radio interference.
10 Front brake and clutch lever pivot blocks each include $5/16$ in threaded hole for handlebar mirrors.
11 Geometry of prop-stand spring attachment point revised.
12 Amal Concentric carbs feature redesigned needle-jet holder, needle jet and needle.
For B25 S:
13 Oil pressure warning light provided.

1971

For B25 SS, B25 T, B25 FS:

1 Wider rear engine mounting lug to suit new frame.
2 Con rods strengthened further, and with Unified Thread bolts.

1972

B25 SS, B25 T, B25 FS, B50 SS, B50 T:

1 Frame now black instead of Dove Grey.
For B25 SS, B25 FS, B50 SS:
2 Spring-loaded foot-rests as for trail models now fitted.
For B50 SS:
3 17-tooth gearbox sprocket and 47-tooth rear wheel sprocket substituted for previous 16 and 52, raising gearing from 6.036, 7.508, 9.935, 16.01 to 5.134, 6.387, 8.451, 13.62.
4 B50 T frame adopted, giving $1/2$ in greater ground clearance at 7.5 in.
For B50 SS, B50 T:
5 $1\frac{1}{2}$ in longer wheelbase at $55\frac{1}{2}$ in.

BSA: The A7 and A10 pre-unit twins

I will probably immediately make enemies but I must declare an interest – for me the A7/A10 parallel twins are the definitive British motor cycles of this period, and possibly of all time. And appropriately enough almost every British designer of stature during the years of their evolution had a hand in their design.

It was not, of course, the original – Edward Turner's trend-setting 500 cc Speed Twin of 1938. But its roots leap-frogged back beyond that to another 360° twin, Val Page's 1933 Triumph 6/1 650. This was an underrated design at the time, perhaps because it was offered for use with sidecars only. It was a commercial failure – less than 100 were sold over three years for which its

1947

500cc O.H.V VERTICAL TWIN

Newcomer of promise. 1947 A7 495 cc vertical twin power unit.

driven camshafts. There were never any heating problems with the BSA twins, and from the start they acquired a reputation for a quiet engine.

Page left Armoury Road to return to Ariel in 1939, during which year Norton's ohc singles wizard, Joe Craig, had a sojourn at the BSA factory where he developed prototypes of both a conventional ohv 350 twin, as well as a sports 500 cc ohc version. He left shortly after, and his influence on the production twins is less clear than that of Edward Turner himself, who came to BSA from Triumph in 1942, and not unnaturally worked on their twin.

Evidence of his efforts can be found in the early Triumph-type 4 separate hexagonal-headed rocker caps, and also in the characteristic and very pretty shape of the timing-side crankcase cover fitted to the A7. Though it was cut off rather abruptly at the bottom, lacking the Triumph's last graceful curve—compare it to the deliberately different and awkward cover on the Ariel Huntmaster, a Selly Oak version of the later BSA 650. From Turner too may have come the plain big ends, though the use of these was current practice at that time. The plain drive side main bearing which acted as a main oil feed to the big-ends, and a two-piece built-up crankshaft, like a Scott's but assembled by a special two-thread through-bolt, were both as found on Turner's 3T 350 which was delayed by the war and finally obliterated in the Coventry blitz. The plain driveside bearing appeared on the A7/A10 twins from start to finish, the timing side bearing initially being a ball journal bearing, but the production crankshaft was to be a one-piece job with bolted-on flywheel.

Turner returned to Triumph at Meriden towards the end of the war, and work on the twin proceeded apace, the man responsible being the Chief Designer, Herbert Perkins, assisted by David Munro of the Technical Department. Perkins has become associated with one or two less than perfect features of the early A7 design, which Bert Hopwood was to revamp extensively in creating the A10 and the new-for-1951 A7, and it is as well to remember that he also did the groundwork on which Hopwood's design was based. Perkins had joined the BSA design office in 1920, and as well as being responsible for several significant improvements to machine-tool design, had the widest motor cycle design experience. Hopwood characterises him as 'a fine man and a first-class engineer', and the 500 cc A7 which was

price, and the Depression, can take some of the blame. Turner, on his arrival at Triumph, according to Bert Hopwood, threw a tantrum, feeling he had been robbed of experimental work which he had done with Page while the two had been working at Ariel, and scrapped the 6/1 entirely.

Page had moved on to BSA where he laid the basis of the post-war singles range (see p55). The instant runaway commercial success of Turner's Triumph twins meant that, even pre-war, BSA were working to come up with a rival version, and Page's contribution to these early prototype efforts included two main features that he had tried on the 6/1, and which were to find their way onto BSA production versions after the war.

One of those was the four-speed gearbox bolted in semi-unit form onto the rear of the crankcase. The other, more fundamentally, was the engine layout, with a single four-lobed camshaft operating all four pushrods, which sloped forward in a cast-in tunnel to the rear of the cylinders. This left the cylinders unobstructed for cooling purposes, and it reduced mechanical noise significantly compared to the Triumph's twin fore-and-aft cams driven by a train of five gears, or to the later Ariel or Royal Enfield layouts with push-rods at the outer ends of twin chain-

announced and marketed during September 1946 was, as Hopwood put it, 'Mr Perkins' baby'.

As well as the features already described, the 495 cc (62 × 82 mm) 26 bhp twin had an iron barrel and cylinder head with separate bolted-on alloy rocker boxes, alloy crankcases, and initially a single carburettor characteristically fitted with a drip-shield to protect the magneto, which was mounted beneath it and behind the cylinder, in the manner of the BSA singles. A chain-driven dynamo sat forward of the motor. Inside the bolted-on gearbox shell was the BSA box, with its centre pair of gears on each shaft, as opposed to other marques' one gear per shaft, and its more numerous engagement dogs. Though tending to crunchiness of action, it was perfectly adequate, and though giving a heavyish change, eliminated the rear chain whip associated with Triumph's finer tooth form. There could be, however, what Hopwood calls 'severe gearshift operation problems' prior to modifications he incorporated for 1950.

The engine was housed in a duplex down-tube cradle frame with a rigid rear end, provided from the outset with the excellent BSA telescopic front fork, again a Val Page design (see page 60) and the best then available. The machine had a top speed of around 85 mph despite the low (6.6:1) compression ratio and Pool fuel, which it sipped at an average 60 mpg even under hard usage, plus good 7 in SLS brakes, excellent road-holding and handling, and good slow tick-over and pulling from low speeds, as well as a stirring deep exhaust note and a mechanically quiet engine. Inevitably with a 360° parallel twin, there was vibration. However, it was not severe, and the engine's rigidity meant there was no particular vibration period to avoid. Among the many rider features, which included touches like rear chainguards on both upper and lower runs, one was outstanding. This was the quickly-detachable rear wheel which came out by simply removing the spindle and knocking out a distance piece, leaving chain, brake and sprocket undisturbed. It was retained into the '60s and acknowledged as the best in the business. As far as the engine was concerned — it may have lacked the zing of a Triumph but its prospects of holding together were already infinitely better.

Teething problems were tackled in 1948 and a sports version, the Star Twin, offered, with twin carburettors and a 7.5:1 compression motor

Herbert Perkins' 1947 A7 twin.

Comp variant. 1947 A7 in trials trim.

giving 31 bhp. This was the only A7/A10 to feature twin carbs, though conversions were later available, and journalist Titch Allen, who owned an early A7, wrote that when he tried the twin carb version it felt little different. Among numerous changes to the standard model were crankshaft modifications, the moving of the speedometer to the fork crown tops from its pre-war style mounting on the tank, with the ammeter and light switch going to the headlamp shell, and the 19 in wheels becoming no longer inter-changeable.

In the alloy rocker box the valve gear, which had previously relied simply on oil mist for lubrication, now benefited from a feed from the oil return pipe to the left end of the rocker spindles, which were drilled to take this. But this was only a partial improvement, and sticking exhaust valves due to the build-up of carbon were always a problem with the pre-1951 A7s. The early cylinder head design was principally to blame, but the later models were prone to a build-up of carbon on the exhaust valve stems too. Amusingly, the trait was to be found not only on the early A50/A65 unit twins, but even apparently on a Japanese version of the A10 from Kawasaki, of which more later. The early cylinder head plus low-octane Pool fuel was also responsible for these A7's habit of 'running-on', or self-ignition, after switch-off.

Another problem inherent in the design, present from the start and never to be remedied, concerned the primary chaincase and the six-spring clutch. If the oil level in the case became too low, the duplex chain and its slipper-type tensioner suffered – if it was too high, oil got on the linings of the dry clutch, causing it to slip. The five plates of the clutch with their fabric inserts were packed in tight, and with the hard-to-adjust six springs the clutch was prone to drag as well

as slip. Stronger clutch springs, or Triumph plates with cork inserts, were possible solutions, but the one that found favour with owners in the light of experience was the substitution of another clutch hub (Part No 42-3170) which allowed the use of the four-spring Triumph clutch in its entirety, thereby eliminating one of the bike's few really irritating shortcomings.

Early in 1949 Bert Hopwood arrived at Armoury Road from Norton, where he had been responsible, among other things, for the basic design of the Dominator Twin. Before the war he had trained with Val Page at Ariel, and then been one of Edward Turner's assistants at Triumph and had been intimately involved with the evolution of the Speed Twin. Both the Dominator and the coming A7/A10 twins were to reflect the lessons he had learned, and the things about the Turner designs which he intended to avoid. These included the twin-cam layout – in his view the cylinders on the original Triumph has been badly obscured by the push-rod tubes, and cooling had suffered. His Norton twin had featured a single cam (though the camshaft in that case had been chain-driven and positioned in front of the cylinder), so with the A7 he was lucky to inherit a design in line with his thinking. His priorities were a compact engine, since production requirements imposed a conventional frame, smoothness and mechanical quietness (the Triumph's train of five gears to the magdyno, plus the twin cams, he thought, condemned it to be 'fundamentally a rattler' forever), with good engine coolness as mentioned, good accessibility, as well as the lower inertia loadings that a shorter-stroke engine brings with its attendant gain of rigidity and oil tightness.

The BSA twin already fulfilled many of these requirements, and although, according to the factory, prototype A7s bored-out to 650 had been circulating since 1948, it was Hopwood's revamping which brought about all these positive factors. Although the main bearings were already sturdy, the ball journal bearing on the drive side was replaced in Hopwood's design by a roller bearing. For rigidity, there was a long (1¼ in) plain bearing on the timing side, the journal of which was induction hardened, ground and polished. It was well equal to the stresses to which it would normally be subjected, and as mentioned, the main oil feed to the big-ends ran through it. Since the crankshaft pinion was immediately next to it, this too benefited from the flow in terms of quietness of the timing gear.

The A7/A10 bottom end was proverbially strong, but with two important provisos. While as Titch Allen wrote, 'no A7 or A10 I have ever known has ever called for a replacement of the main ball race', the plain drive side bearing could be damaged if regular oil changes were neglected, and these were vital for a number of reasons as well. The wide mesh filter system employed, particularly in the pump filter in the sump, allowed grit into the oil. So without clean oil there was not just general wear to the engine, but the plain

bearing was liable both to corrosion and to rapid wear of its lead-bronze bush. This in turn allowed oil intended for the plain big-ends to escape and never reach them. So regular oil changes, preferably every 1,000 miles rather than the 2,000 recommended, were a real necessity.

The other thing to avoid was over-revving. The engine characteristics did not encourage it. About 5,750 rpm was the early A10's recommended peak and 6,000 the absolute limit for the wise, although 6,500 could be risked on a carefully prepared post—57 DA 10 model.

If these conditions were observed, the new BSA twins would go on and on for very high mileages, sometimes as high as six figures, without a major overhaul. And the big-ends with their steel-backed shell bearings of lead bronze with indium flash diffused into their surfaces were long wearing, and easy to replace when the time came. All round, in fact, the pre-unit twins became phenomena of durability. The Rhodesian police force A10s, for instance, operating non-stop over the most rugged terrain imaginable, had a service life of an amazing seven years. The Yamahas which replaced them were only good for three.

Back in the beginning, there was one other priority for the BSA twin at the time of Hopwood's arrival, and that was to beat Triumph. Small Heath knew that Meriden were going

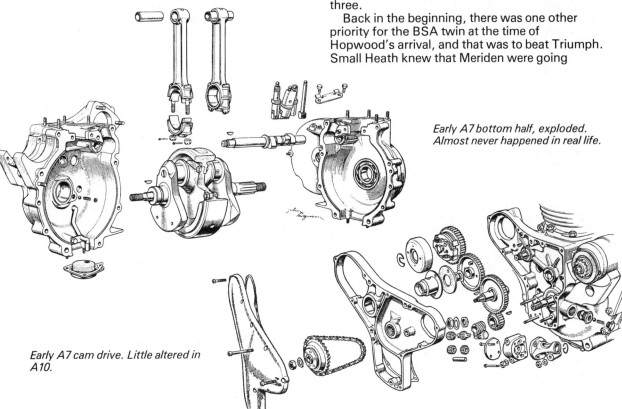

Early A7 bottom half, exploded. Almost never happened in real life.

Early A7 cam drive. Little altered in A10.

Left *Bert Hopwood's 1950 A10 Golden Flash.*

Below right *Flash anatomised, showing one-piece alloy rocker box inspection covers, and larger diameter timing sideshaft. Pistons were soon to have concave crowns.*

to come up with the Thunderbird, a 650 cc version of their twin, for 1950. So Hopwood went right to work in May 1949, and after just four incredible weeks came up with designs for both a 650 and a 500 of new dimensions sharing 95% of parts with the big 'un. The 650's (70 × 84 mm) dimensions were very similar to the coming (71 × 82 mm) Thunderbird, and the size of the new 500 A7 (which was not introduced until 1951) at 66 × 72.6 mm was significantly shorter-stroked than the old version's 62 × 82 mm dimensions. With air passing between the two bores to outlets round the side of the pushrod tunnels, the well-cooled one-piece cylinder barrel casting provided the greater rigidity Hopwood sought. The number of nuts holding the barrel on to the base flange were increased from 8 to 9.

The main area of redesign was the cylinder head. The head was still iron, but the increased bore of both models meant a shallower combustion chamber, and Hopwood opted for narrower angle valve geometry for improved combustion. Unlike the previous combined arrangement, each exhaust valve now had its own well, and with a view to efficient cooling, air guided by curved vertical fins could pass between these. The inlet valves however were still combined. The induction manifold, with a slight downdraught angle, was now included in the head casting, and as mentioned was only ever to be for a single carburettor. The alloy rocker box inspection covers were no longer the screw-in type, but were now of one piece for each pair of

valves, each held down by four nuts. But the joint faces were thin, and the exhaust rocker-box in particular was an exception to the otherwise mostly oil-tight engine.

Rocker and valve design was unaltered, but all four rockers were now in one casting, and the inlet as well as the exhaust valves were now of strengthened austenitic iron with stellite-tipped stems. The disadvantage of this layout was that relocating the push-rods on their rockers during engine assembly became more difficult, and BSA produced a proprietary push-rod comb tool (Pt No 67-9114) to assist the process. Some heavy grease smeared in the rocker-cups to help stick the push-rods in helped, but otherwise, without the tool, it was down to fiddling with a torch and bent wire till they were located.

Standard compression was fractionally raised at 6.6:1 for the standard A7, with an optional 7.2:1, and for the A10 was a modest 6.5:1. These were achieved with BSA own-brand piston, initially concave for the A10, later flat-top for the A7. They were alloy, with semi-split skirt pistons, the split extending upwards only as far as the centre-line through the gudgeon-pin bosses, with 4 in heat gaps, slots cut parallel to the internal webs, running from the base of the gudgeon-pin bosses to the crown, and with each pair joined to the top end by a $\frac{1}{16}$ in slot. This kept heat from the piston skirt and allowed it flexibility, as well as minimising piston slap and reducing clearances by half. Hopwood provides a fascinating insight into how initial problems with the right-hand piston running dry and seizing were solved, not by the outside piston specialist that a worried Hopwood wanted to call in, but by the suggestion from BSA Production Director, Tom Whittington, that they simply cut a perspex window into the engine to see what was happening! The unorthodox method revealed not faulty piston design but inadequate lubrication to the offside, which was quickly corrected.

This was done by a modification to the lubrication system, with oil passing via a small relief valve in the timing chest via oilways directly onto the camshaft, where a trough was now cast beneath it, both for continuous cooling, and to fling lubricant up onto the cylinder bores. The camshaft was also provided with quietening ramps. The timed engine breather on the end of the camshaft was reduced in diameter, and followed a more convoluted path to atmosphere. Other changes from previous A7 practice included alloy not steel con-rods, altered tappet positions and method of casting, and a dynamo of increased output. There were changes to the tooth form of the timing gears, also to reduce noise. As mentioned, a roller main bearing replaced the previous ballrace on the driveside, and the crankshaft, though unaltered, was now allowed a small degree of end float. And early in 1950 there were also modifications made to the gearbox to improve the change. These were effective, but changes could still be clonky unless properly timed, and there was a distinctive whine in third gear.

To get in alongside Triumph with the 650 by the end of 1949, risks were taken and extraordinary efforts made. Management authorised the design and ordering of production tools almost immediately after the engine design had been completed, gambling that there would be few design changes necessary. The BSA in-house facilities made further savings of time possible. Hopwood worked his magic in May, and by August three prototypes were available for testing. This took place round the clock with three riders per machine clocking up 4,000 miles per week. The new motor cycle was ready for the Motor Cycle Show in October, and production quantities were available from November 1. The gamble paid off. Hopwood and the team had got it right, few modifications were necessary and the A10 Golden Flash was a success from the start.

The 35 bhp Flash was offered for 1950 in plunger trim as standard, with a rigid option until 1952, and with a new dual seat, also optional until 1954. It came with sidecar or solo gearing, via a rear wheel sprocket of 49 or 42 teeth (46 solo for the 500 cc), though after 1954 this was standardised for the 650 at 42 teeth for either function, but with a 17 tooth gearbox sprocket for the 500 replacing its solo sprocket of 19 teeth — the merely small variations considered necessary are evidence of the motor's very considerable torque. The plunger system which had been available optionally for the old A7 since 1949 will be found discussed in the BSA *Pre-unit singles* section (see page 61). The handling was not an improvement on the rigid frame, one additional reason to those already stated being variations in manufacturing tolerances which made it possible for the wheel to push or pull the sliding wheel-carriers away from their true positions, so that different frames would have stiff or easy wheel movements. The units clashed audibly and the bike hopped about on poorly surfaced corners, but the rather low clearance given by the centre stand prevented radical angles of lean and hence trouble, and the minimal comfort of the at best 2 in of wheel movement was not to be sneered at on the poor road surfaces of the day.

The plunger frame dictated some styling

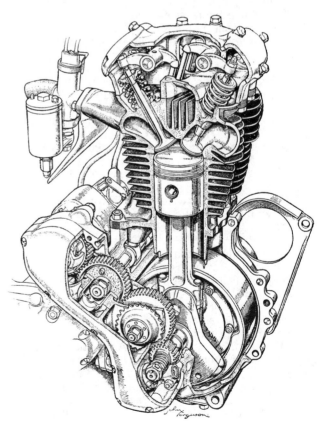

changes, such as a larger petrol tank and more rounded tool boxes. Others, like extra chrome, a deeper front mudguard, modified petrol tank fixing, and an 8 in brake at the front, distinguished the new 1950 650 from its smaller-bore predecessor. It was a while before the plunger system was fully accepted by sidecar men, an important section of the market then. For by the end of the '50s one in every three large-capacity machines was attached to a chair. However, the torque of the A10's motor as well as its speed of well over 70 mph with a chair attached, soon made it a firm favourite with sidecar fans, as did the economy factor — the bike returned 50–55 mpg even with the bike in harness. The only real drawback such enthusiasts faced at this time were the brakes. These were little worse than their competitors, but even the solo brakes faded under hard use, and were barely adequate for the extra weight of a chair. The bearings of the 19 in wheels could also wear out quickly under the strain of prolonged sidecar hammering. Another potential weak point was the single-sided quickly-detachable rear hub with its crinkled edges for straight equal-length spokes — the edges were rivetted to a central sleeve, and the rivets could loosen and shear off with wear.

Otherwise the rugged-twins were purpose-built, and by the time the swinging-arm frame was introduced for 1954, sidecarrists had accepted the plunger frame and the factory could offer the new (and perfectly suitable) frame 'for solo use only' and keep the plunger frame on the market as an option until the end of 1957, by which time stocks were cleared. The plunger frame bumped dry weight up from the rigid version's 380 lb to 395 lb, the first in a progressive but never chronic series of weight rises that culminated in the 1960 A10 which weighed in at 425 lb. But with a seat height of 30 in and a 56 in wheel-base (55 for the plunger frame) these bikes were always compact, and my Flash of '61 vintage never really felt heavy — just solid.

From early 1950 the Golden Flash was offered appropriately enough in polychromatic Golden Beige paint all over, as an option — more recently this shade has been seen as one of the 1979 paint jobs on the T140E Bonneville, but it was shown off to best advantage on the A10's tank which was chromed with beige panels at first, then from 1953 with the very typically BSA red-lined chrome side-panels. From 1958-on the beige was applied to tank, guards, oil tank and toolbox only, the rest being black, and although other colours came and went, the Golden Beige or its black and chrome standard alternative were *the* finishes for the

Flash, just the later A7 Shooting Stars' polychromatic green with dark green frame, the A10 Super Rocket's Royal red or the A10 Rocket Gold Star's metallic silver were all totally characteristic.

Solo, a Flash tested in 1950 was good for 104 mph — the highest speed of any machine tested that year. Though the 650 Triumphs were soon to exceed this, a more relevant comment made by the testers was that A10 average speed could sustain a very high figure over long distances, because of the engine's tirelessness and its excellent torque at medium revs. The A10 was built for the long haul, and was fast in any terms, even the standard Flashes always just exceeding 100 mph—but it was not the fastest, and it certainly didn't have the fastest image.

As Titch Allen pointed out in an excellent series contrasting the Small Heath and Meriden twins (*Motor Cycle Sport*, June 1978), although there was little official Triumph racing at this time, so many Triumph-mounted privateers had been active in the field from the start that both an image of speed, and a large body of tuning lore and goodies, had built up. BSA were definitely not interested in factory level, the pre-1951 A7s could not be tuned to any degree of reliability, and though the situation improved for the 500s, as we shall see, the 650s could not really be tuned to their maximum outputs until the DA10 series which appeared post-1958. However, at the level of club sports, this was often not too important — on grass, for instance, the iron engine single carb BSA could be tuned as fast as the alloy-engined twin carb Triumphs, and they kept their edge for longer.

The Triumph v BSA rivalry persisted throughout the '50s and '60s, and it was largely a question of a different approach. But as Titch Allen pointed out, the BSA offered the qd rear wheel, and the slipper primary chain tensioner against Triumph's tensioning system with its inaccessible gearbox retaining bolts that tended to move forward. The BSA telefork, even with its continued lack of two-way damping, was stronger both in looks and in fact than the Triumph version with its early oil seals made of felt and its tendency to stick. The BSA fork and frame provided more reliable handling than the Triumph and were to continue to do so until the mid-'60s. The silence of the Flash's engine and the deep drone of its exhaust both contrasted with the clatter of the Triumph and its more metallic exhaust note.

And at the most basic level, the over-engineered A10 engine, designed as a 650, not as a scaled-up 500 with flywheels and bottom end in common with the Speed Twin, took 20 to 30,000 miles to bed in before starting to give its best. It could then more often than not run for over 100,000 miles on the same crankshaft. Triumphs, on the other hand, acquired a largely justified reputation for devouring main bearings — '10,000 miles was considered quite good in the early '50s' for Triumph main bearing life expectancy, wrote Titch Allen. It didn't always end up like that of course and the odds improved with sensible driving — but that was scarcely the reason for buying a Triumph, and until the later big-bearing motor, main bearing failure was a definite occupational hazard.

Despite these shortcomings, many continued to prefer and to buy the Triumph twins. Why? Some clue is given by their looks. The BSA's styling was solidly handsome, but the Triumph by its lightness and by a hundred little touches achieved an elegance approaching beauty itself. As without, so within — the A10 was willing, but the T110 was eager. And as with the ladies, liveliness in a bike can blind our judgement to less desirable qualities. Titch Allen concedes that the difference in character was a combination of many factors 'like carburation and valve timing, but a lot of it is due to the balance and rigidity of the bottom half. The Triumph engine had periods of balance and periods of imbalance and it seems to have a natural tendency to seek out the calm periods'. These always seemed to be further up the rev scale, giving the Triumph an aggressive, go-faster quality. The A10 by contrast did what you told it, no more, no less, and went on doing it all day. You could call it uninspiring, but in me it inspired confidence and affection.

I preferred the BSA, but I hasten to add this is a strictly personal value judgement. A list of this author's favourite Ancient Brits would differ almost entirely from that provided by, for instance, Royce Creasey in his seminal 'Alternative Biking' article, *Bike,* March 1976. Royce genuinely loves speed, and as a qualified engineer and mechanic, views any mechanical malfunction in a bike as a problem he will probably be able to solve. I like riding long distances at no more than a fair clip, and as a mechanical ignoramus view the possibility of bits breaking with profound dismay. As Royce has said, there has to be something interesting and satisfying about a bike to compensate for the discomfort of motor cycling, but for some it's going to be adrenalin and for others peace of mind. He judges the Thunderbird and the big Velo to be the definitive British bikes, I'd give the title, with

more conventional wisdom, to the A10 and the AMC singles. It's different strokes for different folks, and always had been.

I have been speaking of the 650 cc BSA, but it would be unfair, though not unusual, to continue to ignore its smaller brother, which as we shall see, was a consistently under-rated machine. The new A7 appeared a year after the first Flash, for 1951. Some 95% of parts were in common with the A10, so much so that the (identical) frames for both were coded A7. There were one or two areas of difference to take note of, such as the exhaust pipes which were assymetrical left and right as on the A10, but also different from the 650 which was a slightly taller bike. As mentioned, the earlier Star Twin's dual carburettors were dropped, but power on the stock A7 was up slightly at 27 bhp, and the sport versions' 31 bhp remained unchanged. The tuned Star Twin like the A10 had the plunger frame as standard, and a silver and chrome tank with its own motif to distinguish it. A lubrication modification for both A10 and A7 of 1951 was effected by the drilling of a small hole in the left hand connecting rod and upper-big end bearing shell to improve oil flow to that big end, and care was needed during reassembly to make sure the correct half went in there. Otherwise the A10s and A7s were much the same, the latter's lower gearing giving even better mid-range torque, with optimum cruising speed at 70 and a top speed of nearly 90 mph.

1952 provided two opportunities for the 500s to cover themselves in their own glory rather than the Flash-reflected kind. Star Twins, with the

A7 Shooting Star's hour of glory, 1952.

manual ignition control that Pool fuel made very necessary for best results, won the Maudes Trophy with an ACU-observed round trip of nearly 5,000 miles through 10 countries, punctuated by successful participation in the ISDT (see page 15 for some details). And on the other side of the pond, West Coast distributor Hap Alzina organised an attempt at Bonneville Salt Flats on the AMAs Class C record, for basically standard current production machines. With an 8:1 compression ratio sports cams, special valve springs, a $1\frac{1}{16}$ in Amal TT carb and a polished and ported engine, the unfaired A7 with a fully clad rider took the record with a flying mile at 123.69 mph. A 650 did the same for the less restricted Class A record, which allowed a 13.5:1 compression engine running on alcohol and bike and rider stripped, with a flying mile of 143.54 mph.

That year's roadster twins, bereft of their tank chrome by the current shortages, had their front fork damping improved by a lengthening of the top bushes, as well as their petrol tank fixing modified. Internally it has been found that at low revs, oil could drip into the outward passage of the ported, timed breather, so a circular shroud was cast round the breather, on the inside of the timing cover, to act as a baffle. An oil seal was also fitted on the gearbox mainshaft. Brakes had their fulcrum pin and cam bearings stiffened. And the Star Twin 500s, in addition to the manual ignition control, were now fitted with higher compression pistons giving a 7.5:1 ratio, a larger Amal TT $1\frac{1}{16}$ in carburettor and a higher lift cam, plus the 650's 8 in brake, though testers of the day found this only adequate. Headlights were changed to the pre-focus type for all and an unpopular underslung pilot light was introduced.

For 1953 came a headlamp cowling, as the fashion of the day dictated. Titch Allen described it as 'a compromise cover-up job', a semi-circular pressing which covered the top of the lamp before flowing back to be clamped in place by the fork top nuts and the lower crown clamp bolts. The speedometer was now mounted in it, as were the light switch and ammeter, but since the latter was at such an angle as to be unreadable from the saddle and the former inaccessible if a screen was fitted, and since the headlamp could only be adjusted when the cowl's rubber beading had been first removed, the whole thing was scarcely a benefit to the rider. There was a new rear light fitting, and chrome tank panels and wheel rims were restored for all, with tank mountings further modified. Finally the Star Twin was resplendent in its polychromatic green livery with large round black tank badges.

This was the year of the first sports 650, the A10 Super Flash, initially for export to the US only, though half a dozen did find their way out in Britain. With pistons that raised compression to 8:1, special cam and Amal TT9 carb, output was up to 42 bhp. There were paired speedometer and rev counter above a shell headlamp, chrome sports mudguard and handlebars, a butterfly filler-cap on the oil tank, and a special finish and tank badges. However, the cycle parts were still basically the plunger frame, which was scarcely up to the 110 mph top speed.

1954 was to see that situation change with a great leap forward — the appearance as an option for both A7 and A10 of the swinging-arm frame, of the type developed for the Gold Star. (The frames fitted to the singles and twins were similar but never identical — for the singles the kink in the right hand lower frame loop, to accommodate their oil pump, was the distinguishing mark, and it meant that though with new engine plates a twin's engine could slot into a single's frame — incidentally the reverse was not possible.) The frame, an immensely strong example of the all-welded duplex-downtube cradle type, had its swinging-arm pivoted on Silentbloc bushes, and Girling 3-position dampers at the rear.

Its single top tube also held the mounting for the excellent rubber-padded single-bolt petrol tank fixing, a great practical improvement which was to feature on most BSAs from then until the end. Oil tank mountings were also modified as they had been on the Gold Stars. The supply pipe from the return pipe for the oil feed to the rocker gear now continued into the tank so that its end fitted into the filter situated therein. The oil tanks were larger and of a new shape. This was matched on the nearside by the tool-box cover, and the battery was now carried out of sight beneath the seat. The new frame also allowed the footrests, still adjustable, to be set further rearwards relative to the seat. The quickly detachable rear wheel and its backplate moved round so that the cam pivot was directly above the wheel spindle and the cam lever hung down, with the brake rod running alongside the swinging fork tube. At the same time the front fork, unchanged externally, had its damping improved internally, with fork oil contents nearly doubled.

The new frame allowed the old bolt-up gearbox to be replaced by a completely separate box, with the shape of the drive side crankcase altered accordingly. Primary chain adjustment was consequently achieved by using draw bolts to move the box backwards. The slipper tensioner was discarded and the primary chain itself reverted to single row. The separate box meant that a full range of internal ratios could be offered, as on the Gold Star—wide for trials, standard, scrambles, close and extra-close, including the legendary RRT2 with its needle roller bearings. The box would also, like the Gold Star, take a reverse cam-plate to allow for reversing the gear-pedal with rear-set footrests, with no alteration in shift-pattern. Ratios on the standard box were slightly reduced from the start, and some pinions were machined with internal dogs, while the mating gears were machined so as to telescope inside, which shortened and stiffened the shafts and reduced flexing. The changes of direction on the cam-track were also made less severe to reduce wear. It was a stronger box than previously, though still potentially clonky in action.

1954 was the first year of the Ariel Huntmaster—Selly Oak's badge engineered version of the A10

(for more details see Volume 1) and the year also saw, after the 500 twins' victory in the Daytona 200 race, (see page 20), the Star Twin being supplanted by a new version of the sports 500, the Shooting Star, which for the first time employed, as well as the pivoted-fork frame, an alloy cylinder head. (The finning on the cast-iron cylinder heads was also increased at this time.) The previous Amal TT carb was replaced for 1955 with an Amal Monobloc 376, compression ratio was 7.25:1 and high-lift cams were fitted. The Shooting Star represented the definitive version of the 500 and though overshadowed in the public eye by the 650s, those who knew, such as journalists with a lot of miles under their belt and an opportunity for comparison with other models, rated it very highly indeed and continue to do so. 'I conceived an immense regard for this model which was easily the sweetest twin on the market', wrote Bruce Main-Smith. 'It was eyeable, handleable and

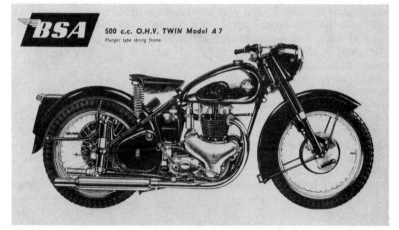

1954 Plunger A7—that year's swinging arm frame was optional.

1954, first swinging arm A10 Flash.

economical,' said Titch Allen, who went on: 'I would add tractable, because with a lower than average top gear of 5.28 it was exceptionally flexible and responsive in mid-range', adding that only its weight (408 lb dry for 1955) let it down. Output was up at 32 bhp. Top speed by 1956 was 93 mph and by 1958, with the wind behind, it was timed at just under 100, yet driven hard it would still return over 60 mpg. Perhaps Edward Turner got it right from the start, and 500 cc is actually the optimum capacity for a parallel twin. In any event, the Shooting Star, the AMC 500 twin and the Triumph Daytona all evoke not only respect but unusually affectionate memories.

Externally, the A7 Shooting Star was still distinguished by the polychromatic green livery inherited from the Star Twin, as well as by the fact that from the start its petrol tank still bore a large round black acrylic plastic badge the same size as the one fitted to the Gold Star—when the other twins traded their winged metal badges for smaller versions of the round jobs, with piled arms motifs (1955 for the A10 Road Rocket, 1956 for the stock A7 and A10), the two types were not inter-changeable, and only the Rocket Gold Star was to revert to the use of the larger diameter badges.

1955 saw only detail changes to the twins. The underslung pilot light was deleted, a steering lock fitted and dipswitch and horn buttons were combined in one control on the left bar. Monobloc carburettors came in throughout the pivoted-fork range, and as on the B-range roadster singles, there was a redesign of the engine-shaft shock absorber with two lobes instead of four. For the pivoted-fork twins, a repositioned rear mudguard

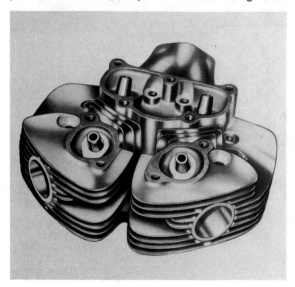

resulted in a more horizontal location of the dual seat, and there was a new one-piece valanced front mudguard.

A pivoted-fork sports version of the 650 could not be long in coming, and indeed was displayed at European shows throughout 1954. It was available for export from the end of that year on, before being released in a slightly modified version for the home market in July 1956. This was the 40 bhp A10RR Road Rocket, tested for 1956 at 109 mph, with an alloy head, raised gearing, a TT9 carburettor and 8:1 compression ratio. Yet though in 1956 only a Vincent had returned a better standing quarter time in the hands of testers, the motor was characterised, with its manual ignition control helping with the inevitable slightly erratic tickover, as still tractable and good in traffic. Since the European model carried not only a flatter handlebar but also a more effective silencer than the US spec, there was felt to be no sacrifice of the bike's unobtrusiveness, while acceleration all the way up to 100 mph was steep and consistent.

That year, however, had seen the change on all the pivoted-fork twins to Ariel-type full-width hub brakes, which meant cable operation of the rear brake giving a spongy action, a fault only partially compensated for by the replacement of the old 8 in SLS front brake by the more efficient (at least in the dry) 7 × 1.5 in number that replaced it. Finish on the Road Rocket included chrome mudguards (sports at the front), a red, chrome-panelled tank and a separate headlamp shell, with speedometer and optional rev counter mounted on the fork top crowns. All in all, it represented a genuinely strong challenge to Triumph's 1954-on T110. Its only major problem was caused by the comparatively thin flange at the base of the cylinder block. Designed with the original compression ratio in mind, it proved a potential weak spot under hard revving with the new higher compression motors, and this was not to be remedied until 1958.

The new-for-1956 full-width hub brakes for all the twins were of cast aluminium, ribbed externally for cooling and webbed internally for strength. The alloy backplate was anchored to a torque stay and carried a lug to the cable adjuster to screw into. There was also a fulcrum adjuster fitted to work on the shoe ends furthest away from the brake cam, for improved adjustment. At the rear, the brake itself was moved to the right, which meant a cross-over operation, by means of a small lever attached to a spindle running through the fork pivot bolt, from the brake pedal on the left to brake cable on the right. The qd rear wheel was modified, with rubber-plugged holes now fitted

Below left *Alloy cylinder head — this one was for 1956 A10 Road Rocket.*

Right *Black Rat's delight. 1957 A10 in police trim with Motoplas fittings.*

giving access to taper-seated dome nuts on the driving studs.

This was the first year that the four-piece full rear chain enclosure, with plugged holes to lubricate the chain, check its tension and get at the rear sprocket bolts, was offered as an option. (The BSA twins particularly benefited from this sensible piece of equipment as there was no oiling arrangement for the rear chain, and wear had been a problem from the start.) And the 1956 Shooting Star, to raise volumetric efficiency, had its carburettor now bolted directly onto the siamesed inlet port of the alloy head.

There were no alterations for 1957, a time of management changeover, but in 1958 there was a welter of substantial modifications. The plunger Flash was no more, and the sports 650 became the 43 bhp Super Rocket. Its compression ratio was raised to 8.5:1 and there was a cylinder head redesign, with the angle and sweep of both inlet and exhaust ports changed, and the Amal TT carburettor replaced by a large bore Monobloc (though the TT was still available as an optional extra). In fact, in many ways the Super Rocket resembled the iron-engined A10 — externally the Road Rocket's chrome mudguards and separate headlamp had gone in favour of sports guards as on the Shooting Star, and the 1958 headlamp nacelle replaced the separate headlamp and speedometer. The A7 Shooting Star's compression was also raised, to 8:1.

In common with the A10 for that year there was

a new one-piece crankshaft of EN 16B steel with a heavier load capacity, a more substantial big-end bearing shell and a strengthened timing-side main bearing. The crankshaft had the flywheel located in a circular centre boss by means of three radial set-screws, not bolted on laterally as previously. The twin-crank throw was hollow and contained an improved tubular sludge-trap, positioned endwise and prevented from rotating by an extension of one of the flywheel set-screws. The cylinder base flange was also increased considerably in thickness.

It can be no coincidence that this strengthening of an already strong motor was carried out in the same year in which a scrambles A10 was released for America. As Hopwood had discovered, the demands both of Stateside sports and of the terrain placed extraordinary stress on components which were quite adequate for everyday European usage. The Brits benefited to the extent that these 1958-on engines are the ones that can be safely tuned for maximum output. There was no distinguishing change of engine number yet for the Super Rocket, but the roadster Golden Flash became identifiable by the DA10 prefix.

All the twins that year adopted cigar-shaped silencers to replace the older square-shouldered type, and comments by 1958 Super Rocket tester, Peter Howdle, suggest that they were marginally less efficient — 'a trifle too sporting on full chat' was how he put it. Brakes front and rear were changed to Triumph-type, still full-width but

Left *1958 A7 in characteristic harness.*
Below left *1958 A7. Full cowl headlamp, cigar silencers, Triumph-type brakes.*

ammeter, was fitted on all the twins. Side-car attachment points were provided now the plunger-frame A10 was no more. As a result of all this, weights were up, with the A7 at 425 lb and the A10 peaking at 430 lb.

From then on there was little fundamental change. 1959 saw the sports and the standard models draw still closer together. The US scrambler was modified and given the name Spitfire, which was to crop up again on the hot A65 of the mid-'60s. Both A7 and A10 acquired the higher-lift camshaft as previously on the sports models only, and the camshaft on the 650s was stiffened. The old type Amal Monobloc 376 was replaced by the 389 for the touring A10 as on the Super Rocket. The carburettors were to change in size for the last time in 1960, the Flash going from $1\frac{1}{16}$ in to the export Super Rocket's $1\frac{1}{8}$ in bore, and the home market Super Rocket going to $1\frac{5}{32}$ in. A more fundamental change for that year was a clutch redesign as part of a not altogether successful effort to sort out the slip and drag, with four-springs replacing the previous six, adjusted by Simmonds self-locking nuts via a screwed plug in the primary chaincase, present on some models since mid-1958 but standardised in 1959. The clutch drum ceased to have inserts fitted to it, the clutch bearing ran on 20 rollers and the method of removing the clutch centre changed.

Also for 1960, on the bottom of the primary chaincase there was a new method of regulating the oil level, a combined drain and oil level, to prevent confusion between the previous two separate screws. Removing the inner screw, which was threaded into a stand-pipe inside, gave the level, while undoing the plug into which the screw threaded, removed the stand-pipe base and drained the oil. It was a fiddly, messy arrangement which is to be found on the Triumph Bonneville to the end. There was a restyling of the front mudguard and its mounting, and a tidying of the rear with revised side stays/grab handles. Seat height was reduced an inch and comfort on the dual seat effectively increased by giving its foam-rubber better air-flow passages. A different battery, a new Wico-Pacy combined handlebar switch to the left, and the moving of the front brake adjuster from backplate to handlebar lever were all modest benefits, while the return of the air lever from the bars to its old home beneath the seat was not. Plain knee-grips (no BSA motif) and pear-shaped tank badges as on the Star 250

with the hubs now heavier, in cast-iron not light alloy, and the back plate was enamelled black but with polished chrome rim bands. The size of the front brake, for all but the touring A7, was increased to 8 in with the front brake torque arm being replaced by a slotted boss on the shoe plates which engaged with a lug projecting from the inner face of the front leg. But its performance was no great improvement and the 7 in rear brake remained cable-operated and spongy. A new roll-on centre stand was a more tangible benefit. The clutch now consisted of five friction plates and the drum was strengthened. A proper full headlamp nacelle, with neat chrome flutings along each side and speedo, lightswitch and easier-to-read

single, were adopted also.

For 1961 there were no changes. The end was in sight for the non-unit twins, caught in a pincer movement between Edward Turner's management policies, Joe Lucas' reluctance to continue to provide magnetos, and the contraction of the bike market, plus the virtual demise of side-cars, in the face of affluence and the Mini. However, two more twists to the tale suggest that with a bit of judicious restyling and weight saving, the mighty Flash might have survived. The first concerns the Japanese Flash (and I am indebted to an excellent article by C.D. Bohon in the BSA Owners Club magazine *The Star* for my information, and to the Club for their permission to use it).

Copies of British iron were much in evidence during the booming bike scene in Japan in the '50s, so it comes as no surprise that in 1960, Meguro, one of the many companies soon to be boiled down to the Big Four, came up with the K-1, a 497 cc twin, with the exact (66 × 72.6) dimensions of the A7. It was advertised as 'English-style', with separate engine and gearbox and right hand gearchange. There was a later and more powerful K-2 version, a 100 mph motor cycle, and the K-series were used by the police, despatch riders and sportsmen.

By 1966 Kawasaki had absorbed Meguro and come up with a bored-out version of the 500, namely the (74 × 72.6) 624 cc W-1. The lower end was redesigned with a built-up crank and roller bearings, compression was 9:1, and the 47 bhp bike, still fitted with a single carb, was good for 105 mph. As the Kawasaki Commander it was imported briefly into the States and in 1967 even appeared at the Earls Court Show. It fared badly for export, but a twin carb, twin-leading shoe version, the 53 bhp 5-gear W-2, with cam lubri-cation improved, the dynamo uprated from 60 to 90W, and with a 112 mph top speed, was launched in Japan, where import restrictions meant that genuine British bikes were rare and expensive. It became a firm favourite with police and riders alike, and even the bad times were good — one fan wrote: 'over 4,000 rpm the vibration tingles your body and you can feel the pistons moving — over 5,000 rpm the W-1 is like a wild horse — it's fantastic!' A twin front disc version with left-hand gear change, the W-3, was produced until the model's demise in, wait for it, 1976.

The arguments used against the Flash (old-fashioned, limited development potential, pre-unit, difficult to convert from mag electrics, etc) clearly didn't hold much water with the Japanese.

Nearly the last A7 Shooting Star, late 1961 model.

A second example of the A10's development potential came in 1962. The A7 and A10 roadsters were scheduled for the chop in mid-year when their new A50/A65 replacements came on stream. The Super Rocket, with redesigned silencers, modified gears and brakes and an optional siamesed exhaust remained available into 1963 while stocks lasted. However, from February 1962 came the definitive sporting version of the A10, the Rocket Gold Star. It was the brainchild of Gold Star specialist Eddie Dow, who had been involved with high performance parts for the twins.

Unable to obtain an extension of life for the beloved Goldie, he suggested the BSA Management produce a hybrid, with the Super Rocket engine slotted into a Gold Star-type frame and cycle parts, thereby producing a flagship to plug a gap for the factory until sports versions of the new unit twins had been developed (and simultaneously use up the pre-unit and Goldie stocks). It could be said that the scheme succeeded all too well, for the RGS was an ultimate, and one that made the forthcoming Rocket and Lightning look somewhat underwhelming.

Chromed fork shrouds, and gaitered front fork stanchions, topped lower fork legs of the Gold Star type, which were necessary to enable use of

the large diameter wheel spindle and hence allow the option of the much-prized 7 ½ in diameter 190 mm Gold Star front brake—incidentally, converting any BSA to that brake means fitting the lower fork legs too. Otherwise the front brake was a conventional alloy 8 in one, with the rear 7 in, but rod-operated like the Gold Star, which meant the use of the early single-sided crinkle-edged quickly-detachable wheel hub with the brake to the left. The frame was as the Gold Star but without the kink in the right-hand side for the oil pump, and all good bikers must by now know that if you're vetting a Rocket Goldie (and at the time of writing they are fetching up to £10,000, or £6,000 to £7,000 more than a stock A10), the presence or absence of the kink is the first thing you check to make sure you're shelling out for the real thing rather than a later hybrid Gold Star-framed/Super Rocket-engined homebrew.

Another means of idenification are the chrome mudguards—sports efforts unique to the RGS, distinct from both the Gold Star and the later A65, and identifiable by a beaded flare on the lower edge of the six-stay front guard, and the trailing edge of the rear guard—where the registration and light fitting is open-sided, like the Bantam. A third is the silver 4-gallon petrol tank with butterfly nut racing snap-filler cap, and chrome side panels outlined in maroon, as well as the big badges as on the A7 Shooting Star/Gold Star. The exhaust pipe was siamesed and the single silencer either the cigar shape A10/Super Rocket type or the Gold Star's. The dual seat came from the standard A10.

The engines were the cream of those used for the Super Rocket, selected after bench-testing, but with a larger exhaust valve (which the Super Rocket was itself to acquire for 1963), 9:1 compression and, initially, the very close-ratio RRT2 gearbox, but with ratios widened slightly for 1963. Top gear in standard trim was low due to a 46-tooth rear wheel, which together with bad weather at the time of the test, accounted for the rather low 103 mph top speed next to a figure of 101 mph in 3rd—Bruce Main-Smith reckons 108 mph is a more realistic top speed. But this and the use of the same Monobloc 389 (though with the air lever returned to the handlebar) as the Road Rocket, and the manually-controlled ignition, were praised in a 1962 *Motor Cycle* test as the source of sweetness of carburation, clean pick-up from low revs and excellent acceleration, all of which made it a rarity, a powerful bike that was tractable in traffic—much more so than the Gold Star single. Vibration from the 9:1 cr motor was noted ('not in the turbine-smooth category'), as was progressively lighter steering from 90 mph, culminating in slight front wheel wander above the 'Ton', which stiffer front fork internals would have been needed to cure. In both those respects the unit twin could probably, as it stood, be seen to be reaching the limits of its development. But below those limits it was a joy.

It also followed the Gold Star in offering a variety of options, with an eye particularly to production racing. A track silencer was claimed to increase output to 50 bhp, and the headlamp wiring featured plugs and sockets to give easy removal. The touring handlebar was reversible,

Far left *Late sporting A10 which supplied RGS engines — the 1962 Super Rocket.*

Left *Mighty road warrior — the 1962 A10 Rocket Gold Star.*

Right *One to seek out. Cutaway of the 1961 A7 Shooting Star.*

the gearbox still featured the reversible camplate, and rear-sets, clip-ons, alloy wheel rims and the TT carburettor, (as well as a later twin carb conversion from an accessory company) were all optional extras. The whole lot was available in the guise of the factory Clubman model. Eddie Dow, too, provided sports goodies like a 5 gallon alloy tank and Superleggera alloy fork yokes. But during its brief life the RGS never shone in production racing — pre-unit sports honours for 1962 went to Chris Vincent's side-car twin which, with a single $1\frac{5}{32}$ in carburettor and a publicly available 358 cam, won that year's sidecar TT. Perhaps it's preferable to think of the Rocket Gold Star as firmly in the A10 tradition, as a fast, tractable, reliable and stylish road-going motor cycle. 1963 saw the last of it, of the Super Rocket and of the pre-unit twins. Gone but not forgotten.

If the RGS should turn your thoughts to tweaking a stock A10 or A7, and you first make sure it is a 1958-on DA10 motor the following might be of use. The Rocket Gold Star and the late Super Rocket's camshaft was derived from the pre-DA10 sports engine (Part No 67-356). The 356 can also be fitted to an A7 with 8:1 pistons (the highest they went) but preferably to use it with an alloy head 500. The Spitfire cam from the scramblers and the later unit twins was Part No 67-357 and is strictly for 650 alloy-head DA10 motors only — it requires valve clearances of .010 (inlet) and .012 (exhaust). 67-358 is a waste of time; if you raise the compression (and for the 650s the RGS's 9:1 is high enough for road use), a thicker, copper head gasket is advisable. As Bruce Main-Smith has pointed out, the 500 and 650 cylinder heads

are interchangeable, and even carry the same foundry casting numbers, but the hemispheres of the 500 are smaller than for the 650 and play havoc with the compression. As a means of identification it's worth remembering that the head fins on the 500 will be narrower than those on the 650 barrel.

The larger exhaust valve that went in the 1962 A10 variants will fit the whole A10 range from 1950 onwards. The inlet valve can be increased from a $\frac{7}{16}$ in to $1\frac{1}{2}$ in diameter if a larger carburettor is fitted, and the larger exhaust valve and '56-on inlet valve from the Shooting Star will fit any Shooting Star from '51 onwards. As to carburettors, although a $1\frac{3}{16}$ in throat Monobloc was the biggest made, Eddie Dow recommended only the $1\frac{5}{32}$ size, as this allowed normal carburation settings. He also recommended a number 3 throttle slide and a larger 420 main jet, but some have found the latter a plug-clogger in everyday use and prefer a 360. If you go to a later Concentric carb, rough settings are a 250 main jet, a 3½ throttle slide and a 0.016 needle jet, with the needle in No. 3 position.

The twins, as stated, were reasonably oil-tight if carefully assembled — the alloy heads in particular can be distorted by overtightening or tightening out of sequence — with the exception of the exhaust rocker box joint. So if you suffer from leaks it is wise to check the state of the piston rings and in particular of the timed breather. Ignition timing on the A10 is important, and as with any Lucas magneto-equipped machine, the slip ring on the mag if nicked on one or two places can cause misfiring on one cylinder. Wear to the

Another ultimate. 1961 A10 and massive Carmobile side-car. You could do it with a Flash.

ignition cam can also cause the points to open more on one cylinder than the other.

Further points to watch are the big-end bolts, which can stretch, the cork washer on the end of the breather sleeve, which came in various thicknesses and should be just nipped by the breather sleeve, and the cork washer sealing the dynamo to the crankcase. A last thought from Dow was to drop the size of the engine sprocket on the late 650s to obtain full benefit, since the standard engine tended to be overgeared. I would only suggest the substitution of one of the later BSA or Triumph 8 in TLS front brakes, which are still fairly readily available, and pretty well mandatory for today's traffic conditions.

BSA: A7/A10 pre-unit twins—dates and specifications
Production dates
A7 495 cc—1946–50
A7 Star Twin 495 cc—1948–50
A10 Golden Flash—1950–61
A7 497 cc—1951–61
A7 Star Twin 497 cc—1951–54
A10 Super Flash—1953–54
A7 Shooting Star—1954–61
A10 Road Rocket—1955–57
A10 Super Rocket—1958–63
A10 Rocket Gold Star—1962–63

Specifications
A7/A7 Star Twin (1946–50)
Capacity, bore and stroke—495 cc (62 mm × 82 mm)

Type of Engine—ohv twin
Ignition—Magneto
Weight—A7 Rigid (1946) 365 lb

A7/A7 Star Twin/A7 Shooting Star (1951–61)
Capacity, bore and stroke—497 cc (66 mm × 72.6 mm)
Type of Engine—ohv twin
Ignition—Magneto
Weight—A7 plunger (1951) 382 lb, A7 Shooting Star (1955) 416 lb.

A10 Gold Flash/A10 Super Flash/A10 Road Rocket/A10 Super Rocket/A10 Rocket Gold Star
Capacity, bore and stroke—646 cc (70 mm × 84 mm)
Type of Engine—ohv twin
Ignition—Magneto
Weight—Golden Flash Plunger, A10 (1951) 395 lb, A10 Road Rocket (1956) 418 lb, A10 Golden Flash (1959) 430 lb, A10 Rocket Gold Star (1962) 395 lb approx.

BSA: A7/A10 pre-unit twins—annual development and modification
1950
For A10 Golden Flash:
1 Early 1950, gearbox internal modifications and new-design of gear cluster.

1951
For all pre-unit Twins:
1 Lubrication system modified by drilling of small hole in left hand connecting rod and upper big-

end bearing shell to improve oil flow to that big end.

2 From late 1951, previously chromed petrol tanks, and other portions, now painted matt silver.

For A7/A7 Star Twin

3 For details of new 497 cc engine, with 95% of parts common with A10, see text.

4 A7 carburettor slide altered from 6/3 to 6/4.

5 A7 Star Twin's carburettor enlarged from 275 ($\frac{7}{8}$ in bore) to 276 (1 in bore), but single not previous twin carbs fitted.

1952

For all pre-unit Twins:

1 Engines adopt breather of ported, timed design, with circular shroud cast round breather on inside of timing cover to act as a baffle and prevent oil dripping into outlet passage at low speeds.

2 Spring-loaded synthetic rubber oil seal fitted on gearbox mainshaft.

3 Horns changed to Lucas HF1234 type.

4 Damping on tele forks improved by lengthening the bushes, since on the BSA fork the oil reservoir was the annular space between the bushes.

5 Only plunger versions of all twins available.

6 Optional dual seats available for all.

7 Brake fulcrum pin and cam bearing stiffened.

8 Petrol tank fixing modified by addition to tie bars.

9 Headlamps change from adjustable focus to pre-focus type.

10 Underslung pilot lamp adopted.

11 Late September, portions chromed prior to previous year's restrictions now chrome again, with wheel rims now totally chromed without prior painted and lined centres, and chromed side-panels extending to rear of knee-grips on tank as opposed to prior chromed tank with painted top and (smaller) side panels.

For A7:

12 From March, new winged metal tank badge in yellow and chrome.

For A7 Star Twin:

13 Manual ignition control adopted as standard.

14 Change to special higher lift camshaft.

15 New pistons raise compression from 7 to 7.5:1.

16 Optional Amal TT carburettor.

1953

For All pre-unit twins:

1 New headlamp and semi-cowling, carrying speedometer and incorporating lightswitch and ammeter.

2 Redesigned number plate, incorporating Lucas stop and tail light, blended into lines of mudguard by a steel fairing, with a red reflector at the bottom of the plate.

3 Another new petrol tank mounting with horizontal through-bolts at each end and slightly larger petrol tank.

4 Finned collars for the exhausts.

5 Prop-stand lugs now brazed, not clipped, onto frame.

For A7, A7 Star Twin:

6 8 × 1.37 in front brake as fitted on A10.

1954

For A10 Golden Flash, A10 Road Rocket, A7 Shooting Star:

1 Export only except A7 Shooting Star, these machines now feature front forks with internals allowing nearly double the oil content, and all-welded duplex cradle frame with pivoted fork rear suspension, separate gearbox, redesigned engine-shaft shock absorber, new-shaped $5\frac{1}{2}$ pint oil tank and matching toolbox, single-bolt tank fixing for 4 gallon tank with round red piled arm badge (Road Rocket) or larger bright red Gold Star badge (Shooting Star)—Golden Flash retains previous winged badge. Battery mounted under seat, footrests further to rear, dual seat as standard and rev counter drive (where fitted) from magneto gear. Also back brake plate now has cam pivot above wheel spindle, and cam lever hanging downwards.

2 For pivoted-fork models, finning on cast-iron heads increased.

3 For pivoted-fork models, gear ratios reduced slightly (A7 Shooting Star now 5.28, 6.38, 9.28, 13.62—A10 Golden Flash now 4.52, 5.47, 7.95, 11.67 to 1).

For A7 Shooting Star

4 Alloy cylinder head (for further details see text).

5 Petrol tank now with large chrome sidepanels as on A10, and large round bright three-dimensional plastic tank badge as on Gold Star.

1955

For all pre-unit twins:

1 As 1954 (1), as standard for home market, with plunger option retained for A10.

2 Steering-head lock fitted.

3 Underslung pilot light discontinued.

4 Combined dip-switch/horn button mounted on left handlebar.

5 Amal Monobloc Type 376 carburettors with plastic pipes, including as replacement for Amal TT, etc, on A7 Shooting Star, but not A10 Road Rocket.

For all pivoted-fork twins:

6 Repositioned rear mudguard, resulting in a more horizontal dual seat, and new one-piece valanced front mudguard.

7 Girling units slimmer than previously.

For A7:

8 Round red piled-arms tank badge on new tank.

For A7 Shooting Star:

9 Ignition advance-retard control lever operated by outward instead of customary inward movement to retard.

1956

For all pivoted-fork twins:

1 New Ariel-type full-width alloy hubs front and rear, with 7 × 1.5 in centrally disposed brakes, ribbed externally for cooling, webbed internally for rigidity. Fulcrum brake adjusters. Quick-detachable rear wheel arrangement modified with

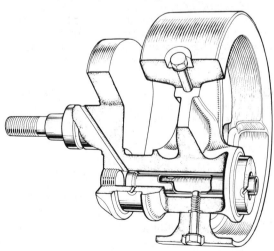

1956 Ariel-type full-width alloy hub brake.

rubber-plugged hole fitted in hub to give access to taper-seated domed nuts on the driving studs. Hole-and-tommybar rear wheel removal replaced by spindle which is a bolt. Rear brake operation by cable.

2 4-piece full rear chain enclosure as option.

For A7 Shooting Star:

3 Siamesed inlet ports cast integrally with the alloy cylinder heads, and carburettor now bolted directly on to head.

A10 Road Rocket:

4 Released for home market July 1956. Alloy head (for further details see text).

1957

No changes.

1958

For all twins:

1 Sidecar connections fitted at rear and under seat, as plunger A10 option no longer available.

2 New full-width Triumph-type cast-iron hubs with straight-pull spokes, back-plates enamelled with polished rim bands, 8 × 1.12 in diameter front (for all but standard A7), 7 × 1.12 in rear. Front brake's torque arm replaced by a slotted boss on the shoe plates which engages with a lug projecting from inner face of front leg.

3 Revised full headlamp nacelle.

4 New silencers of elongated oval pattern.

5 New roll-on centre stand.

6 New 5-plate clutch with strengthened drum.

For A10 Golden Flash, A10 Super Rocket (available from July, for details see text):

7 New crankshaft. One-piece forging of EN 16B steel with a circular middle web. Flywheel retained in web by 3 radial set-screws. Twin-crank throw was hollow, and contained a circular sludge trap positioned end-wise, prevented from rotating by extension of one of the flywheel set-screws.

8 More substantial big-end bearing shell.

9 Steel-backed, lead-bronze bush replaces previous white-metal timing-side main bearing.

10 Thickness of cylinder base flange increased from $\frac{3}{8}$ in to $\frac{1}{2}$ in.

For A7 Shooting Star

11 Compression raised to 8:1.

For all twins:

12 Toolbox lid, previously flat, now with more domed shape, oil tank domed to match.

1959

For A10 Golden Flash and standard A7 twins:

1 Camshaft as on A7 Shooting Star, A10 Super

A7/A10 1958 revised method of flywheel location by radial set-screws.

Rocket, adopted for A10 Golden Flash.
2 Round tank badge, as standard A7.

1960
For all pre-unit twins:
1 Primary chaincase redesigned. Now includes an aperture, closed by a screwed plug, so each of clutch springs can be adjusted in turn without removing cover. Simmonds self-locking nuts fitted on the spring studs to simplify adjustment. Clutch now 4-spring not 6, runs on 20 rollers and features different method of clutch centre attachment. At base of chaincase, new combined drain and level-plug assembly, screwed into base.
2 Cam-action cable adjusters abutting handlebar pivot blocks for clutch and front-brake levers.
3 Rear brake cam lever repositioned to provide increased initial pressure on the leading shoe.
4 New valanced front mudguard, without registration facings, but with reinforced attachment to fork legs.
5 Appearance of rear mudguard tidied by fitting of side-stays with forged ends resting snugly against valances, secured from inside the guard.
6 On left of handlebars a Wico-Pacy Triconsul ring-type fitment fitted incorporating dipswitch, horn and engine cut-out.
7 Seat height reduced 1 in, and foam-rubber filler given better air-flow passages for greater resilience.
8 All (except A7 Shooting Star) adopt pear-shaped three-dimensional plastic tank badges as on C15 Star single.
9 All adopt plain rubber knee-grips without BSA logo.
10 New-type Lucas batteries.

For A10 Golden Flash:
11 Bore of Monobloc carb increased to $1\frac{1}{8}$ in (as previous Super Rocket).
For A10 Super Rocket:
12 Bore of Monobloc carburettor increased to $1\frac{5}{32}$ in.
13 Rev counter drive now fitted on the oil-pump mainshaft.
14 Amal TT9 carburettor option again.

1961
No changes.

1962
For A10 Super Rocket:
1 Brakes redesigned front and rear (as B40's) with self-servo effect from floating action of shoes, leading edge of each friction surface chamfered back $1\frac{1}{4}$ in to avoid excessive bite.

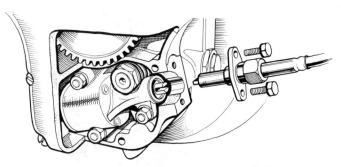

1960 A10 Super Rocket with revised rev counter drive.

2 New Burgess silencer with 25 per cent greater capacity, and optional siamesed exhaust, with left pipe passing between engine and front down tubes.
3 1st, 2nd, 3rd gears lowered.
4 July 1962, compression ratio raised from 8.3 to 9:1.
For A10 Rocket Gold Star:
5 Introduced February 1962. For details see text.

BSA: The A50/A65 unit twins

From the start the A50/A65 range was a victim of the troubles through which the BSA company was passing during that decade of its existence. After an unusually brief development period of around two years, it was rushed out by a production-hungry US market-oriented management and suffered from both fundamental flaws, and teething troubles, particularly in the electrical department. The spares situation was poor and the bike emerged as a victim of the much vaunted new approach known as 'value engineering'. As a result of this system modifications were no longer incorporated smoothly but were sometimes lost in the system. Declining standards of workmanship and of finish, and poor quality control, also took their toll. All this is discussed in greater detail in the introductory section (see page 25).

Further problems ensued as the company attempted to wring more power out of a fundamentally dated design, with inevitable consequences—namely drastically increased vibration, oil leaks and blow-ups. Finally came the oil-in-frame models for 1971, when the 650 cc engine with many of its problems intact was slotted into a frame that was too high. All this was going on while, setting aside the Oriental tidal

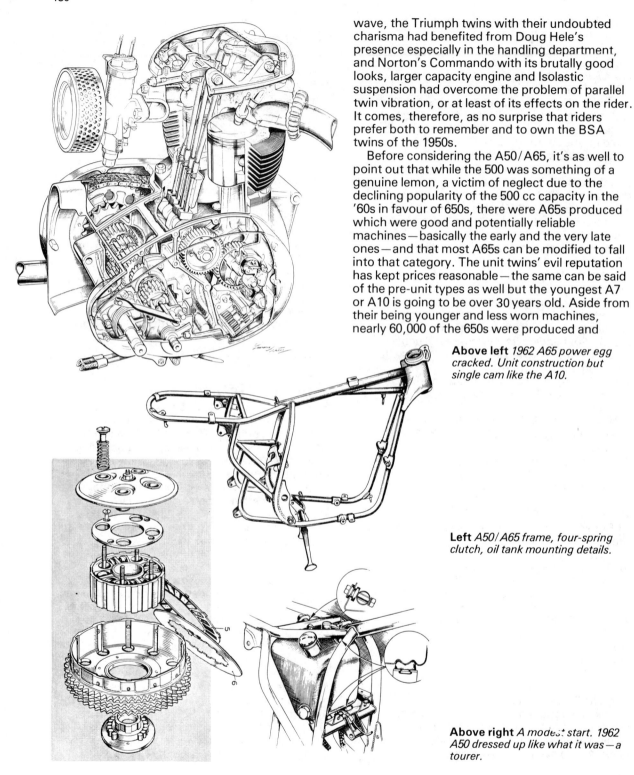

wave, the Triumph twins with their undoubted charisma had benefited from Doug Hele's presence especially in the handling department, and Norton's Commando with its brutally good looks, larger capacity engine and Isolastic suspension had overcome the problem of parallel twin vibration, or at least of its effects on the rider. It comes, therefore, as no surprise that riders prefer both to remember and to own the BSA twins of the 1950s.

Before considering the A50/A65, it's as well to point out that while the 500 was something of a genuine lemon, a victim of neglect due to the declining popularity of the 500 cc capacity in the '60s in favour of 650s, there were A65s produced which were good and potentially reliable machines—basically the early and the very late ones—and that most A65s can be modified to fall into that category. The unit twins' evil reputation has kept prices reasonable—the same can be said of the pre-unit types as well but the youngest A7 or A10 is going to be over 30 years old. Aside from their being younger and less worn machines, nearly 60,000 of the 650s were produced and

Above left *1962 A65 power egg cracked. Unit construction but single cam like the A10.*

Left *A50/A65 frame, four-spring clutch, oil tank mounting details.*

Above right *A modest start. 1962 A50 dressed up like what it was—a tourer.*

spares are plentiful. The Triumph 650s are expensive, and Commandos can have their problems. Some unfortunate A65 features, such as the vibration, can never be entirely cured, but as working bikes rather than collectors' items they can still make sense.

At the time of their introduction in 1962 they were said to be 30 lb lighter than the older pre-unit twins, and were a little more expensive at around £280. The advantages of unit construction were pointed out, and the convenience and clean lines of the 'power egg' engine shape which alternator electrics allowed, were emphasised. The first A65's 38 bhp was admitted to be on the low side compared to the 46 bhp A10 Rocket Gold Star, but it was stressed that this model was just the initial roadster version, with power enough for everyday use. But that power derived from an engine whose short-stroke, near-square layout (the A65 oversquare at 75 x 74 mm, the A50 65.5 x 74 mm) allowed room for a good-breathing cylinder-head design, with valves which were well-positioned and large, and could be larger. And unlike the A7/A10, twin carburettors were no problem, with the manifold a separate attachment once again. Given a compression hike from the original 7.5:1, the A65 at least had considerable tuning potential, and in fact 52 bhp was claimed for the final versions. These early A50 and A65's valve sizes differed.

Under Bert Perrigo as Chief Development Engineer, the engine as a whole had been the last assignment of foreman Len Crisp (one-time Humber works rider) of the Experimental Department, who retired early in 1962. The cylinder head was the principal area of redesign and had been developed by Bill Johnson. It was of die-cast light alloy and had the rocker box formed with it, as well as the three pillars supporting each rocker spindle. Though rocker gear wear was to be a problem, this was a rigid assembly, and since the rocker cover carried no load, an oil-tight joint was made more likely. The inlet valves were parallel once again. Overall it was a superb design both for easy gas flow and for combustion, with the hemispherical combustion chambers deeper than those of its predecessors.

Both the iron barrels and the bottom end were similar to the A7/A10. Con rods were alloy, with bushes in the small end and bearing shells in the big end. The push-rods were still behind the cylinder, inclined forward in a cast-in tunnel and operated by a single camshaft. The latter was still gear-driven, and hollow, with a timed breather at the left end opening at the point of maximum crankcase pressure. The tappets were changed to simple round pins with block feet which worked

against each other to prevent rotation. Each ran in an unbushed hole in the barrel, and the previous problems of assembly were eased by the fact that each was now retained by a circlip to hold it in place during assembly so that it could not drop out when the cylinder block was raised.

A50 and A65 bottom ends were the same, and the crankcase on both was in two halves and bolted together along a vertical split down the centre line. The left-hand side featured a bolted-on flange, which when removed gave access directly to the gearbox sprocket, while the right embodied the gearbox casting itself. The gearbox was similar to that on the C15/B40, with a 'Triumph'-type up-for-up shift pattern — for production considerations the BSA Group wanted a standard box. While this led to the A50/A65 box being considerably less substantial than its predecessors in terms of components like the selector plate, the gears themselves were exceptionally wide, and though changes remained clonky, a 5-plate 4-spring clutch with Ferodo friction material eliminated some of the problems associated with the pre-unit clutch, though introducing one or two of its own — a minor one was a tendency for clutch cables to snap, as on the Triumphs of the '70s, and they were awkward to replace, even after the introduction in mid-1962 of a 'quick release' mechanism for the clutch cable end.

On the drive side there was a Triplex primary chain, aimed, like the short-stroke engine, at the demands of US short-track dirt racing. (In fact the A65 was the shortest stroke of any 650-and-over British twins offered after the war. It was also probably the worst vibrator, the two facts not being unconnected.) Chain adjustment was by slipper tensioner, and could be checked via a hollow bolt projecting from the base of the crankcase. Arguing for the unfamiliar unit construction, it was claimed that with the short chain run and the increased rigidity of the connection between the engine and gearbox, alignment of the primary drive could be held to very close tolerances. As we shall see, this was not always to be so again.

The crankshaft was the same as on the pre-unit twins, but the drive-side main bearing was now a ball journal bearing, while on the timing side, the bearing though still plain, was increased in size, now being of $1\frac{1}{4}$ in diameter and copper lead, with the crankpin diameter increased to suit. While knowing that crowded rollers would have been preferable, the BSA designers felt that they were not commercially practical, and also hoped that the chosen combination of bearing would allow

Close-up of the 1962 engine-gearbox unit. The star soon went.

for some flexing of the crankshaft. But there were to be other less happy and commercially fortunate effects from their choice, and judging by the motor's vibration, the flexing too was not all they could have desired.

Front forks were as on the later A7/A10s, but with modified geometry, and the rear suspension was again by Girling 3-position units. The frame, though modified, was still of duplex down-tube cradle type, and even the silencers were as on the late A10 Super Rockets. But the wheelbase at 54 in was 2 in shorter than previously, and together with 18 in wheels this made for a pair of exceptionally compact twins. Early styling was generally in line with the previous bikes, with headlamp cowl, chrome-sided petrol tanks sporting pear-shaped badges, generous mudguarding and full width hubs, the A65's 8 in SLS front brake being the only difference from the 500 which had 7 in brakes front and rear.

One departure was the fitting of unduly bulky pressed steel side panels, with their early A10-type winged badges. These panels were extended forward to conceal the carburettors, giving a lumpy look to the middle of the bike and obscuring the clean lines of the 'power egg' — the dilemma, common to other designers at the time, was what to do about the acres of space left around the cylinders with the advent of alternator electrics, but though BSA avoided the temptation of full enclosure, there must have been more elegant solutions than those panels. Ironically even the slot in their fasteners was too narrow, and the space they provided for tools, behind the oil tank, was less than adequate. But the tool-kit in a zip-up case was at this stage of good quality, and even included the necessary clutch adjustment tool, something later owners would sometimes have to improvise by sawing the handle of a beer can opener across the middle of the hole.

Problems inherent in the design were not slow in emerging. The most fundamental concerned the main bearings. Early on, the drive side ball race was found inadequate and was quietly replaced for 1966 by a lipped roller bearing of the same size. But a ball-bearing will naturally act as a thrust-race as well as taking unusual stresses. With the roller, the crank needed positive location, and this was achieved by shimming the rollers tight against the lip, and by putting a thrust washer between the crankweb and the plain timing side bearing. But this was no cure, and indeed aggravated the situation. The lipped roller and its shims would start to turn together. It then didn't need much side pressure to make the rollers act as very blunt drill bits against the side lip of the outer race. The cage would begin to fragment, savage the crankcase, eject the shims and overstress the thrust washer, so that the plain bearing too would turn in its housing and cut off the oil feed to the big ends, causing a symphony of destruction at the bottom end.

A solution was hit on during the preparation of the 500s for the 1966 and 67 Daytona, but never implemented. The racers at least had an answer to another of the unit twins' problems, which came from the use of an oil pump made of alloy rather than the high performance machines' iron pump. The alloy pump could malfunction, with unhappy results. Even when it was working, oil changes were still as vital as they had been on the A7/A10, and like the unit singles, oil leaks would occur on the timing-chest joint when the oil pump's ball valve in the sump became unseated by grit particles. Another problem arose from one of the unit bikes' supposed strengths, the absence of primary chain misalignment. In practice it was found that this could occur, and if it did, the triplex drive chain wore out very rapidly. One way to check, assuming that the tensioner was not worn paper-thin, was to see if the tensioner bolt beneath the casing had reached the end of the travel on its thread. If it had, it was time to renew the chain. Further problems involved the clutch which was still prone to slip, and its pushrod which, lacking positive location on the pressure plate, could misalign and cause drag.

For all that, these early low compression single carb twins could settle in and provide pleasant mounts. A *Motor Cycle* report on the A50/A65 up to mid-1965 gave 92/94 per cent marks respectively for reliability. As intended, handling and steering of these lighter machines were an improvement on the pre-unit twins and they were eminently chuckable through bends, the angle of lean on the left still being limited by the centre-stand. And at speed on bumpy bends the front end, still with no two-way damping, was prone to wallow, the only cure being to fit side-car strength springs and endure a harder ride.

Starting was easy, due both to the alternator and to the fact that there were a few more teeth on the starter pinion and a few less on the kick-starter quadrant than previously, so for each depression of the kickstart the engine was turning over less, and so less effort was involved. Acceleration was excellent, with top speed around 90 for the 500 and between 95 and the ton for the 650. The latter could be cruised at 80 and the motor's fat power curve meant that the new twins were still very suitable for side-car work,

though for any application the brakes left something to be desired, especially on the 500. A rather hard seat was one drawback, and accessibility was only fair, as the tank had to come off to get at the rockers, and many found difficulty in getting the qd rear wheel clear of the mudguard. Petrol economy was still good, with the A65 returning over 60 mpg under hard general usage and the A50 over 65 mpg.

The A50 had its compression raised from 7.5 to 8:1 in mid-1962, and that year a version of the 500 competed in the ISDT and took a Gold. This was to be the last real European sporting success for the A50, though versions of the motor were used by side-car ace Chris Vincent, along with the 650 in standard or overbored form, which he and fellow practitioners like Terry Vinicombe and Mick Boddice found well suited to their purpose. In the States, as intended, the 650 was a strong contender on the dirt track well into the '70s, and some of the dirt track machines were adapted to take a magneto. The 500's Dayton. .orts in 1966 and 1967 were not successful, however.

As the last of the old brigade A10 variants were phased out, the new twins continued into 1963 with optional 12-volt electrics rather crudely provided by two 6-volt batteries in series. Early in the year the cable-operated rear brake was happily supplanted by rod operation, initially still via cross-over on the right hand side, until for the following year's single-sided brakes it shifted to the left.

It was not until 1964 that the promise of increased power was fulfilled for home market customers with the advent of the A65R Rocket (the plain A65 was called the Star). Still with single carburettor, but with 9:1 compression, high-lift cams, strengthened valve springs, and clutch plates faced with heavy-duty friction material, the A65R boasted a claimed output of 45 bhp and a top speed of over 105 mph. Styling too, for the first time, was distinctly sporty, with rubber bellows on the front forks, siamesed pipes and, in common with the rest of the range, a new silencer with a series of steel baffles replacing the previous glass wool absorption internals. There were chrome sports mudguards (from which 'you cannot expect really effective shielding', as one tester philosophically put it) and a separately mounted headlamp, as well as an optional rev counter to match the new Smiths magnetic speedometer. The rev counter had to be specified when ordering as it was no bolt-on goody — the drive was taken from the oil-pump spindle and called for modified inner and outer timing-side crankcase covers (see Engine No table for distinguishing prefixes). Another optional extra

Mick Boddice's 1965 A65-powered kneeler outfit.

The pace quickens. 1964 A65R, as used by that year's TT Travelling Marshals.

was the 12-volt electrics, the twin batteries being concealed behind even more bulbous side-covers. The A65R was to be in production only for 1964 and 1965. It was an extremely tractable and good-handling bike, with lightness of the front end only evident above 90 mph. A tester called it 'one of the most desirable BSAs ever produced', and even allowing for hyperbole, it seems to have been a good 'un.

The next year saw some previously export-only high-performance machines appear on the home market. These were the twin carburettor A65L Lightning and A50C Cyclone variants, with sports camshafts and siamesed exhausts. Both were also offered in A50CC and A65LC Clubman's racing versions. The engines used in the Clubman models were bench-tested, and they came with racing seat and bars, rear-sets and a reversed camplate gear pedal on close ratio boxes. All twins had the benefit of stub-form gear teeth. On the roadsters,

each of the twin carburettors was fitted with a chrome-plate covered cylindrical pill-box type air cleaner and the side-panels, in fibreglass, were abbreviated, with two fastening bolts each. Single-sided brakes, 8 in at the front, were fitted on 19 in wheels (18 in rear for the Clubman's 500 and the 650s), with the rear brake changeover as mentioned. The headlamp shell was chromed, likewise the mudguards and fork top shrouds, and a rev counter was standard. A kickstart and a centre stand modified for greater cornering clearance were benefits for the whole range of twins also, and the A65s now featured 12-volt electrics as standard. All the twins acquired a new method of setting the ignition timing, with a timing plug which fitted into the front of the crankcase, via a blanked-off hole and locked the crankshaft into position.

motor cycle, but both vibration from the motor, experienced through handlebars and footrests, and the slightly forward position of the footrests themselves, showed themselves as drawbacks at about 5,000 rpm/80 mph, while the front end weave at about 90 mph persisted.

Testers also found the lights below average, the horn lousy and the voltage control inadequate — the batteries boiled during high-speed cruising. In practical terms it seemed that with the increased output the bike was being asked to live beyond its limits. But 1965 did see Mike Hailwood's win on an A65L in a rain-soaked 15-lap production race at the Hutchinson 100 at Silverstone, beating two Triumphs and setting the fastest lap time.

For 1966 the floodgates opened and a plethora of variants aimed at the US appeared on the home market as the factory merged the UK and export ranges, much to the disgust of practical-minded British enthusiasts. The A50 was now offered as the Royal Star single carb roadster and the Wasp twin carb as a 'large capacity scrambler of a sort'. The 650s went from the standard A65T Thunderbolt, but now with 9:1 compression a 100 mph motor cycle, to the twin carb A65L Lightning, with its larger ($1\frac{1}{8}$ in choke) Monoblocs with each float chamber turned towards the outside and the inlet tracts coupled by a balancer pipe. Balancing two carburettors is hard enough, and sensibly, on all the twin carb models, the previous throttle cable junction box was dispensed with and an individual cable carried from each carburettor to a

Above right *Fast and tractable 1964 A65R on test.*

500 Cyclone 650 Lightning

New two carburetter high performance twins

Fresh from a successful conquest of the American market come these sparkling new twins. We've even retained the American names—Lightning for the 650, Cyclone for the 500. High compression pistons, special camshaft, two monobloc carburetters with cylindrical air cleaners, twin-mounted speedometer and tachometer, chromium plated headlamps, fork covers, mudguards and fuel tank are just some of the features to make these models the undoubted leaders in their class. As for performance, it's breathtaking—coupled of course with the traditional BSA standards of braking, steering and handling.

Speed . Sparkle . Stamina

CYCLONE CLUBMAN
LIGHTNING CLUBMAN

For production sports models racing both the Lightning and Cyclone may be specified (at a small additional charge) with rear mounted footrests, brake pedal and gearchange, racing seat, special silencer and low-set racing handlebars, as shown in this photograph.

BSA

Model A65L

Right *For 1965 home market, first A65 Lightning, handsome twin-carb model.*

double drum twistgrip. The Lightning sported a 'humpy rump' seat 'of racing appearance', and its speedo and rev counter were carried on the fork tops in a new cast-alloy bracket. Twin silencers were fitted from this year onwards and there were to be no more siamesed exhausts—and no more optional fully-enclosed rear chaincases either.

Then there was the A65H Hornet, another twin carb 'scrambler of a sort'. Like the Wasp it had a 10.5:1 compression engine, energy transfer ignition, large section tyres, a crankcase under-shield and a tiny 1¾ gallon fibreglass tank decorated with a Star transfer. Unlike the Wasp with its standard silencers, matching rev counter and speedo, and dual seat, the Hornet had a rev counter only, open exhaust pipes and racing seat.

Top of the range was the 54 bhp Spitfire Mk II Special—there never seemed to have been a Spitfire Mk I, unless it was the '65 Lightning Clubmans, or 1964's export-only Spitfire Hornet street scrambler. The Mk II was certainly the heir to the previous year's Lightning Clubman, but with the Hornet's 10.5:1 compression engine and tiny tank (there was a 4 and later a 5 gallon fibre-glass option), close gear ratios, twin Amal GP2 1 5/32 in choke carburettors, alloy rims and a full width hub for its 190 mm front brake. It was light at 382 lb and very fast, with wheel-lifting acceleration limited only by a clutch that got overworked and then slipped. One was tested at 120 mph, but they were very, very fragile, and both lumpy low speed running and the level of vibration above 4,500 rpm (see the 'Wimpey fist' anecdote on page 34) made it really an irrelevance for the road rider.

Of greater interest were that year's changes shared by all the twins. Principal among these were frame modifications, which came in conjunction with a new front fork based on the one Jeff Smith developed for his scramblers, and featured for the first time 'some semblance of two-way damping', though it still topped out on a hard rebound. (This was designed for use with the 8 in single-sided front brake, so it could be used as a direct replacement on the A7/A10 models which had featured this, according to tester David Dixon, and on the 1965 A65 Lightning, but other existing forks could not be modified to it). The

1965 Lightning Clubman being ridden by Peter Perrigo, development chief Bert Perrigo's son.

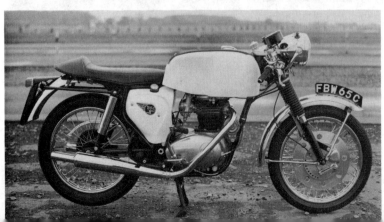

1965 Lightning Clubman with a variety of Eddie Dow goodies.

Girling rear units also had a somewhat softer action. These changes gave a riding position with slightly more forward lean, and definitely improved the roadholding at speed. A 1966 Lightning on test had lost its tendency to weave above 90 mph and on bumpy bends, and steered steadily to its near-110 mph maximum speed. A lower bottom gear eliminated the need to slip the clutch, and an overall reduction in gearing plus better silencing gave more usable performance, while enlarged inlet valves (for all models) ensured no loss of power.

The lights were improved, the new humped seats (on all but the A50 Royal Star) more comfortable, a new 6-plate clutch coped with the increased outputs, and the 8 in front brake, on all, with a 25 per cent increase in drum width, helped the stopping. 12-volt electrics with Zener diode were standard for all, as was a bracing strap linking the exhaust pipes and keeping them tight at the ports. Together with several other detail changes, it added up to the fact that amongst the mid-Atlantic claptrap there were some solid gains for the rider.

1967 saw the Wasp and Hornet dropped for home, but in this year of the Queen's Export Award for the company, most of the changes were US-oriented. There were blade-type chrome rear mudguards, and in tacit admission of the vibration problem, cushioned handlebar grips and rubber cups for the new 150 mph speedo and matching rev counter, between which the rotary light switch nestled inaccessibly. Facilities were provided for timing by strobe, with an aperture in the timing cover exposing a point on the inner face on the case, to align with a timing mark on the alternator. The mounting of the alternator stator itself was modified. An O-ring gas seal was fitted inside the exhaust ports, and the front fork oil seal holders were lengthened to improve the fitting of the gaiters, as well as sealing arrangements at the top of the fork being modified.

Rear tyre size went up to 4 in section for all, and as well as further detail improvements there was a new, heavily-finned rocker-box cover (a straight replacement for the previous type) which nicely echoed the old Harleys at that time so coveted by chopper freaks — except that for the moment it

With US short circuits in mind. A50 Hornet for 1966.

Flaming red monster. First Spitfire roadster, 1966 Mk II.

Above *Spitfire Mk III, 1967. Twin Concentrics and chromed upper fork stanchions.*

Below *1968, and US spec for all is in full flood. Heavily chromed A50 Royal Star with new tank, badges and finned rocker cover.*

was invisible beneath the petrol tank, unless the pretty chrome panelled 2 gallon option was fitted. The Zener diode was now mounted in a finned die-cast heat-sink and located under the steering head, not its previous sheet-aluminium sink under the seat, for better cooling. This was particularly necessary now that some of the twins' wiring-circuits included capacitor ignition. The Spitfire of that year, the Mk III, had chrome-plated upper fork stanchions and alloy control levers. With twin 32 mm Amal Concentrics (it was the first of the twins to feature these) and a 10:1 compression ratio it developed a claimed 55 bhp.

For 1968 there were further US-oriented moves, with high-rise bars, no front registration plates and side reflectors fitted beneath the nose of the dual seat and to the side of a new streamlined cast-alloy tail lamp housing at the rear. The Lightning's rear damper springs were now exposed and chromed, and the linking pipes between the exhausts were no longer fitted. There was restyling of the pear-shaped tank badges and these, for this year only, were fitted on a slimmer, smaller (2¾ gallons not 4) petrol tank with snap-action filler cap and larger chrome side panels, with dual seats narrower at the nose to suit. All now changed to Concentric carburettors, but petrol consumption was not improved, the Lightning's falling below 50 mpg overall. There was a change to a toggle switch (still inaccessible) on the headlamp shell, and to clipless rubber gaiters.

But there were also important steps forward. The Lightning and Spitfire Mk IV fitted the excellent twin leading-shoe front brake, in a full-width hub, as developed for Triumph production racers, with Triumph-type fork-end caps to suit. (This meant that it was not interchangeable with the previous brake without the forks as well.) And previously all the twins had fitted the old Lucas 4CA points, with two sets mounted on a common backplate, so that when the timing was done it was necessary to assume the timing was the same for both cylinders, which in practice frequently led to different ignition timing on each cylinder. These were now replaced by the improved 6CA points assembly, which had two separate backplates so that each cylinder could be timed separately, as well as two separate condensers moved off the contact breaker plate and now located in a waterproof cover close to the ignition coil, which acquired modified mountings. Adjustment was made easier and more accurate. There was a conversion kit from one to the other (see the 1968 modifications for Part Nos).

A new crankcase casting embodying a deep

Last of the Spitfires, the 1968 Mark IV.

spigot afforded a still firmer and more accurate location for the alternator stator than the earlier stud mountings or the previous year's centralising housing. Head gaskets, particularly on the Spitfire, had been prone to blow as compression went up and were replaced with solid copper ones. The oil supply to the rockers was taken from a point near the crankcase rather than the oil tank, and the oilways to the head modified. The gearbox oil level now had to be checked by means of a dipstick attached to the filler cap.

1969, after two poor selling seasons for the company, saw some back-pedalling on the US styling for Europe, and a determined assault on oil leaks, as well as modifications on the 650s which sacrificed top end slightly in the interests of tractability. The frames on all the twins were redesigned again—from now on top-heaviness was noticed and commented on by testers, seat height was raised to 32 in, and vibration apparently worsened, probably quite badly, as both the latter factors were actually commented on unfavourably in Lightning and Thunderbolt tests of that year. (These were now the only BSA 650s available at home, as with the coming of the Rocket III, the Spitfire had been dropped.) In the new frame, the pivoted rear fork was fitted with phosphor-bronze bushes giving greater rigidity than had been possible with the earlier bonded-rubber bearings. To fit them the fork cross-tube was of larger diameter, equipped with a grease nipple, and enlarged spacers and O-ring grease seals were fitted.

Flat bars replaced the previous year's cowboy curls, and petrol tanks reverted to chrome-panelled steel and $3\frac{1}{2}$ gallon size, and again included two taps, the left-hand with a lower stand-pipe to provide a reserve supply. Grab rails were fitted to some machines. The side panels too were again steel not fibreglass, whereas the 650's contact breaker cover, previously steel, was now a polished light-alloy casting carrying a sunken winged-BSA motif. The move from the mixed BSF and CEI thread forms got underway, but as with the singles, was never to be properly completed. All models gained a front brake cable with a switch operating the rear brake light, and the 8 in twin leading shoe brake was adopted by all.

This brake featured a new nave plate for the left of the hub, in which concentric ribs replaced the previous slotted panels. There was also a revised front brake linkage, involving the cable laying parallel to the front legs, and a second arm set at an angle to the short arm and linked to the second cam lever, rather than the previous set-up with the cable coming down directly to the external front lever. And in their third change so far, all the twins adopted Triumph lower members for the telescopic fork, which was thereby slightly shortened. Internally there was Triumph two-way damping by shuttle valves and restrictors in the lower end of the fork stanchions, as on the Rocket III.

In the battle to contain lubricant, the width of crankcase and primary chaincase joints was increased by 15 per cent. The chaincase oil filler and the clutch adjustment plug were fitted with rubber O-rings. Another seal was added on the idler pinion spindle bearing to stop oil leaks into the inner timing cover. And an oil pressure warning lamp was also fitted should this Canute-like endeavour, or the pump itself, have occasion to fail. Unfortunately the switch itself could give trouble, being prone to breaking down or causing short circuits, and staying on when the oil pressure was in fact all right. The internals of the silencers were again completely revised for a quieter exhaust, and on the 650s balance pipes linking the two exhausts near the ports were again introduced for a slight gain in power and secure fixing. The Lightning was alone in at last tackling the problem of its horn, previously characterised as 'a bee's mating call' — this was replaced with a pair of powerful Windtone horns, and there was provision on the wiring harness of all the twins to fit these.

As well as the silencing, the faces of the valve collets now tapered at 20°, not 15°, and the valve-spring collars were modified to suit. With

1969 Home market A65 Thunderbolt on test, with flat bars, steel tank and side panels, and grab rail.

the valve-springs' lengths already shortened from 1966, this brought a slight drop in top speed, but the added tractability and low speed punch were appreciated by testers. Handling, the good damping of the new front fork, brakes, lights and the good riding position with the new flat bar were all praised, but inescapable vibration was still there, causing numbed hands, blown bulbs and a fractured horn bracket — one Thunderbolt even needed five-star petrol to avoid pinking!

For 1970, with panic up at the factory and the 'new' range in their oil-bearing frames imminent, another expensive effort was launched to make the twins' engine viable. There had already been a fretful stab at an ohc version (see page 37), as well as an experimental A65 with a 180° crank and the engine mounted in Silentbloc bushes. Now the cylinder blocks were modified, with the base flange area increased, which permitted the enlarging of the retaining studs' diameter from $\frac{5}{16}$ to $\frac{3}{8}$ in, with differently designed nuts. The crankcase mouth was modified to suit, the oil drain holes repositioned, a new gasket provided, and none of this was interchangeable with the old.

Internally the crankshaft and flywheel assembly were machined all over to permit more accurate balancing. The section of the alloy con rods was increased, and piston skirt dimensions were modified to reduce engine noise. Clutch thrust-rod operation was now a Triumph-pattern three-ball camplate mechanism on the inside face of the gearbox end cover, which meant another redesign. And the oil pump, while still of the unreliable alloy type, was changed, becoming common on both twins and singles. It was externally similar to the previous one, but its driven spindle now spigotted to the scavenge gear, and the sections of the casing were dowelled, so preventing any chance of air leaks.

Among other detail changes, the front fork stanchions were given a hard chrome-plated micro-finish. Capacitor ignition was fitted, and provision also made in the wiring harness for direction indicators. The Amal Concentrics (twin 30 mm for the Lightning, single 28 mm on the Thunderbolt, 26 mm on the A50) had a redesigned needle-jet holder, needle jet and needle, and this was to improve petrol consumption figures, though the Lightnings stayed below 50 mpg overall under hard usage. The Lightning alone adopted a new $3\frac{1}{4}$ gallon steel petrol tank with a similar scalloped shape to the singles' tank.

The engine changes seemed to have had the effect of improving the vibration situation for the rider, but not the machine — one tester lost the use of both speedometer and rev counter as well as having his horn attachment brackets fracture. There was evidently no one at Small Heath or Umberslade Hall in a position both to know what to do and to implement the necessary detail changes, as Doug Hele had done at Meriden during the '60s to improve the Triumph Bonneville's handling. While the basic problem of the shakes was inescapable, with the increased power matched by more vibration some, quite small changes around the swinging-arm and frame loops, as 1972 was to show, could have brought substantial improvements—if they were the right changes.

Then with the November 1970 launch came the 1971 oil-in-frame range. This was a 650's only benefit however, as the Royal Star was dropped, caught commercially in a pincer between the more popular 350 and 750 capacities. There were three 650 variants, Lightning, Thunderbolt and Firebird scrambler, the latter being heir to the Hornet and having been export-only since 1968, but a few of the new type were now released in the UK. The cycle parts of all were new from stem to stern, and their appearance was very Californian, with ultra-skimpy chrome guards, naked fork stanchions, high rise 33 inch wide handlebars, indicators, chrome rear fork springs and grab rail, and, revealing the finned rocker box covers, slim two-tone 2½ gallon petrol tanks.

The off-white lower colour of the tank picked up the impractical colour, variously described as dove-grey or cream, of the oil bearing frame, and the tank's slim line, together with the resculptured die-cast alloy side-panels with their dummy louvres, revealed the clean lines of the engine, as well as the carburettor(s). The off-white paint was an unsuccessful attempt to emulate the look of the Rickmans nickel-plated frames. Hopwood was later to dismiss this P39 frame, an Umberslade creation, as unnecessary, 'heavier, more costly, and [with] with accessibility problems than its [Triumph] predecessor'.

BSA claimed it was 25% lighter, with twice the torsional stiffness and double the test life—but curiously, the actual overall machine weight was virtually unchanged, going up fractionally from 391 lb to 393 lb. However the overall appearance was undeniably striking. There was, however, the matter of the excessive seat height—at 33 in, better than the Triumphs 34½ in, but still limiting its uses to 6ft-plus mortals only, as the factory testers had pointed out that it would.

Mounted on new Timken taper-roller bearings, the new front fork, developed from the BSA

New wave. 1971 oil-in-frame A65 Lightning. High and wide.

moto-cross fork, was now the same general design as on all the BSA/Triumph machines bar the Bantam and the Triumph 500s. Internally the two-way hydraulic damping was revised, and 6½ in of movement provided. Like the BSA singles the forks featured cast-alloy sliders with four-stud cap fixings for the new conical wheel hub (likened at the time to a blancmange mould) with its powerful 8 in brake. (For details of this and of the rear hub, see Singles page 103). The upper parts of the precision-ground fork stanchion were exposed, and as on the singles and the Rocket III, particularly vulnerable to wear on the sliders, with water and grit continuously passing the seals which were in need of frequent replacement. The headlamp was supported on shaped brackets of chromed rod rubber mounted to the lower fork yokes. The single front mudguard stay was also supported in rubber mountings attached to the fork sliders.

The handlebars were now rubber-mounted too, and with bulbous soft rubber grips, and light alloy levers for the Lightning and Firebird. Secured by the front fork cap nuts were separate carrier plates for the rubber binnacles of the speedo and rev counter. There was revised Lucas switchgear, with impractically stubby thumb switches. On the left hand pivot block was the dipswitch, horn and headlamp flasher button, and on the right the indicator switch and the ignition cut-out. Mounted to the rear of the louvres beneath the seat on the right-hand side was a four-position ignition switch interlocked with the lighting. With the key detached the lights could not be switched on, but in one position the rider could remove the key while leaving either pilot-light or headlamp in operation as a parking light. The whole system was common, with minor variations, to the Triumphs and to Norton Commandos.

The frame had a massive 3 in × 16 gauge tube extending rearward from the steering head, then striking downward beneath the seat nose. A duplex cradle of $1\frac{1}{4}$ in × 14 g tubes descended from the steering head, passed beneath the engine unit and rose again at the rear sub-frame. At the base of the seat-tube section of the main spine, a pressing linked the duplex cradle tubes. Raising the seat gave access to the oil filler cap with its loose dip-stick, serving the 5 pint oil reservoir formed by the main tube's upright section. Secured to the underside of the base pressing was an inspection plate embodying a gauze filter and with a drain-plug at its centre. (A similar frame but with different mounting brackets

appeared for the Triumph 650 twins.) To the frame were attached new centre and prop stands.

The two die-cast louvres flanked the vertical frame tube, and it was as well that the unridged dual seat was hinged and gave access to the area beneath, as the louvres were fiddly to remove — you had to unscrew the masterswitch bezel, take off the air filter box, slacken the two attachment bolts from inside the air filter box and draw the panel, front edge first, off its locating peg on the frame. The size of the louvres themselves varied from the single to the twin carb model. Behind the louvres were twin element air filters, which were found effective in suppressing induction noise, as well as the relocated Zener diode which now used the aluminium body of the air cleaner for its mounting point, and behind that the battery, coils and tool kit. Below, the two roadsters had new conical megaphone silencers, very lusty, while the Firebird's twin high-level matt black exhausts led back to matt-black cigar-shaped silencers mounted high to the left behind a flimsy-looking wire heat-shield. This system plus lower gearing, a sump bash-plate, and its orange and cream colour scheme were all that distinguished it from the other two.

The snail cam adjustment for the rear chain, and the new rear hub, were as for the singles (for details see page 103). Like them, the rear wheel was no longer qd. It should be mentioned, though, that all rear wheel bearing retaining rings had a left-hand thread — this had already occurred sometimes on previous rear wheels, when the only distinguishing mark had been a 'L' stamped on the retainer.

Inside the 650 engines there was one important and overdue change — a new oil pump, as previously used on production racers, with a cast-iron body and a 30% increase in oil flow. A piston-type pressure release valve was also substituted for the previous spring-loaded ball.

A 1971 *Motor Cycle* tester enjoyed the new Lightning, which was fast, at over 110 mph and with a 14.5 second standing quarter, climbed hills effortlessly, yet with no sacrifice of low-down punch. Clutch and gearbox action were light, though heavier springs in the former required a strong wrist. The brakes stopped it in $29\frac{1}{2}$ ft from 30 mph and it handled excellently, the steering feeling light at low speeds up to 30, but taut and responsive from there on up. After all, this was virtually the Triumph frame which was to maintain the British reputation for good handling over the next ten years. In 1971 terms it was not the most practical machine though, the small tank with its centre line cap only gave a range of about 110

BSA FIREBIRD SCRAMBLER 650

Below left *1971 A65F Firebird scrambler version of the oil-in-frame 650s.*

Right *1972 Lightning with black, lowered frame courtesy of Hele and Hopwood.*

miles, and the wide bars limited speed to the medium range.

As the year progressed the company's financially disastrous position emerged and the management mainly responsible departed. Bert Hopwood became a director and with other more motor cycle-oriented colleagues realised that lowering the seat height of the group's twins was of paramount importance. After unnecessary delays he and Hele went to work, and the 1972 BSA 650s, reduced to just the Lightning and Thunderbolt, presented a very different appearance from the year before, with a 4 gallon steel tank (of the type to be found on the UK Triumphs throughout the '70s) with thin knee-grips for the Thunderbolt but not the Lightning, more sober colour schemes, more substantial chrome mudguards, short flat pulled-back bars, the top surface of the dual seat now cross-hatched and the frame stoved black. Subtle changes including rear dampers $\frac{1}{2}$ in shorter at $12\frac{1}{2}$ in, had lowered the seat height by nearly 2 in, and according to the *Bike* magazine test (early summer 1972) of a straight-from-the-crate Lightning, handling was an improvement on previous years, and the A65 'transmitted tolerable vibration' which was 'definitely down on the previous year'. (Ironically this was in contrast to the Japanese twin tested alongside it, the Yamaha XS2, on which the high-speed vibration was rather worse and 'at a hundred miles an hour all you could hear was the rider's teeth chattering', as they put it.) The Beeza was also oil-tight. They said of it: 'clearly a viceless machine in practically any situation'. BSA had got it right at last—but tragically too late.

The changes to the 'lower, slightly more compact frame' according to Hopwood were completed by April 1972; that would be from engine numbers A65L and A65T with DG onwards prefixes to numbers (see the engine number tables at the end of the BSA section), D being April, G being 1972, and production ceasing at the end of that year. Some of the 1972 engines suffered from timing-side bearings inserted the wrong way round by contract labour.

Amid the confusion of BSA's collapse there was a further postscript to the saga of the twins, in the shape of the A70, or Lightning 75, 750 cc variant. 202 of these engines were produced with just the stroke increased to 85 mm to give 751 cc, and compression raised to 9.5:1. The majority were shipped to the United States for homologation and then used for $\frac{1}{2}$-mile flat track dirt racing. The idea had been that of factory side-car racer ace Peter Brown, but according to Doug Hele, with its increased power there were considerable vibration problems with the machines, particularly around the swinging arm and footrests. Some of these engines left the factory one way and another and ended up in the UK. Unfortunately their appearance is identical to an A65, they carry 'Lightning 650' transfers and even have A65L engine number prefixes. Some found a new home at the premises of ex-tester Les Mason's Staffordshire-based firm, Devimead. (Today Devimead's A65 improvements are provided by SRM.)

Mason was a long-time fan of the twins, and while at Small Heath and working on the Daytona racers had already suggested a cheap and simple cure for the crucial main-bearing problem, which the management characteristically chose to ignore. Since setting up on his own in the early '70s, he had been able to offer answers to this and to most of the twin's other problems. His most indispensible item was the roller ball conversion for the plain timing side main bearing. This consists of a roller bearing but with a ball-race built in for positive location. The existing shimmed roller on

A disc-braked Devimead 750 conversion of the A65. 'Gemello' is wop for 'twin' — geddit?

the drive side is then replaced by a lipped roller with space between lips and rollers, and this provides a complete set of workable roller mains, and an end to crankshafts punching their way out through the cases, as well as to the associated big end lubrication problems when the plain bearing's clearance became too great.

The new roller bearing itself needs only a trickle of oil, and although SRM will provide an iron oil-pump for increased circulation for pre-'71 twins, they claim this is not strictly necessary if, in conjunction with the roller/ball conversion, they fit a new oilway. One half of this is a block fitted with an oil seal and welded on to the timing side inner case, and completing the feed is a hollow quill-shaft in the end of the crankshaft. In this way the oil to the big ends is pumped straight in through the end of the mainshaft. Problems with the clutch are also dealt with, by means of an alloy clutch cover using an ingeniously simple little roller thrust bearing at the end of the clutch pushrod, operating onto a hardened thrust pad on the cover. But the A70s are not the only 750 BSA twins around. Ian Kennedy (GB) used to offer a conversion for the earlier twins, and now SRM do likewise, claiming cooler running and better balance from their own thicker flange barrels. Even an A50 500 can be thus transformed, though for that you will need to provide a 650 head.

The stigma of the short-stroke unit twins remains, but the options outlined above hopefully go some way to removing it. If you come by one, of whatever vintage, the 7.5:1 pistons are a sound move, as is replacing the pre-'68 contact breakers and coils with the later set-up, or with Lucas Rita

or Boyer electronic ignition. The single carb bikes always came very close to the Lightnings in performance, and were a lot less bother to keep adjusted. A despatch rider I know did 25,000 City of London miles on a second-hand Thunderbolt with the low compression pistons, and swore by it rather than at it. And Bob Currie, a self-confessed Triumph man, recently wrote of borrowing a friend's A65 with 40,000-odd miles on the clock, and soon settling down to it as a good solid Brumagem workhorse.

'Can you tune a bike,' he wondered, 'not by laying a single spanner on it but merely by riding it, day in, day out in the same way?' If you find a bike that's been well treated like that, and do the same yourself, perhaps the late BSA twins, while they will never qualify as classics, could make good sense.

BSA: The unit twins — dates and specifications
Production dates
A50 Star — 1962–65
A50 C Cyclone — 1964–65
A50 Cyclone Clubman — 1964–65
A50 W Wasp — 1965–66
A50 R Royal Star — 1965–70
A65 Star — 1962–65
A65 Rocket — 1963–65
A65 Lightning Rocket (USA) — 1964–65
A65 L Lightning — 1964–73
A65 Lightning Clubmans — 1964–65
A65 T Thunderbolt — 1965–73
A65 Spitfire Hornet (USA) — 1964–65
A65 H Hornet — 1966–67

A65 SS Spitfire Mk II, III, IV—1966, 67, 68
A65 ES/F Firebird—1968–71
A70 Lightning 75—1972

Specifications
A50 Star/Cyclone/Wasp/Royal Star
Capacity, bore and stroke—499 cc (65.5 mm ×
74 mm)
Type of engine—ohv Twin
Ignition—Coil (A50 Wasp, Energy Transfer)
Weight—A50 Star (1962) 385 lb, A50 Royal Star
(1965) 391 lb

A65 Star/Rocket/Lightning Rocket/
Lightning/Thunderbolt/Spitfire Hornet/
Hornet/Spitfire/Firebird
Capacity, bore and stroke—654 cc (75 mm ×
74 mm)
Type of engine—ohv twin
Ignition—Coil (Spitfire Hornet/Hornet/Firebird to
1971, Energy Transfer)
Weight—A65 Star (1962) 390 lb, A65 Lightning
(1966) 398 lb, A65 Spitfire Mk II (1966) 382 lb, A65
Thunderbolt, oil-in-frame (1971) 390 lb

A70 Lightning 75
Capacity, bore and stroke—751 cc (75 mm ×
85 mm)
(otherwise as 1972 Lightning)

BSA: A50 and A65 Roadster twins—
annual development and
modifications
1962
For A65 Star models:
1 Early 1962, compression raised from 7.25 to
7.5:1.
For A50 Star models:
2 Mid-1962, compression raised from 7.5 to 8:1.

For A65 and A50 models:
3 Mid-1962, from engine numbers A65-1307,
A50-396, quick-release device for clutch cable
provided within crankcase.

1963
For A65 and A50 models:
1 12-volt electrics provided by two Lucas
MKZ 9E batteries connected in series offered as
optional extra, with side panels enlarged to suit.
2 Early 1963, from frame numbers A50-2701 (A50
frame numbers were applied to both A65 and A50)
rod-operated rear brake on right hand side
replaces previous cable operation. Brake worked
by two linked rods and cross-shaft.

1964
For A65, A65R and A50 models:
1 Previous Smiths chronometric speedometers
replaced by Smiths magnetic type.
2 New silencer internals with a system of steel
baffles replacing previous glass wool absorption
material.
3 Lucas type 2DS 506 rectifier replaces previous
FSX 1849 type.
4 In clutch cable quick release mechanism, starter
spring retaining plate now secured to spindle by
small screw.

1965
For all A65 and A50 models:
1 Folding kickstart pedal.
2 Modified centre stand giving greater ground
clearance.
For A65L, A50C models:
3 Lh side brake at rear with straight-through rod
operation. Rh side brake at front with pull-out
spindle, not end-caps as previously.
4 Twin carburettors and cylinder head (previously

*1964 A65. Not pretty, but still quite
reliable.*

available for export only) with chrome plated cylindrical air cleaners for each.

5 Fibre glass side panels, of modified shape. (For further A65L, A50C details, see text.) Now with two fixing screws per panel.

6 12-volt electrics now standard.

7 Mid-year, from engine nos. A65A-1625, A65C-1986, A65D-3456, A65B-410, A65E-1149, A50B and A50BC-524, A50A-1271, A50Ap-330, A50D and A50DC-102, A50P-142, special aperture provided in front of rh half of crankcase, with detachable plug allowing insertion of BSA tool (Part No 68-710) to register with a slot machined in flywheel, and place first the right hand piston and then after one revolution of the engine, the left-hand piston, in the correct positions for timing the ignition. (Timing plug must be fitted with 'A50' symbol uppermost, ie, with 'cut-away' portion at the top, for both A50 and A65.)

For A50C:

8 Inlet valve sizes larger (1.45 inch diameter) than A50 Star (1.41 inch diameter).

For all A50 models:

9 Front brake became 8 in.

1966

For all A65 and A50 models:

1 Ignition switch moved to nearside of head-lug, and emergency start position no longer incorporated. New Yale-type tumbler.

2 Oil tank capacity reduced from $5\frac{1}{2}$ to 5 pints.

3 Primary chaincase modified so that two inspection caps (clutch adjustment and clutch spring adjustment), previously concealed beneath a single oval outer cap, are now exposed. Clutch spring adjustment now requires removal of chaincase. Threaded screwed-in filler plug placed at top of chaincase in the middle.

4 Oil tank filler cap acquired dipstick.

5 Inner valve springs shortened from $1\frac{5}{8}$ to $1\frac{7}{16}$ in, outer valve springs shortened from $2\frac{1}{32}$ to $1\frac{3}{4}$ in, with close-wound coils nearest to cylinder head base.

6 Air cleaners' previous felt element replaced by 'surgical gauze' type, and previous screw-on method of air filter attachment replaced by clip-on method.

7 Clutch now changed to three not four springs, and carries six not five plain, and six not five compression plates. Clutch no longer has a fixed inner plain plate, so first friction plate to be inserted bears directly on chainwheel.

8 Number of clutch chainwheel bearing rollers reduced from 21 to 20.

9 Front fork internals modified to provide two-way damping, now fitted with a damper rod attached to fork cap nuts. Externally fit rubber bellows. Softer action springs in Girling rear units.

10 Primary chain adjuster was previously a hollow screwed sleeve, in the top of which a sliding thrust button bore against the chain slipper, with the plunger moving freely within the screwed adjuster once a feeler rod has been inserted. Now modified so that the thrust button was part of the adjuster, and there was no provision for insertion of a feeler rod, adjustment being effected only by screwing in the adjuster.

11 Control cable inners treated with molybdenum-based grease.

12 New Lucas ht cables with inbuilt supression.

13 Ball-ended handlebar levers.

For A65R, A50RS:

14 Blade pattern mudguards at front, valanced at rear, as 1965 Lightning, but not chromed.

15 Single-sided brakes at front and rear, fork end caps and nearside brake rod, as 1965 Lightning and Cyclone. Fully enclosed rear chaincases no longer available.

16 Previous year's Lightning-pattern frame adopted.

For A65L, A65SS:

17 (And for all twin carburettor models), recommended spark plugs changed from Champion N4 to N3.

18 A65L twin carbs now Amal $1\frac{5}{32}$ in Monoblocs with each float chamber turned towards outside, and inlets tracts coupled by balance pipe. A65SS Mk II's Amal GP $1\frac{5}{32}$ in.

19 Racing type dual seat but with rear hump soft to allow passenger to be carried, with gold-embossed BSA badge on rear and chrome strip around edge.

20 Matching speedometer and rev-counter in new cast light-alloy bracket.

21 Earlier throttle cable junction box replaced by individual cables carried from each carburettor to a double-drum twistgrip.

22 Chromed sports mudguards.

23 Linking bar between exhaust pipes.

For A65SS Mk II:

24 Alloy wheel rims, 4.00 × 18 in rear wheel, 190 mm front brake, closer ratio gears, folding footrests, optional 4 gallon fibreglass tank with snap-action filler cap, knee recesses, transfer not badge. Early 1966, 5 gallon fibreglass tank option.

For A65L:

25 Overall reduction in gearing, lower bottom gear.

For all A65 and A50 models:

26 Drive side main bearing became a lipped roller race.

1967

For All A65 and A50 models:

1 Single 12 volt battery replaced two 6 volt in series.

2 Heat-sink for Lucas Zener diode now located

Right *1966 A65T Thunderbolt, single-carb 650, on test.*
Below right *A Mr William Eccles, Milk Race enthusiast, and his milk-white steed, a 1966 Lightning. The side-car spec was available to special order.*

under steering head, replacing sheet-aluminium sink mounted under dual seat.

3 New cast light-alloy support bracket for rear light.

4 New blade type rear mudguard.

5 Speedometers calibrated up to 150 mph.

6 New timing arrangements. A circular aperture in the primary chaincase covered by a new bolted-on plate exposes a point on the inner face of the case. Under strobe light, this pointer coincides with timing mark on the alternator rotor when timing full-advance correct.

7 Alternator-stator, previously mounted on three studs projecting from the crankcase, now fitted into an independent centralizing housing.

8 Valve guide material changed from cast iron to non-ferrous material.

9 Two rearmost central cylinder head bolts enlarged.

10 Finned rocker cover replaces previous smooth one, interchangeable with it.

11 O-ring gas seals fitted inside exhaust ports.

12 Front fork oil seal holders lengthened to improve bellows fitting. Sealing arrangements at fork leg tops modified.

13 Speedometers and rev counters fitted with new rubber cups.

14 Cushioned handlebar grips.

15 4×18 in section rear tyre (as on Spitfire Mk II).

16 More tools of better quality in tool kit.

For A65T, A50:

17 Racing-type dual seat with rear hump as 1966 A65L, A65SS.

For A65SS Mk III:

18 Twin 32 mm Amal Concentric, 10:1 compression, alloy control levers, chrome-plated upper fork shrouds.

1968

For all A65 and A50 models:

1 Export specification styling, ie, $2\frac{3}{4}$ gallon steel petrol tank with no knee grips, with larger chrome side panels, and snap-action filler caps centrally positioned, high rise 33 in-wide handlebars, side reflectors under fuel-tank nose and on side of new streamlined alloy tail lamp housing, slimmer dual seats, no front registration plates, chrome mudguards now for A65T but not A50.

2 Latest Lucas 6CA contact-breaker assembly replaced old 4CA type, providing independent adjustment of points gap and points positioning.

Redesigned assembly no longer housed condensers within contact-breaker compartment. These were now located in waterproof cover close to the ignition coils. Modified mounting for coils gave increased clearance between coils and machine side-panels. Conversion kit from 4CA to 6CA as follows: (Triumph) Part No CP209, consisting of Lucas Parts 54419340 Auto Advance Unit, 54419097 Contact Breaker Plate Assembly, 2 × 54420128 Condensers/Capacitors, 54418526 Condenser/Capacitor base plate, 54418528 Moulded Rubber Cover for Condensers/ Capacitors.

3 New crankcase castings with a deep spigot giving firmer and more accurate location for alternator stator, which abandons previous year's independent centralising housing to become integral with the crankcase. Lucas RM21 alternator replaces RM19.

4 3-position toggle lightswitch replaces rotary type on headlamp shell.

5 New tank badges, similar pear-shaped as previous acrylic moulding but now three-dimensional ribbed moulding in anodised light alloy.

6 Dipstick on gearbox filler plug.

7 Clipless rubber gaiters for front fork legs.

8 Oil supply to rockers taken from point near crankcase, and oilways to head modified.

9 Cross-flag transfers replace previous winged badges on side panels.

10 Amal Concentric carburettors (as already on previous A65SS Mk III) replace Monoblocs.

11 Head gaskets now of solid copper.

For A65L, A65SS Mk IV:

12 8 in twin leading-shoe full-width hub (Triumph-developed) front brake unit, with Triumph-type fork end caps. Main adjuster midway in the cable. (Fork end caps were not identical on different models and should be assembled with identifying letters/figures, or drill-point holes, matching.)

For A65L:

13 Exposed chrome-plated rear damper springs.

14 Link between exhausts no longer fitted.

1969

For all A65 and A50 models:

1 Partial changeover of BSF, CEI, etc, thread forms to Unified thread for all bolts, studs and screwed components, ie, oil pressure relief valve thread changed to Unified, not interchangeable with previous. But changeover incomplete.

2 Front brake cable fitted with switch to actuate rear brake light.

3 Revised and improved silencer internals.

4 Width of crankcase and primary chaincase joint faces increased 15%.

5 Tubular connectors, welded to steering-head gusset plates allow fitting of fairings.

6 Blue oil pressure warning light fitted in headlamp shell, with switch, rubber-covered, at front of timing chest below rev-counter drive.

7 Footrest rubbers of more wear-resistant material, bearing revised BSA emblem in a rectangular panel.

8 All twins adopt 8 in TLS front brake, Triumph pattern as A65L/A65SS Mk IV previous year, but with revised linkage, and with a new nave plate for left of hub in which concentric ribs replace slotted panels. Also Triumph lower members for telescopic fork which is thereby shortened. Revised internal damping, front fork damper rod no longer attached to fork cap nuts. Two-way damping via shuttle valves and restrictors in lower ends of fork stanchions. Forked joint at end of front brake cable now connected to brake lever by pivot pin and locknut, replacing spring clip pivot pin. Modified front mudguard mounting.

9 Grease nipple fitted in clutch cable casing.

10 Contact-breaker cam spindle now treated with special dry lubricant and no oil to be applied to it for fear of seizing it on its bearing.

11 Timing plug for aperture in front of right side of crankcase now with a cylindrical plunger, and screws rather than slides into crankcase once blanking plug has been unscrewed. Now registers with hole, not slot, in flywheel. Later versions had the plunger as a sliding fit in the body of the plug, to allow its location to be felt more easily with the fingers.

12 Slotted adjustment sleeve on the steering head adjuster no longer fitted, cap nut alone now serves as adjuster.

13 Chaincase oil filler and clutch-adjustment plug fitted with rubber O-rings.

14 Idler pinion spindle bearing and wall of inner timing cover fitted with oil seals.

15 Frames redesigned. Seat height raised from 31.5 to 32 in. In pivoted rear fork, phosphor bronze bushes now fitted replacing bonded-rubber bearings. Fork cross tube is of larger diameter and equipped with a grease nipple, with enlarged spacers and O-ring grease seals fitted.

16 Side-panels become steel not fibreglass. Side panel transfers changed to names of models.

17 Steel $3\frac{1}{2}$ gallon petrol tanks with reserve supply and rubber knee grips (as for all unit twins, horizontally ribbed but without BSA name), replace previous.

18 Flatter handlebars fitted.

19 Grab rails on some machines.

1969 Export spec. A65 Thunderbolt with new front brake.

20 Contact breaker cover now a polished light alloy casting carrying sunken winged BSA motif, as does circular cover in primary chaincase now.
21 Faces of valve collets now tapered at 20° not 15°, and valve-spring collars were modified to suit.
22 Balance pipes link the exhaust pipes near the ports.
For A65L:
23 Pair of Windtone horns mounted ahead of cylinders.
For A65T, A50:
24 Exposed chrome-plated rear damper springs as A65L 1968.

1970
For all A65 and A50 models:
1 Modified cylinder block, with base flange increased in area. Retaining studs respaced, and stud diameter increased from $\frac{5}{16}$ in to $\frac{3}{8}$ in. Crankcase mouth modified to suit, oil drain holes repositioned, new gasket. Not interchangeable with previous. Crankshaft and flywheel assembly now machined all over. Light alloy con-rods' section increased. Piston skirt dimensions modified to reduce engine noise.
2 Clutch thrust-rod now a (Triumph-pattern) 3-ball camplate mechanism on the inside face of the gearbox end cover, so a new cover design featured.
3 Design of alloy oil pump changed. Externally previous similar to, but driven spindle now spigoted to the scavenge gear, and sections of the casing dowelled, to prevent air leaks. Oil pressure relief valve changed from ball to plunger type.
4 Heavier gauge gear pedal return spring with larger diameter coils and longer locating arms adopted.
5 Front fork stanchions with hard chrome micro-finish to increase oil seal life.
6 Front brake and clutch lever pivot blocks each include $\frac{5}{16}$ in diameter hole for handlebar mirrors.
7 New small Lucas ignition coils.
8 Wiring includes provision for capacitor ignition and indicators.
9 Amal Concentrics have redesigned needle jet holder, needle jet and needle.
For A65L:
10 New $3\frac{1}{4}$ gallon steel petrol tank with scalloped sides similar to singles.

1971
For all A65 models:
1 For oil-in-frame model cycle part details, see text.
2 In engines, alloy oil pump replaced by racing-pattern iron type. Piston type pressure release valve substituted for previous ball-valve.

1972
For all A65 models:
1 Frames now black.
2 4 gallon steel tank with twist-off cap substituted for previous $2\frac{1}{2}$ gallon.
3 Larger chrome mudguards.
4 Shorter, flatter Triumph-type pull-back handlebars.
5 Top surface of hinged dual seat, previously plain, now cross-hatched.
6 Changes to frame lowers seat height nearly two inches. Rear suspension units $\frac{1}{2}$ in shorter at $12\frac{1}{2}$ in.

BSA: The A75R Rocket III triple
The Rocket III's engine was a Triumph design pure and simple, the work of Bert Hopwood, Doug Hele and Jack Wickes, Edward Turner's old drawing-office anchor man. The full story of its evolution will be found in the appropriate Triumph

Trident section of the later volume. But to their credit the Group avoided total badge engineering, and there were substantial differences between Trident and Rocket III. The engines for both machines were built at Small Heath — 'in 56 time-consuming stages' as Bob Currie was to write later of T160 Trident construction, which also took place at Armoury Road.

The transverse triple formula, brought to prominence by the MV Agusta racers of that era, was basically achieved by a 'Tiger-and-a-half' configuration, that is a 500 cc Triumph with an extra cylinder. The contemporary Tiger 100/Daytona 500, though, had a 69 mm bore as opposed to the triples' bore of 67 mm, but the basic engine layout was the same as the twins, with twin camshafts, ahead and behind the cylinder block, driven by gears and working vertical pushrods in tubes located between the cylinders, which were even prone to leak oil in the traditional way. Timing gear and valve layout were also similar, while the gearbox internals were the same type as the current Triumph 650.

The alloy crankcase consisted of a vertically split centre section — the necessity of using existing machine tools where possible meant that horizontally split cases were not a possibility. The rear of this carried the four-speed gearbox, with the outer sections of the crankcases bolted to this centre section on either side. These outer cases, again like the Triumph twin, carried the twin camshafts in plain bearings. The car-type Borg and Beck diaphragm clutch ran on an outrigger bearing for greater rigidity, though there was in fact no inner bearing.

But the BSA was distinct from the Trident in having not the entire engine but only its cylinders inclined forward at a 15° angle. (The later T160 Trident was also to adopt this configuration.) This meant that not only cylinders but also the crankcase and chaincases were different, the latter on the BSA presenting smooth, almost 'power-egg' contours while on the Trident, as with the Bonneville, the shape of the gearbox was still clearly discernible.

The cylinder head of the 9.5:1 compression engine was a one-piece aluminium casting, with two separate well-finned rocker boxes bolted to it. There were also three separate bolted-on inlet stubs for the trio of Amal 626 Concentric carbs, which were actually of 27 mm bore (and too big for a 750, in the opinion of ex-Triumph factory development engineer and triple expert Norman Hyde). The throttle was worked by a single cable from the twist-grip to a shaft bearing three short operating levers directly connected to the throttle slides. A single adjusting screw on the shaft permitted the setting of tickover without individual adjustment of all three. Back on the head, the exhaust stubs were screwed in. Within the generously finned barrels the pistons ran on alloy con-rods with plain big end bearings.

The crankshaft was a product of the Small Heath forge, and a special feature. It was forged in one plane and then reheated and twisted to provide the 120° crank throws, which meant that only one piston reached the top of its stroke at a time, which gave excellent balance and a comparative lack of vibration. The crank was carried in two plain main bearings on the inside, with the ends of the shaft running in ball bearings on the drive side and roller bearings on the timing side. In the interests of slimness there were no flywheels, and the shaft was balanced by bob-

Right *A new thing. The A75R Rocket III arrives late in 1968.*

Above far right *Power egg contours of BSA triple engine seen from the drive side.*

Above right *3 into 4 into 2 exhaust bracketting BSA duplex down-tube frame.*

weights only. For one of the design problems with the triple had been the potential width of the engine, and for this reason the Lucas 100-watt alternator was, unusually, positioned on the right-hand end of the crankshaft. The resulting engine was only $3\frac{1}{2}$ in wider than the Bonneville twin.

The BSA frame in which this engine was housed was a duplex down-tube affair, while the Trident was carried in a single-down-tube frame similar to the Bonneville. The Rocket III frame was an inch taller than the Triumph with a seat height of 32 in, and made for a big, though not unduly bulky machine. The BSA frame's saddle tubes connecting the end of the top tube to the duplex tubes by the swinging-arm pivot, plus its rear mudguard loop, contrasted with the Trident's bolt-on sub-frame. Opinions varied as to which handled best. A *Motor Cycle* Rider's Report on both triples in 1972 found that the BSA seemed to have a slight edge on the Trident for steering. But in 1969, tester David Dixon felt that the Triumph steered steadier than the Rocket III. In practice there seems to have been little in it. Both were excellent long-distance fast tourers, unaffected by the weight of a passenger and luggage.

The BSA's cycle parts included some good, useful old-fashioned items like a steering-damper, gaitered front forks, a handlebar-mounted air lever and an ammeter in the instrument panel along with oil pressure and main beam warning lights, and matching speedo and rev counter. The machine's overall styling, however, was conceived after American importers had asked for something different from the Triumph, and after the project had been taken over by Umberslade Hall and 'minced about by huge committees', as Bert Hopwood put it.

In charge of overall design were Ogle, famous for their car design work with Reliant. This work not only added about 25 lb to its weight, but delayed its release fatally close to that of the Honda-4 (see page 41). Since 1969 I have become sufficiently fixated on BSAs to see the appeal of the Rocket III, but at the time it seemed a bizarre mixture of the old and the new. The high-rise bars and the four exhausts (two from the centre cylinder) leading to the twin Dan Dare ray-gun silencers with their three stubby tail-pipes, braced by long stay-rods from the rear grab rails, all contrasted with the big side-panels coming forward to half-conceal the air cleaners, the wide ribbed and polished aluminium hubs, the slab-sided 4.5 gallon petrol tank and the substantial look of the bike as a whole.

In the end, I suppose, I was as conservative as the average biker, and there was simply too little

continuity with what had gone before. After a steady diet of twins, the three-pot set-up was difficult to swallow, as was the weight (468 lb dry was a heavy motor cycle in those days), let alone the tales of high petrol consumption and — just possibly — more performance than one could handle. The fact that the bike looked as though it couldn't decide whether it was a dray-horse or a spaceship, meant that in many cases the A75 was elbowed in favour of a Commando when it came to buying. Only about 7,000 Rocket IIIs were built over a $3\frac{1}{2}$ year production run, against averages of 6,000 a year for the A50/A65 twins of those years. Though factory disruption must have played a part in this, the bikes were clearly not a spectacular sales success. Tridents, in contrast, were always closer in appearance to the Meriden twins, and for 1972, again, somewhat contradictorily, at American insistence, they reverted to the 'conventional' look that Hele and Hopwood had wanted from the start. Around 45,000 T150s were made between 1969 and the end of 1974, when the T160 version arrived.

Further detail Rocket III styling differences with the Trident included a smooth, hump-backed seat against the T150's ribbed one, rear dampers with the springs unshrouded and chrome top covers, more ornate ribbed side panels with their alloy 'ROCKET 3' name strips, and a different front mudguard, white-lined, with a blunt arrow shaped front. An oil cooler was a standard item on both triples, with the plain bearings causing oil temperature to rise, and lubricant circulating $3\frac{1}{2}$ times as fast as on a 650 twin. The Trident's cooler was unshrouded, the Rocket III's tucked away beneath the tank nose behind alloy side covers with side reflectors.

The few that were released in America towards the end of 1968 confirmed that the triple was the fastest production street multi in the world that year. British road tests in May the following year described a 120 mph plus potential, with smoother power delivery than would ever be possible on a parallel twin, thanks to the 240-degree firing interval as well as the rubber cush-drive in the clutch sprocket. There was vibration between 4,500 and 6,000 revs but it then smoothed itself out up to the peak recommended revs of 7,250.

These early testers were understandably so impressed with the all-round performance of the

Above left *Massive ribbed and polished aluminium hubs.*
Left *'Be the first on your block.' In late 1968 this dude was the first in the world to own a Rocket III. British punters had to wait for the New Year.*

machine that they made no mention of something which was to emerge from comparative experience later, namely that there was less positive pick-up at lower revs from the engine, than from either the new transverse 4-cylinder bikes spearheaded by Honda, or from a traditional twin like the Commando. An attempt was made to remedy this on the 1971 BSA triples by the replacement of the No 3 throttle slides with No $3\frac{1}{2}$, and NVT, on later T160 Tridents, also recommended richer slides than the No 4 items which were fitted as standard. Progressively lower gearing was also applied, but the characteristic seemed endemic to the engine, at least in its 750 cc form. (Norman Hyde was to say that not only the carburettors but also the ports and valves were too big for a 750, since the motor was developed at a time when top speed was all. He believes his larger capacity conversions, which the factory had hoped to achieve, realised the engine's true potential and tractability.)

However, when the power really came in, from 4,500–5,000 rpm, the triple was unbeatable, accelerating particularly well from 80 mph on. And though not effortless, for being heavy machines they needed a determined rider to get the best from them, the Rocket IIIs had the solid feel and the handling to match its high speeds. Obviously only high-speed runners could enjoy these bikes to the full.

The machine as a whole provoked mixed reactions. The overwhelming impression was favourable—this was a new thing, a genuine superbike. There were detail points of criticism—the valves clattered like a Triumph, the prop stand with no extension foot was inaccessible, as was the light switch which had to be reached for under the bars to its mounting on the left side headlamp support. The Windtone horns, being mounted low down by the rear dampers, were less than effective. The high bars were, as usual, found not suitable for speeds over about 70, and the alternative lower-level pull-backs were recommended. There were minor oil leaks even on test, and these would be part of owners' experience—the legendary Trident racer Slippery Sam acquired that tag from the time when its engine ''wet-sumped'' at the 1970 Bol d'Or. On Rocket IIIs, trouble spots were the rocker boxes, pushrod tubes and gearbox spindle housings, as well as, initially, inside the gearbox between the mainshaft and the high-gear pinion sleeve—this was remedied for 1970 by a new mainshaft nut and clutch hub. More serious was the problem of leaking or blown head gaskets, and a solid copper gasket was only a sometime solution. Fitting breather pipes on the rocker boxes was another.

Working on these problems was aggravated by the fact that headbolts, rocker-bolts and barrel base-nuts, though now of United Thread throughout the machine, were inaccessible to the necessary torque wrench. Even the tappets were awkward to set until the introduction of a slightly longer ($\frac{15}{16}$ in) tappet adjuster. This was distinguishable only by a cross milled on its end. Other maintenance was not easy either—the exhaust pipes had to come off to remove the sump filter, for instance. Finish was not very good, and poor quality control aggravated another potential problem area, starting, which required a definite knack. It involved, from cold, generous flooding of the outer carbs (the tickler on the middle one being inaccessible) and sensitive use of the choke—not too much—and even when hot, gentle tickling, and the throttle set for fast tickover. The ignition timing and carburation also had to be well-maintained for easy starting, and owners were to find that there could be an absence of careful factory strobe setting of the three sets of points behind their chromed cover on the timing side, as well as of checks on the contact-breakers themselves. Some BSA owners also found Champion N4 plugs to be more suitable than the recommended N3s.

Erratic slow tickover also meant that the machine could be stalled quite easily. This turned out to be caused by the return springs in the advance-retard unit. On earlier models light springs were fitted which tended to allow the timing to wander. When heavy springs were fitted to cure this they worked well except that the ignition then tended to be too retarded at high engine rpm, and the ultimate solution was one heavy and one light spring. Another answer now available is electronic ignition, which though occasionally not without its own problems, is of particular benefit to the triples.

Another setback for riders that was marginally affected by ignition timing was the petrol consumption. While 5-star was always a must, early magazine tests returned reasonable figures—over 50 mpg at a steady 70 for the *Motor Cycle*, and a 39 mpg average under hard driving for *Motorcyclist Illustrated*. But riders found that the real average, with the sort of driving the engine encouraged, was 30–35 mpg, a strikingly low figure at the time and one which meant that even the $4\frac{1}{4}$ gallon tank gave a range of well under 150 miles. It should be noted that the better figures achieved on test were achieved with the machines carefully set up, and with the earlier 'European' gearing—a 52-tooth rear sprocket and

Vic Willoughby tests a 1969 Rocket III.

a 19-tooth gearbox sprocket giving overall 4.98, 5.95, 8.42 and 12.15 to 1 ratios. These were lowered twice in the interests of low-down stomp and great flexibility. Oil consumption was generally low on these early machines, although the situation would deteriorate with later Tridents. The oil level, incidentally, always had to be checked immediately after a run, as something like a pint remained suspended in the oil cooler and pipework.

One last, less than perfect, point for the rider was braking. Drum brakes on a 480 lb, 125 mph projectile were a dubious proposition, and a test machine only stopped in $32\frac{1}{2}$ ft from 30 mph. The Triumph 8 in TLS front brake with its airscoop was reasonably efficient, but the 7 in SLS rod-operated rear brake less so. There was a Triumph modification which involved fitting the brake shoes with different linings (Part No 99-0043) modified fulcrum pads, with the linings then ground in and a new cam lever (Part No W4034) and return spring (Part No W4049), but it was

stressed that the work should be done by a competent engineer.

All this emphasises the negative, but there were many rider plus points about the Rocket III — excellent lights, a comfortable riding position for both pilot and pillion, and gear-changing that was clean if clonky. However, the heart of the matter was the performance — a 13.9 second standing quarter, 50 in first, 80 in second, 110 in third and 125 mph in top, on a *Motorcyclist Illustrated* test machine. And at those speeds, the ray-guns were wailing in a distinctive and blood-stirring way. Medium and high speed acceleration, from say 80 to 110 mph, was a particular strong point. There had been nothing like it since the demise of the Vincent vee-twins. New tyres had been developed by Dunlop to match the performance. Based on their triangular racing design, the 4.10 × 19 K81's front and rear were well up to the job. The rear chain only lasted 4,000 miles but meanwhile was well served by a metered oiler from the oil return pipe in the tank. Handling was more than adequate, though described by the Rider's Report as not superlative — in contrast to the praise heaped on the later Tridents — but the report rated the 1971-on cast alloy front fork a definite improvement.

There were teething troubles on the early machines, and some of these were quite serious. The most frequent involved the triplex primary chain and clutch getting out of alignment, which was due to incorrect machining of the shock absorber sprocket teeth leading to power loss, to mashing of the transmission sprockets, and to early main bearing failure. A specialist check on alignment, and the use of a clock gauge and a special tool to shim the sprocket into line was the only cure. Doug Hele had wanted a wider-type duplex primary drive and this was eventually adopted on the T160 Trident. Less seriously, clutch slip could also be a problem. Another clutch-related hassle concerned the shock absorber rubbers, which could expire rapidly when the plate retaining them worked loose. The gearbox, too, largely based on the Triumph twins', sometimes proved inadequate.

There were also problems with crankshaft lubrication, with some early crankshaft breakages at the drive end overhang, though it is doubtful whether these were caused by lubrication problems. Hele would have preferred roller bearings on both sides. The situation was improved when the original feed pipes carried by the main bearing caps to the tappets and cams were removed, as the latter were found to be adequately lubricated by splash. The extra oil

drained into the crankcase instead, and a small
ledge that was built up in the crankcase to trap oil
and give an additional feed to the bearings was a
further benefit. The somewhat devious oilways
with their $\frac{1}{4}$ in holes were not always entirely
satisfactory, and could be improved on by
opening out between the tank and the pump,
though not between the pump and the crank. In
the meantime, pistons occasionally burned out.
Piston rings took 1,000 miles to bed in on the
triples, and during this time oil consumption was
heavy. Ironically, if the running-in was done too
carefully, it was possible that the rings would
become scuffed. Another lubrication problem was
caused by leaking or improperly seated oil non-
return valves.

For 1970, the first year of the triples' racing
glory (see page 46), there were only detail
modifications to the Rocket III. Gearing was
lowered slightly in the hope of improving low-
down acceleration by the adoption of a 53-tooth
rear sprocket as against the previous 52-tooth
item. This reduced top speed to around 115 mph.
second gear was also lowered internally from 8.3
to 8.42 to 1. Wider tooth faces were used in the
gearbox, and the gear ratio between the kickstart
and the crankshaft lowered slightly in the interests
of easier starting. Efforts were made to counter oil
leaks, both by increasing the size of the joint
faces, and by fitting gaskets between the gearbox
outer and inner covers, and inner cover and main
casing. There was also a new mainshaft nut
incorporating an O-ring, and a new clutch hub.
The new gaskets and the crankcase gaskets were
of new asbestos and synthetic rubber material.
The rear brake operating cam was modified, and a
flatter pull-back Triumph-type handlebar fitted on
European models. Also, early in the year, the
clutch housing was said to have been ventilated
and holes drilled in the casing to let it breathe, in
an effort to stop the clutch slip — though triples
expert Norman Hyde has never encountered a
clutch housing of this type. Mid-year, too, there
was a change in the shape of the shock-absorber
rubbers, and of the type of bolt used to hold the
plate retaining the rubbers.

There were a few other changes, but as the
racers with their very close to standard engines
were to demonstrate, the use of tried and
perfected twin cylinder tooling and techniques

Above right *Winner. 1971 Triple racer.*
Right *With a track record like theirs, you could even
forgive the ties. Don Castro, Gary Nixon, Jim Rice,
Dave Allard, Dick Mann, and Don Emde, the 1971
American Match race team.*

had resulted in something that was very nearly right from the start. The basic strength of the engine is demonstrated by the way the racers used roadster con rods for a whole season and standard cranks which were simply reground at the end of the season and used again and again—all the more impressive when the 12:1 compression ratio was taken into account. This made it all the more tragic that they should be winners on the track but not the road.

The great racing year of 1971 merely saw the roadster Rocket III embarrassingly restyled, as part of the BSA new range extravaganza. A tiny white and chrome petrol tank with a pear-shaped tank badge was roundly loathed for the ludicrously short range its 2¾ gallon capacity gave in combination with the triples' thirst, as well as for being too narrow between the knees. The new Lucas electrical switchgear was less than perfect and resulted in the Rocket III on test with *Bike* magazine experiencing electrical failure while overtaking at night in a motorway fast lane, thus unleashing a justified stream of invective from Mark Williams. The handlebars reverted to the high and (33 in) wide variety, with the air lever no longer on the bars, but down by the left end of the carburettor manifold. Direction indicators were a standard fitting.

The mudguards were the same skimpy size and chrome finished as for the rest of the range, with the same single rubber-mounted fixing at the front. The seat's hump lost its white piping, the oil cooler lost its alloy end caps, the rear damper

springs lost their chrome top cover and were now fully exposed, the shape of the side panels with their revised badges was cut away so that they were no longer covering the now separate pillbox-type air cleaners, and the frame was painted cream/dove grey. The new cast alloy front fork, with its 6½ in of movement, and the conical hub brakes front and rear, were fitted (see page 103 for details).

If riders found the new brakes (which were still not really up to the bike's weight and speed) and the fork an improvement on the predecessors, they had to swallow the fact that a combination of the air-cleaners, a drop in compression back to 9.0:1, slightly lower gearing again, 3½ throttle slides in the Amal Concentrics, and the new chrome megaphone silencers, had restricted the engine's output and top speed further. There was some gain in engine flexibility, with better acceleration between 40 mph and 70 mph in top gear. But overall, the 1971 Rocket III was a far from practical machine, and top performance requires a reversion to the rather odd ray-gun silencers or to a new item giving greater flexibility (such as the one devised by Norman Hyde). Fitting the ray-guns just requires a small adaptor at the end of the existing pipes. They are only fully effective, however, with the earlier one-piece air-filter box, and a number 3½ throttle slide.

For 1972 the styling of the Rocket III, like the remaining twins and single, was revised in more sober fashion, and gearing was lowered by the use of an 18-tooth not 19-tooth gearbox sprocket. The tank reverted to the previous larger size and style, the seat lost its hump and became cross-hatched on top, and even lower and narrower pull-back handlebars returned. Frames were black again as were the bottom halves of the side-panels, above which a white transfer replaced the previous badge, and the front brake backplate was also coloured black. Everything else, including the megaphone silencers and tiny mudguards, stayed until the finish of production at the end of that year. The Trident continued the saga for another four years, and though one version, the ultra-stylish Hurricane of 1973, was a Rocket III in disguise, all the Triumph-named versions will be dealt with later.

In the same way as for the Trident, there are some specialists concerned with keeping this authentic British superbike alive. Rights for the original Rob North-designed racer frames and its ancillary equipment have gone to Norman Miles, and Anglo-Bike produced a North-framed triple-engined special, the Tristar-3. Improving on the original is Norman Hyde, with his experience at

BSA ROCKET 3 750

Below left *Restyled 1971 Rocket III, somewhat excessive.*

Right *Last Rocket from Small Heath, more soberly styled 1972 model.*

Meriden, and later NVT's Kitt's Green, as one of Doug Hele's four development engineers, of working on the racers, and of building and running a 975 cc triple-engined dragster on which, in 1974, solo and sidecar, he had taken more short distance world and national speed records than for any other rider. His right-hand man was Jack Shemans, 28 years at Meriden and again heavily involved with the development of the racing bikes. They offer a range of large-bore conversions, as well as solutions to many of the triples' other problems, such as new-design more deeply-spigoted cylinder liners to seal the cylinder head gasket effectively, and a sintered iron clutch friction plate to banish slipping. The ex-Meriden team of L. P. Williams are another quality triple specialist outfit. For advice, rebuilds and updates, they must be the men to see about these road machines which, though tragically cut off in their prime, were good enough still to be competitive 10 or 15 years later.

BSA: The A75 Rocket III — dates and specifications

Production dates
A75 Rocket III — 1968–72

Specifications
Capacity, bore and stroke — 740 cc (67 mm × 70 mm)
Type of engine — Transverse ohv triple
Ignition — Coil
Weight — (1969) 468 lb

Rocket III — annual development and modifications

1969
1 Mid-year, oil feed pipes carried by main bearing caps to the tappets and cams were removed.

1970
1 53-tooth rear wheel sprocket replaced previous 52-tooth.
2 3rd gear lowered internally from 8.3 to 8.42:1.
3 Wider tooth faces in gearbox.
4 Gaskets fitted between gearbox outer and inner covers, and between inner covers, and between inner cover and main casing. These, and the crankcase gaskets, were of new material made of asbestos and synthetic rubber.
5 New mainshaft nut incorporating an O-ring, and a new clutch hub. (New nut can be used on older machines if old clutch hub is machined in by $\frac{1}{64}$ in at an angle of 45° to the back so that the nut can sit slightly into it.)
6 Lower kickstart ratio.
7 Rear brake operating cam's form modified.
8 Clutch cable now nylon-lined.
9 Front mudguard mounting stays changed.
10 Early 1970, clutch housing ventilated and holes drilled in casing to let it breathe.
11 Mid-1970, change in shape of clutch shock-absorber rubbers which had extruded between the outer edge of the paddles and the inside of the hub, and of type of bolt used to hold the plate retaining the rubbers.

1971
1 For cycle part changes, see text.
2 New Lucas switchgear and indicators.

1972
1 Gearing lowered by use of 18-tooth not 19-tooth gearbox sprocket.
2 Petrol tank changes from 1971 $2\frac{3}{4}$-gallon type to previous $4\frac{1}{4}$ gallon.
3 Dual seat top ribbed, and no longer humped at rear.
4 Frame colour changes from 1971 dove grey back to black. Front brake backplate also now black.

BSA: engine and frame numbers

Model	Engine	Frame

1950

Singles

Model	Engine	Frame
C10	ZC10-4001	ZC10-10001
C11	ZC11-8001	ZC10-10001
B31	ZB31-9001	
B32	ZB32-3001	ZB31-9001
B32 alloy engine	ZB32A-3001	rigid or
B33	ZB33-4001	ZB31S-5001
B34	ZB34-2001	plunger
B34 alloy engine	ZB34A-2001	
M20	ZM20-4001	ZM20-7001
M21	ZM21-5001	ZM20-7001
M33	ZM33-3001	ZM20-7001
Gold Star 350	ZB32GS-2001	ZB31-9001 rigid
500	ZB34GS-2001	and ZB32S-2001 plunger

Twins

Model	Engine	Frame
A7	ZA7-7001	ZA7-4001
A7 (S/F)	ZA7-7001	ZA7S-6001
A7 Star Twin	ZA7S-4001	ZA7S-6001
A10	ZA10-101	ZA7-4001
A10 (S/F)	ZA10-1-1	ZA7S-6001

1951

Singles

Model	Engine	Frame
C10	ZC10-7001	ZC10-21001 rigid or ZC10S-101 plunger or ZC10S4-101 plunger frame and four speed gearbox
C11	ZC11-16001	
B31	ZB31-15001	
B32	ZB32-4001	
B32 alloy engine	ZB32A-4001	ZB31-14001
B33	ZB33-7001	rigid or
B34	ZB34-3001	ZB31S-10001
B34 alloy engine	ZB34A-3001	plunger
M20	ZM20-6001	ZM20-10001
M21	ZM21-8001	rigid or
M33	ZM33-4001	ZM20S-101 plunger
Gold star 350	ZB32GS-3001	ZB31-14001
500	ZB34GS-3001	rigid and ZB32S-3001 plunger

Twins

Model	Engine	Frame
A7	AA7-101	ZA7-6001
A7 (S/F)	AA7-101	ZA7S-14001
A7 Star Twin	AA7S-101	ZA7S-14001
A10	ZA10-4001	ZA7-6001
A10 (S/F)	ZA10-4001	ZA7S-14001

1952

Singles

Model	Engine	Frame
C10	ZA10-10001	ZC10-29001 rigid or ZC10S-2601 plunger or ZC10S4-2001 plunger and 4-speed
C11	SC11-25001	
B31	ZB31-21001	
B32	ZB32-5001	
B32 alloy engine	ZB32A-5001	ZB31-19001
B33	ZB33-11001	rigid or
B34	ZB34-4001	ZB31S-17001
B34 sand cast alloy	ZB34A-4001	plunger
B34 die cast alloy	ZB34A-5001	
M20	ZM20-10001	ZM20-14001
M21	ZM21-10001	rigid or
M33	ZM33-5001	ZM20S-301 plunger
Gold Star 350	ZB32GS-4001	ZB31-19001
350 Clubman	ZB32GS-6001	rigid and
500 Sandcast	ZB34GS-4001	ZB32S-4001
500 die cast	ZB34GS-5001	plunger

Twins

Model	Engine	Frame
A7	AA7-5001	ZA7-8001
A7 (S/F)	AA7-101	ZA7S-26001
A7 Star Twin	AA7S-101	ZA7S-26001
A10	ZA10-12001	ZA7-8001
A10 (S/F)	ZA10-12001	ZA7S-26001

1953

Singles

Model	Engine	Frame
C10	BC10-101	BC10-101 rigid or BC10S-101 plunger or BC10S4-101 plunger and 4-speed
C11	BC11-101	
B31	BB31-101	B31-101 rigid or
B32	BB32-101	
B32 alloy engine	BB32A-101	BB31S-101
BB33	BB33-101	plunger
B34	B34-101	
B34 alloy engine	BB34A-101	
M20	BM20-101	BM20-101 or
M21	BM21-101	BM20S-101
M33	BM33-101	plunger
Gold Star 350	BB32GS-101	BB31-101 rigid
500	BB34GS-101	or BB32S-101 plunger or BB32A-101 s/a

Twins

Model	Engine	Frame
A7	BA7-101	BA7-101

A7 (S/F)	BA7-101	BA7S-101
A7 Star Twin	BA7S-101	BA7S-101
A10	BA10-101	BA7S-101

1954
Singles

C10L	BC10L-101	BC10LS-101
C11G	BC11G-101	BC11-101 rigid or BC11S-101 plunger or BC11S4-101 plunger and 4-speed
B31	BB31-6001	BB31-1386 rigid or BB31S-5895 plunger or CB31-101 s/a
	B33/BB33-2001	
B32	BB32A-201	BB32R-121 rigid or CB31-101 s/a
B34	BB34A-201	
M20	BM20-1001	BM20-1502 rigid or
M21	BM21-1601	BM20S-1192 plunger
M33	BM33-501	
Gold Star 350	BB32GS-1001	CB32-101
350 new Clubman	CB32GS-101	
500	BB34GS-1001	
500 new Clubman	CB34GS-101	
500 Daytona	BB34GSD-101	CB32D-101 rigid (very few made)

Twins

A7	BA7-2001	BA7S-8950
A7 Star Twin	BA7S-2001	BA7S-8950
A10	BA10-7001	BA7S-8950
A10 Super Flash (S/F)	BA10S-701	BA10S-701
A7 (S/A)	CA7-101	CA7-101
A7 Star Twin	CA7S-101	CA7-101
A7 Shooting Star	CA7SS-101	CA7-101
A10 (S/A)	CA10-101	CA7-101
A10 Super Flash	CA10S-101	CA7-101
A10 Road Rocket	CA10R-101	CA7-101

1955
Singles

C10L	BC10L-4001	BC10LS-4501
C11G 3-speed	BC11G-11501	BC11S-4001 plunger
C11G 4-speed	BC11G-11501	BC11S4-8001 plunger
B31	BB31-15001	BB31S-12001 plunger or CB31-6001 s/a
B33	BB33-5001	
B32	BB32A-251	BB32A-201 rigid or BB31-6001 s/a
B34	BB34A-301	
M20	BM20-2501	BM20-4001 rigid or
M21	BM21-4501	BM20S-4001 plunger
M33	BM33-1301	
Gold Star 350	BB32GS-2001	CB32-1501
350 Clubman	CB32GS-501	
500	BB34GS-2001	
500 Clubman	CB34GS-501	
350 new	DB32GS-101	CB32-4001 1956 models produced in 1955
500 new	DB34GS-101	

Twins

A7 (S/A)	CA7-1501	CA7-7001
A7 Shooting Star	CA7SS-501	CA7-7001
A10 (S/A)	CA10-4501	CA7-7001
A10 (plunger)	BA10-11001	BA7S-15001
A10 Road Rocket	CA10R-601	CA7-7001

1956
Singles

C10L	BC10L-7001	DC10S-101
C12	BC11G-23001	EC12-101 s/a or BC11S4-18001 plunger 4 speed
B31	BB31-22001	EB31-101
B33	BB33-7301	EB31-101
B32	BB32A-301	CB34-101 s/a or B32R-301 rigid
B34	BB34A-351	
M21	BM21-7501	BM20-7001 rigid or BM20S-8001 plunger
M33	BM33-2101	BM20S-8001 plunger
Gold Star (1956-57) 350	DB32GS-501	CB32-4001
500	DB34GS-501	
500 new head	DBD34GS-2001	
500 USA	DB34GS-501	BB32R-301 rigid

Twins

A7 (S/A)	CA7-2701	EA7-101
A7 Shooting Star	CA7SS-2301	EA7-10T

A10 (S/A)	CA10-8001	EA7-101
A10 (plunger)	BA10-14001	BA7S-18001
A10 Road		
Rocket	CA10R-2001	EA7-101

1957
Singles

C10	BC10L-	DC10S-
C12	BC11G-	EC12-
B31	BB31-	EB31-
B33	BB33-	EB31-
B32	BB32A-	CB34-
B34	BB34A-	CB34-
M21	BM21-	BM20 rigid or
		BM20S plunger
M33	BM33-	BM20S plunger

Twins

A7 (S/A)	CA7-	EA7-
A7 Shooting		
Star	CA75S-	EA7-
A10 (S/A)	CA10-	EA7-
A10 Road		
Rocket	CA10R-	EA7-
last A10		
(plunger)	BA10-16036	BA7S-20289

1958
Singles

C12	BC11G-4001	EC12-16001
B31	GB31-101	FB31-101
B33	GB33-101	FB31-101
M21	BM21-11001	BM20-10001
		rigid or
		BM20S-11001
		plunger
Gold Star 500	DBD34GS-3001	CB32-7001

Twins

A7	CA7-5001	FA7-101
A7 Shooting		
Star	CA7SS-4501	FA7-101
A10	DA10-651	FA7-101
A10 Super		
Rocket	CA10R-6001	FA7-101

1959
Singles

C15	C15-101	C15-101
C15S	C15S-101	C15S-101
C15T	C15T-101	C15S-101
B31	GB31-1909	FB31-2572
B33	GB33-662	FB31-2572
M21	BM21-12033	BM20-10313
		rigid or
		BM20S-12031
		plunger

Gold Star 350	DB32GS-1501	CB32-7873
500	DBD34GS-3753	
500 Catalina	DBD34GS-3753	CB32C-101

Twins

A7	CA7-5867	FA7-8522
A7 Shooting		
Star	CA7SS-5425	FA7-8522
A10	DA10-4616	FA7-8522
A10 Super		
Rocket	CA10R-8193	FA7-8522

1960
Singles

C15	C15-11001	C15-11101
C15S	C15S-301	C15S-501
C15T	C15T-301	C15S-501
B33	GB33-1001	GB33-101
M21	BM21-12901	BM20-10451
		rigid or
		BM20S-12031

Gold Star 350	DB32GS-1601	CB32-8701
500	DBD34GS-4601	
500 Catalina	DBD34GS-4601	CB32C-351

Twins

A7	CA7-7101	GA7-101
A7 Shooting		
Star	CA7SS-6701	CA7-101
A10	DA10-7801	GA7-101
A10 Super		
Rocket	DA10R-101	GA7-101

1961
Singles

C15	C15-21251	C15-22001
C15S	C15S-2112	C15S-2701
C15T	C15T-1056	C15S-2701
SS80	C15SS-101	C15-27644
B40	B40-101	B40-101
M21	BM21-14301	BM20S-14201
M21 alternator	BM21A-14301	BM20S-14201
Gold Star 350	DB32GS-1741	CB32-10101
500	DBD34GS-5684	
500 Catalina	DBD34GS-5684	CB32C-601

Twins

A7	CA7-8501	GA7-11101
A7 (generator)	CA7A-8501	GA7-11101
A7 Shooting		
Star	CA7SS-8001	GA7-11101
A10	DA10-13201	GA7-11101
A10 (generator)	DA10A-13201	GA7-11101
A10 Super		
Rocket	DA10R-3001	GA7-11101

1962
Singles

C15	C15-29839	C15-31801

SS80	C15SS-1101	C15-31801
C15S	C15S-3101	C15S-3601
C15T	C15T-1451	C15S-10001
B40	B40-3601	B40-3511
SS90	B40 BSS-101	B40-3511
M21	BM21-15453	BM20S-15061
M21 alternator	BM21A-15453	BM20S-15061
Gold Star 350	DB32GS-1794	CB32-11001
500	DBD34GS-6504	
500 Catalina	DBD34GS-6504	CB32C-741
Twins		
A50 Star Twin	A50-101	A50-101
A65 Star Twin	A65-101	A50-101
A50 Star (rod brake)	A50-101	A50A-101
A65 Star (rod brake)	A65-101	A50A-101
A10	DA10-17181	GA7-21120
A10 Super Rocket	DA10R-5958	GA7-21120
A10 Rocket Gold Star	DA10R-5958	GA-10-101
A7	CA7-9714	GA7-21120
A7 Shooting Star	CA7SS-9277	GA7-21120
A7 (generator)	CA7A-9714	GA7-21120
A10 (generator)	DA10A-341	GA7-21120

1963
Singles

C15	C15-41807	C15-38035
SS80	C15SS-2705	C15-38035
C15S	C15S-4001	C15C-101
C15T	C15T-2001	C15C-101
B40	B40-4506	B40-5017
SS90	B40SS-180	B40-5017
M21	BM21-15588	BM20S-15159
M21 (with alternator)	BM21A-15588	BM20S-15159
Gold Star 500	DBD34GS-6881	CB32-11451
500 Catalina	DBD34GS-6881	CB32C-857
Twins		
A50 Royal Star (cable brake)	A50-823	A50-2288
A50 Royal Star (rod brake)	A50-823	A50-2701
A65 Star (cable brake)	A65-1947	A50-2288
A65 Star (rod brake)	A65-1947	A50-2071
A10 Golden Flash	DA10-17727	GA7-23643
A10 (generator)	DA10A-17727	GA7-23643
A10 Super Rocket	DA10R-8197	GA7-23643

A10 Rocket Gold Star	DA10R-8197	GA10-390

1964
Singles

C15	C15D-101	C15-42211
SS80	C15SS-3633	C15-42211
C15S	C15S-4373	C15C-853
C15T	C15T-2116	C15C-853
B40	B405275	B40-6668
SS90	B40SS-426	B40-6668
Twins		
A50 Royal Star	A50A-101	A50-5501
A65 Star	A65A-101	A50-5501
A65 Rocket (less rev counter)	A65B-101	A50-5501
A65 Rocket (with rev counter)	A65C-101	A50-5501
A65 Thunderbolt Rocket	A65B-101	A50-5501
A65 Lightning Rocket	A65D-101	A50B-101
A65 Spitfire Hornet	A65E-101	A50B-101

1965
Singles

C15	C15F-101	C15-45501
SS80	C15FSS-101	C15-45501
C15S	C15FS-101	C15C-1601
C15T	C15FT-101	C15C-1601
B40	B40F-101	B40-7775
SS90	B40FSS-101	B40-7775
Twins		
A50 Royal Star	A50A-101	A50-8437
A50 Cyclone (road model)	A50D-101	A50B-4001
A50 Cyclone Competition	A50B-507	A50B-4001
A65 Star	A65A-134	A50-8437
A65 Rocket (less rev counter)	A65B-334	A50-8437
A65 Rocket (with rev counter)	A65C-1082	A50-8437
A65 Lightning Rocket	A65D-1742	A50B-4001
A65 Spitfire Hornet	A65E-701	A50B-4001

1966
Singles

C15	C15F-2089	C15-49001

C15 Sportsman	C15SS-2001	C15-49001
B40	B40F-1149	B40-9973
B40 modified engine	B40G-101	B40-9973
B44GP	B44-101	B44-101
B44VE	B44E-101	C15C-3137

Twins

A50 Royal Star	A50R-101	A50C-101
A50 Wasp	A50W-101	A50C-101
A65 Thunderbolt	A65T-101	A50C-101
A65 Lightning	A65L-101	A50C-101
A65 Hornet	A65H-101	A50C-101
A65 Spitfire Mk II	A65S-101	A50C-101

1967

Singles

C15	C15G-101	G15G-101
C15 Sportsman	C15SG-101	C15SG-101
C25 Barracuda	C25-101	C25-101
B25 Starfire	C25-101	B25-101
B40	B40G-201	B40G-201
B44GP	B44-131	B44-267
B44VE	B44EA-101	B44EA-101
B44VR	B44R-101	B44R-101

Twins

A50 Royal Star	A50RA-	101
A50 Wasp	A50WA-	101
A65 Thunderbolt	A65TA-	101
A65 Lightning	A65LA-	101
A65 Hornet	A65 HA-	101
A65 Spitfire Mk III	A65SA-	101

1968

Singles

B25	B25B-101	B25B-101
B44 Victor	B44B-101VS	B44B-101VS
B44 Shooting Star	B44B-202SS	B44B-101SS

Twins

A50 Wasp	A50WB-	101
A65 Thunderbolt	A65TB-	101
A65 Lightning	A65LB-	101
A65 Firebird Scrambler	A65FB-	101
A65 Spitfire Mk IV	A65SB-	101

From 1969 onwards, frame and engine numbers of all BSAs should coincide (though exceptions have been found), and conform to the following code:

(first letter)	Month
(second letter)	Year
(five numbers)	Production numbers (beginning at 00100 each season)
(letters and numbers)	Model designator (always suffix)

First letter Month codes were as follows:

A — January	**H** — July
B — February	**J** — August
C — March	**K** — September
D — April	**N** — October
E — May	**P** — November
G — June	**X** — December

Second letter Year codes were as follows:

C — August 1968/July 1969
D — August 1969/July 1970
E — August 1970/July 1971
G — August 1971/July 1972

A sample Engine/Frame number might be:
DC 12345 A75R — which would denote a Rocket III of April 1969.

BSA: colour schemes

1950 Singles: All cycle parts black. M20, M21, M33, C10, C11, B31, B33, petrol tanks chromed, with top and side tank panels in frosted silver, outlined in black. Wheel rims chrome plated with centres matt silver, black lined, except standard M20, M21, which had matt silver tank lined in black and black wheel rims, but option as others. B31 alternative finish as above but tank panels, wheel rim centres, green, both outlined in gold. B33 alternative as B31, but colour maroon. C11 de luxe chrome plated tank with blue panels and wheel rim centres. Gold Stars; as standard B-Range but with chrome mudguards, chainguard, etc, and special maroon lining and Star transfer on tank. Twins: all cycle parts black. A10 petrol tank chromed with black top and side panels in front of knee grips, lined in gold, wheel rims chrome-plated with black centres gold lined, and circular winged red tank badge with lightning flash in gold beige. A7; as A10 but with colour optionally maroon and different badge. A7 Star Twin; as Gold Stars, with same tank transfer. Early 1950 at extra cost, A10 available in polychromatic beige for all cycle parts. Petrol tank chrome with beige tank panels lined in maroon.
1951 Singles: as 1950, but nickel shortages led to announcement in May that C11 would have blue and beige tank finish, not blue and chrome, and similar changes would occur for the B and M range 'when the next batch was produced', ie, previous chrome portions matt silver. Twins: no

change, but from mid-year previously chromed portions now matt silver.

1952 Singles: as 1951, with petrol tanks plain lined green (B31), red (B33), both with gold lining, silver (M-range, C10) with black lining, silver (Gold Star) with maroon lining, blue (C11) with beige lining. From March, new winged BSA tank badge for all 250 cc and over except Gold Star. From end of September, plating restrictions at an end and new colour schemes announced, see 1953. Gold Stars till then, previous chrome portions matt silver including mudguards, handlebars, chaincase, all matt silver with maroon lining. Twins: as 1951 until late September.

1953 Singles: C10/C11, all cycle parts dark maroon, petrol tank maroon with chromed panels at side, only now extending to the rear of the knee grips, and winged circular BSA badges with 5 chrome bars extending rearwards as far as knee grips. Optional black finish. B31/B33; as C10/C11. M20/21/33 cycle parts black, but tank maroon and chrome as C10/C11. Gold Stars, black cycle parts, chrome mudguards and chainguard, petrol tank matt silver with chrome side panels, maroon lined, and large round bright red badge. Twins: A10, colours and badge as 1952 but now with large chrome tank panels, at side only, extending to the rear of knee grips. A7 all maroon, tank as A10 but maroon with round red 'piled arms' badges. A7 Star Twin; frame dark green enamel, mudguards, front fork and chrome-panelled petrol tank polychromatic green, large round badge as Gold Star but black. *All models* have fully chromed wheel rims from now on.

1954 Singles: C10L, two-tone finish, all cycle parts dark green enamel, except for light green mudguards, forks, headlamp shell, oil tank, tool box. Tank panels light green and gold lined. C11G, all cycle parts dark maroon, tank panels chrome. Both with round plastic 'piled arms' tank badges, but C11G's 1953 chrome tank bars deleted. B31/B33; as C11G. M-range; as 1953, with the new round badges. Gold Stars; as 1953. Twins: as 1953.

1955 Singles: C-group; as 1954, but now with twin chromium-plated beadings running lengthways down the tank top concealing welded joints. B31/33, M-range, Gold Stars; as 1954. Twins: as 1953.

1956 Singles: C10L; as 1955, C12 all maroon with gold-lined cream petrol tank panels. M-range as 1954 but tank panels now gold-lined cream. B-range, Gold Stars; as 1954. Twins: A10 Road Rocket, black cycle parts, chrome mudguards, tank silver with maroon-lined chrome side panels and red round piled-arms badge, or colour

optionally bright scarlet. A10, A7, A7SS; as 1954.

1957 Singles: C10L, C12; as 1956, but C12 colour now optionally black, and both with chrome tank panels as optional extras. M-range; as 1956 but chrome-plated tank panels optional extra. B-range Gold Stars; as 1956. Twins: as 1956, but A10 Road Rocket standard tank colour now bright scarlet, and A7's colour optionally black for first time.

1958 Singles: *All* frames black. C15, black cycle parts, but mudguards, oil tank, tool box and centre section, and petrol tank with chrome strips and pear shaped plastic badge, either blue or fuchsia red. C12, petrol tank black or maroon with gold-lined cream tank panels, chrome tank panels optional extra. B31, cycle parts all black, mudguards and petrol tank polychromatic almond green. B33, as B31 but colour dark gunmetal grey. M21, Gold Stars; as 1957. Twins: *all* frames black. A10 Super Rocket (Home) black cycle parts, with mudguards and chrome panelled petrol tank either brilliant red or silver, with A7-type round badges. A10, if in beige option, has only mudguards, oil tank/tool box and petrol tank in beige. A7 Shooting Star; as 1957 but frame black. A7, mudguards, toolbox/oil tank, petrol tank, now Princess Grey.

1959 Singles: as 1958, but C15 colours either fuchsia red or light turquoise green. Twins: as 1958.

1960 Singles: as 1958, but B33 now with pear-shaped tank badges, and C15 optional colour almond green. Twins: as 1959, but A10 optional sapphire blue for tanks, mudguards and tool box/oil tank.

1961 For *all* (except A10 Super Rocket) silver sheen finish for hubs/brake plates; Super Rocket's polished light alloy brake plates and chromed hubs. Singles: B40 royal red mudguards, oil tank/toolbox, and petrol tank (with chrome side panels), black cycle parts. SS80 black for all cycle parts, petrol tank black with chrome side panels, chrome fork crown pressing. C15; as 1960. Twins: as 1960, but A7 colour fuchsia red, and A7SS offers black alternative for first time. (From August) pear-shaped tank badges adopted, A7SS black, others red. A10 Super Rocket colours Royal Red or Princess Grey.

1962 Singles: B40; as 1961, SS90 black cycle parts, flamboyant red for petrol tank (with chrome plated tank panels and pear-shaped badges), oil tank/toolbox/centre panel, chrome mudguards; optional colour black. C15; as 1961, but alternative sapphire blue with ivory tank panels. SS80; as 1961 but colour polychromatic blue. M21; as 1957. Twins: A7, A10, A10 Super Rocket;

as 1961. A7SS Polychromatic green. A10 Rocket Gold Star black cycle parts, chromed mudguards, petrol tank silver sheen with chrome side panels lined in maroon and large round red Gold Star-type badge. A50 Star cycle parts black, polychromatic green for mudguards, side panels, petrol tank, with chrome side panels and black pear-shaped badge, plus Golden Flash type badge on side panels. Alternative finish black. A65, as A50 but colour polychromatic blue, and pear-shaped tank badges blue. Alternative finish black, or flamboyant red at extra charge.

1963 Singles: as 1962. Twins: as 1962, plus A65 Rocket; as A65 but colour flame red, top fork shrouds and mudguards chrome, pear-shaped tank badges red.

1964 Singles: as 1963, but C15 colour listed as Royal red not fuchsia red. Twins: as 1963.

1965 Singles: as 1964. Twins: as 1964. A65L; as A50 but colour metallic pale gold with red lining tank and on side panels and with chrome headlamp shell and mudguards and fork crown tops. A50C as A65L.

1966 Singles: as 1965, but C15 now with chrome-plated petrol tank panels. New C15 Sportsman; as SS80 previously, but with chrome-plated headlamp. Twins: A50 Royal Star; as previous A50 but colour flamboyant red, and tank now with white lining. A65T; as A50 Royal Star, but colour flamboyant blue. A65L, A50C; as 1965. A65 Spitfire Mark II Cycle parts black, side covers and petrol tank flamboyant red, lined in ivory and gold, with star transfer badge, chrome mudguards, headlamp shell, and top fork shrouds. A65 Hornet; as Spitfire but colour mandarin red. A50 Wasp, as Hornet but colour sapphire blue.

1967 Singles: C15; as 1966. C25 black cycle parts, chrome mudguards and headlamp, tank and side panels Bushfire orange with white panels. Mid-year, changed to blue and white. B44 VR, as C25 but colours royal red and ivory. Twins: A50 as 1966 but colour flamboyant blue. A65T; as 1966 but colour black, A65L; as 1966 but colour flamboyant red, A65 Spitfire Mk III; as 1966 but colour royal red.

1968 Singles: B25; as previous C25, B44SS, as B44VR but petrol tank red. Twins: A50; as 1967 but colour flamboyant red, headlamp chrome, white lining on tank and mudguards. A65T, A65L colours; as 1967, headlamp and mudguards chrome, tank white lining as A50. A65 Spitfire Mk IV, as 1967 Mk III. Rocket III: cycle parts black. Tank, mudguards and side panels red, latter with aluminium badges. Chrome headlamp shell. Alternative finish lime green with red lines on tank and panels.

1969 Singles: B25, B44SS as 1968 but B25 petrol tank all blue. B25 Fleetstar black and white, petrol tank with chrome panels. Twins: A50 as 1968 but colour flamboyant aircraft blue and side panel transfers 'Royal Star'. A56T as 1968 but colour black and side transfers 'Thunderbolt 650'. A65L as 1968 but colour flamboyant red and side transfer '650 Lightning'. Rocket III as 1968.

1970 Singles: as 1969. Twins: as 1969. Rocket III: as 1969.

1971 Singles: B25SS, B50SS, cycle parts dove grey/ivory. Headlamps chrome. Petrol tank flamboyant red or blue with BSA transfers, centre and side stripes black, side panels and mudguards matching, latter with black centre stripe. B25T, B50T petrol tank polished alloy with black centre and side stripes, side panels and mudguards in red and striped as on SS. All exhaust system matt black with stainless steel heat shields. Twins: A65T, A65L, A56FS: cycle parts dove grey/ivory, headlamps and mudguards chrome, tanks two tone with metal BSA badge, A65L sterling moss green and ivory, A65T bronze and ivory, A65FS orange and ivory, side covers same colour. Rocket III. Cycle parts white. Petrol tank white and chrome with pear-shaped badge. Plain side covers with Rocket III badges. Chrome headlamp shell and mudguards.

1972 *All* frames black and brake back plates matt black. Singles: B50SS, B50T; as 1971 but tank colour, side panels and mudguards Hi-violet. Twins: A65L, A65T, chrome mudguards and headlamp. Tank, side panels, A65L Firebird red, A65T Etruscan bronze. Rocket III: chrome mudguards and headlamp. Tank as 1969, colour Burgundy, side cover uppers Burgundy, lower in black, white outline 'Rocket' white solid 'Three' side transfer.

Some approximate modern colour equivalents:

Gold Star RGS, etc, Silver sheen — VW Beetle silver.

C11G, A7, B31/33, etc, maroon — Ford Imperial Maroon.

A10 golden beige — Chrysler Champagne Metallic (Berger 7440), or BL Metallic Golden Beige, or Chrysler Golden Sand.

A7 Star Twin/Shooting Star, polychromatic green — Toyota Altair Metallic Green.

D1 Bantam — Ford Mist Green, Mercedes Green.

C15, A7, fuchsia red — Vauxhall 230S.

B40, red — Jaguar Carman.